THE EDUCATION OF SELVES

The Education of Selves

HOW PSYCHOLOGY TRANSFORMED STUDENTS

Jack Martin

and

Ann-Marie McLellan

OXFORD
UNIVERSITY PRESS

OXFORD

UNIVERSITY PRESS

Oxford University Press is a department of the University of Oxford.
It furthers the University's objective of excellence in research, scholarship,
and education by publishing worldwide.

Oxford   New York
Auckland   Cape Town   Dar es Salaam   Hong Kong   Karachi
Kuala Lumpur   Madrid   Melbourne   Mexico City   Nairobi
New Delhi   Shanghai   Taipei   Toronto

With offices in
Argentina   Austria   Brazil   Chile   Czech Republic   France   Greece
Guatemala   Hungary   Italy   Japan   Poland   Portugal   Singapore
South Korea   Switzerland   Thailand   Turkey   Ukraine   Vietnam

Oxford is a registered trademark of Oxford University Press in the UK and certain other
countries.

Published in the United States of America by
Oxford University Press
198 Madison Avenue, New York, NY 10016

Library of Congress Cataloging-in-Publication Data
    Martin, Jack, 1950-
    The education of selves : how psychology transformed students / Jack Martin, Ann-Marie McLellan.
    p. cm.
    Includes bibliographical references and index.
    ISBN 978–0–19–991367–1 (hardback: alk. paper)
    1. Educational psychology.   2. Transformative learning.   3. Self-actualization (Psychology)
    I. McLellan, Ann-Marie.   II. Title.
    LB1051.M311 2013
    370.15—dc23
    2012023861

9 8 7 6 5 4 3 2 1
Printed in the United States of America
on acid-free paper

Contents

Preface

THIS BOOK EXAMINES the role played by scientific and professional psychology in transforming ideals for student conduct, experience, and goals in American and Canadian schools during the second half of the twentieth century. This was a period and context within which psychological conceptions, measures, research, and interventions related to students' "selves" became highly influential and enshrined in school and classroom rhetoric and practices. In consequence, educational goals, policies, and practices became targeted increasingly at the personal development of students as individuals with high levels of self-esteem, self-concept, self-efficacy, and self-regulation. No longer were school and classroom activities aimed solely at assisting students to develop the knowledge, skills, and attitudes that would allow them to become productive, responsible members of their societies. Schools and teachers now became responsible for ensuring that all students developed as psychological selves—as individuals with the kinds of inner psychological resources that would enable them to lead fulfilling lives, replete with high levels of self-regard, self-understanding, self-confidence, and strategically directed self-interest.

Fueled by the enthusiasm for self-expression and self-actualization that typified the 1960s in the United States and Canada, humanistic, cognitive, developmental, and educational psychologists began to publish more and more academic and professional articles reporting the power of their research findings and intervention procedures to enhance the self-esteem and self-concepts of children and adolescents in general and in schools in particular. They also (especially in subspecializations like school, counseling, community, and consulting psychology) began to promote their expertise as psychoeducators, in possession of knowledge and a practical understanding of how to ensure the positive personal development of schoolchildren through the implementation of a wide range of scientifically supported psychoeducational programs and methods. By the late 1970s, new programs and methods for enhancing students' self-regulation and self-efficacy joined the previous generation of programs and methods geared to elevating self-esteem and enhancing self-concept. Psychologists working in schools now claimed to be capable of enhancing both self-expression and self-management in ways that would allow students to develop the self-confidence and ability to become enterprising lifelong learners in pursuit of their own interests and concerns.

We begin with a general description of the critical historical approach we take to our examination of the ways in which disciplinary psychology changed students during the last half of the twentieth century. Of particular importance here is the way in which a critical history of psychology challenges traditional claims and portrayals of psychology as a natural science, with applications that can be understood as straightforward and predictable instances of social engineering. We then trace the longer-term historical development of psychological conceptions of selfhood and examine those conceptions that have been of particular interest to educational psychologists. Using a combination of historical, theoretical, and methodological critique, we go on to examine psychological theory, measures, research, and interventions in the areas of self-esteem, self-concept, self-efficacy, and self-regulation as these have been implemented within educational contexts. The transformation that emerges from our critical analyses is a movement toward an increasingly psychological version of student conduct and experience—one in which students are helped and encouraged to cultivate heightened concerns and techniques for exploring, expressing, and strategically managing inner psychological causes and motives for their actions and school performance. Students' orientation to their inner psychological selves and concern in this regard are aided by methods of self-description, self-expression, and self-management taught them by psychologically minded teachers encouraged by expert psychological consultants. The result, we argue, is the creation and implementation of a new ideal to guide the personal development of children and adolescents in schools—what we term the "triple-E" student: expressive, enterprising, and entitled. We describe this kind of studenthood by giving examples of how the triple-E concept has been implemented and how it functions in practice; we also examine its consequences for students, schools, and the broader society. Although the individualism and instrumentalism evident in this way of being a student have come in for sharp criticism from many commentators during the first decade of the twenty-first century, there has been no previous detailed examination of the role of educational psychology in the creation and promotion of the psychological or triple-E student. In the last chapter of our book, we discuss an alternative approach to educational psychology and teaching that retains what we think is valuable about self-understanding and self-development but recasts these important social and psychological processes in a way that transforms them into social, communal virtues of benefit to both societies and selves.

A number of individuals have assisted us in compiling the information reported and interpreted herein. In particular we would like to thank Rob Klassen, Michael Levykh, Nathalie Lovasz, and Lauren McNamara, all of whom worked as research assistants with us at various times over the past 10 years. Another group to whom we owe particular thanks is made up of several of our valued colleagues who have been good enough to read previous versions of our manuscript and provide critical commentary, which has been invaluable in helping us to sharpen and shape our ideas, arguments, and presentation. These colleagues include Jeremy Burman, David Burns, Mike Maraun, Kate Slaney, and Jeff Sugarman. We also would like to thank the Social Sciences and Humanities Research Council of Canada and the Burnaby Mountain Endowment Foundation at Simon Fraser University for their support of our work over this same period of time. We also thank archivists at the Bibliothèque Publique et Universitaire in Geneva and at the Archives of the History of American Psychology in Akron, Ohio, for their kind assistance in compiling various segments of the historical records we have used in our text. Finally, we have benefited significantly from the support and expertise extended to us by Abby Gross, Joanna Ng, Emily Perry, and other members of the editorial and production team of Oxford University Press, including the supportive and constructively critical commentaries offered by three anonymous reviewers.

Permission to use portions of our text that have appeared previously, but in different form, in a small number of articles and chapters has been granted by the following publications and publishers: *The Educational Psychologist*/Lawrence Erlbaum Associates, Publishers [parts of Chapter 3 that appeared previously in Martin, J. (2007). The selves of educational psychology: Conceptions, contexts, and critical considerations. *Educational Psychologist, 42*, 79–89], the *Journal of Thought*/Caddo Gap Press [parts of Chapter 4 that appeared previously in Martin, J. (2007) A case against self-esteem as an educational aim. *Journal of Thought, 42*, 55–70], *Advances in Motivation and Achievement*/Emerald Group Publications [parts of Chapter 5 that appeared previously in Martin, J. (2010). Self-concept as persons' understanding and evaluation of their own actions and experiences: Looking backward and forward from where we are. In T. Urdain & S. Karabenick (Eds.), *Advances in Motivation and Achievement* (Vol. 16, pp. 167–198). Bingley, UK: Emerald Books], *Studies in Philosophy and Education*/Springer Science & Business Media [parts of Chapter 7 that appeared previously in Martin, J., & McLellan, A. (2008). The educational psychology of self-regulation: A conceptual and critical analysis. *Studies in Philosophy and Education, 27*, 433–448], and *Educational Theory*/Blackwell Publishing [parts of Chapter 9 that appeared previously in Martin, J. (2007). Educating communal agents: Building on the perspectivism of G. H. Mead. *Educational Theory, 57*, 435–452]. We are most grateful for these courtesies.

Our primary hope is that those who read what we have written will be encouraged to think critically about the complex relationships between disciplinary psychology, in both its research and professional guises, and social institutions such as schools. In particular, we think it's important not to confuse the ways in which psychologists think and talk about us as psychological beings with either our natural state, whatever that might be, or with what is progressive with respect to human flourishing, both individually and collectively.

Jack Martin, Ph.D., Burnaby Mountain Endowed Professor of Psychology, Department of Psychology, Simon Fraser University

Ann-Marie McLellan, Faculty, Department of Educational Studies, Kwantlen Polytechnic University

THE EDUCATION OF SELVES

1 An Introduction to a Critical History of Psychology in Education

AS A SOCIAL institution, public education in North America is designed to produce particular kinds of citizens. This mission is explicit in a wide range of educational documents and curricula that emphasize responsible, participatory citizenship in a liberal democratic context. More informally, numerous school projects and events are designed to educate children about the rights, duties, and responsibilities of citizenship (e.g., learning national and international history, studying contemporary national and world affairs, commemorating important historical figures and occasions, following democratic rules and principles in classroom and school activities). Nonetheless, liberal democracies and their school systems typically have experienced considerable tension between education for citizenship and education for personal development, with the latter reflected not just in educating the intellect but also in pedagogical concern for individual students' self-esteem, self-concept, and self-regulation. A certain amount and kind of student self-development may be relatively easy to reconcile with the idea of students as future citizens; for example, the cultivation of self-discipline, knowledge, and intellectual ability. However, other facets of self-development—for example, self-esteem and self-promotion—may just as readily be associated with self-interest as with the common good. In this book, we provide a critical conceptual history of a particular facet of public education in the United States and Canada during the twentieth century (especially from 1950 to 2000). We examine ways in which disciplinary psychology contributed to the development of students as radically autonomous selves, arguably more attuned to their own self-interest than to responsible community participation.

In particular, we study the ways psychology[1] contributed to the educational development of children as psychological selves. To do so, we employ critical, conceptual, and theoretical methods (Danziger, 1997a,b; Hacking, 1995, 2002; Krantz; 2001; Rose, 1998, 1999) developed recently in the history of psychology to investigate the past—in this case the recent past—in ways that enable us to think differently about the present. By examining the historical conditions that made possible distinctively psychological ways of being students, we hope to penetrate the highly complex relationships between disciplinary psychology and education that came into being during the latter part of the twentieth century in the United States and Canada. Specifically, we explore relationships between psychological theory, research, and intervention practices and the education of students as particular kinds of psychological persons. To do so, we focus on major research and intervention programs of educational psychologists that led to heightened concerns and greater efforts to ensure that pupils in schools experience and achieve certain kinds of self-understanding and act in ways consistent with these self-conceptions. In short, to use Ian Hacking's (2006) apt phrase, this is a book about how psychology participated in the "making up" of students as particular kinds of psychological beings—that is, selves. Our central claim is that scientific and professional psychology in the latter half of the twentieth century, especially in the United States and Canada, transformed the ways in which students understood, experienced, and conducted themselves and the ways in which teachers, parents, and the broader society thought about and interacted with them. Previous generations had thought about students as apprentices, who learned by observation and imitation, or as "knowledge sponges," who soaked up the facts, principles, and rules that enabled the mastery of subjects such as mathematics and history. However, by the 1990s, the scientific and professional knowledge and practices of psychologists afforded a distinctively psychological conception of students as self-expressive, entrepreneurially self-managing, and entitled participants in their own education. Such students required new forms of education that placed as much or more emphasis on the personal development, interests, and entitlement of students (understood as uniquely capable and valuable psychological individuals) as on their intellectual development or transformation into productive citizens and members of their communities. At its best, students' development as psychological selves has been linked to higher levels of student confidence and motivation. At its worst, it has been linked to dysfunctional levels of self-absorption and self-interest. Although the first decade of the twenty-first century has witnessed a mounting reaction against the "education of selves," which we will consider, our main purpose is to understand better some of what happened at the interface of

---

[1] The noun *psychology* refers to the discipline, science, and profession of psychology.

psychology and education in the last 50 years of the twentieth century in American and Canadian education and schooling. In particular, we will attempt to describe and explain how and why psychology became sufficiently influential in the schools of the United States and Canada that it was able to foster the transformation in student understanding, experience, and conduct that occurred between 1950 and 2000. It is our conviction that such knowledge will enrich current and future discussions about the role of education in the development of citizens and persons and the role of psychology in education.

The Idea of an Applied Psychological Science

Central to psychology's influence on education and schooling is its claim to scientific status, a status that has been enshrined in conventional histories of psychology and trumpeted in psychologists' proclamations of scientific discovery and advance, which promise to enhance our individual and collective well-being. In North America, psychology is widely understood as the scientific study of mind and behavior, including areas such as human development, personality, cognition and learning, emotional adjustment, cognitive neuroscience, and sociocultural studies, with applications in psychotherapy, health psychology, forensic psychology, industrial/organizational psychology, and, of course, educational psychology. According to the American Psychological Association (APA), "in every conceivable setting from scientific research centers to mental health care services, 'the understanding of behavior' is the enterprise of psychologists" (2008, p. 1). The basic model of psychological training and practice endorsed by the APA is a "scientist-practitioner" model, in which professional psychologists are considered to be applied scientists with unique expertise in the application of scientifically based psychological knowledge to almost any area of human activity. It is the widespread acceptance of the scientific status of psychology and its applications in education that we consider the key to understanding how psychology changed students during the twentieth century. After all, this was a century, especially in the United States and Canada, of unprecedented scientific discovery and technological innovation that dramatically altered people's lives, and many became enthralled with the power and promise of science as a source of solutions and advances in face of the challenges of everyday family and working life.

The modern discipline of psychology is founded on an Enlightenment understanding of human individuality, one that treats individuals as distinct from others and self-governing (Danziger, 1997b; Fay, 1996; Popkewitz, 1998). In the eighteenth century, the British nations embraced Enlightenment liberal ideals of representative government, individuality, and scientific reason (Popkewitz, 1998; Rose, 1998, 1999). Western psychology, despite an initial flirtation with German intellectual traditions during the late nineteenth century, mostly descended from this British empiricist tradition and replaced older, religiously based moral discourses about "revealed truth" and "character" with a new discourse about "human nature" and "personality." From its inception as a distinctive discipline in the late 1800s, psychology has tended to treat human experience and behavior as governed by natural laws that describe and explain our mental lives in terms of our conscious sensory experience (Leahey, 1992).

At the outset of the twentieth century in North America, there was a growing interest in applying a scientific approach to social problems. Given the obvious success of natural physical science in early-twentieth-century industry and medicine, what was thought to be needed was a social science based on the physical sciences. From this point of view, psychology occupied a key place among the sciences. It provided an important link between the natural and social sciences, and its investigations were expected to yield knowledge of basic laws about both animals and humans (Brennan, 1986)—laws that could be applied to individual and collective life for the general benefit of humankind.

In psychology, the scientific method has been assumed to be the best way to uncover universal laws of human nature, and the natural sciences have been assumed to provide methodological standards for the study of mind and behavior. The scientific method adopted by psychologists emphasizes the systematic observation and measurement of phenomena of interest and stresses the importance of objective testing of hypotheses to determine which ones fit relevant facts. Studies and experiments centered on the impartial assessment of hypotheses are thought to allow psychologists to grasp the laws governing our psychological lives. The conviction that such nomological understanding can be achieved with the objectivism of natural science assumes that mind and self exist independently as psychological objects that scientific psychologists can know as such. In practice, such objective knowing frequently requires considerable theoretical and methodological flexibility.[2] Nonetheless, the stated purpose of psychological research is to test objectively hypotheses and theories about human experience and behavior that assume law-like relationships. To this end, psychological constructs, like self-concept, are treated as variables that can be measured to enable specific research hypotheses to be tested (e.g., individuals with more favorable self-concepts will be more successful in school than individuals with less favorable self-concepts).

In the period of behaviorism and neobehaviorism during the first part of the twentieth century, scientific objectivity was safeguarded by a strong emphasis on the behavior of humans and other animals. Animal learning experiments supported the view of behavior as something that "individuals" did (Danziger, 1997a). The focus of study in these experiments was the behavior of isolated animals within highly constrained physical environments (e.g., rat mazes and Skinner boxes). The study of behavior as an activity of individual organisms in such quarters effectively restricted the environment to a small number of external "stimuli." Over time, the vocabulary employed in descriptive studies of

---

[2] For example, "self-concept" may be scaled as one or more dimensional variables and measured for research purposes by respondents' ratings of items on self-report questionnaires, even though the self-concept itself is assumed to be an inner psychological state of individual persons.

behavior in stimulus–response psychology expanded to include terms such as *independent, dependent,* and *intervening variables*. For example, Edward Tolman's work, as described in his 1932 book *Purposive Behavior in Animals and Men*, introduced intraindividual events as intervening variables that functioned as "behavior-determinants" (p. 412).

By the mid-twentieth century, talk about stimuli was being replaced by talk about independent variables, and talk about responses was giving way to talk about dependent variables. Objects of investigation now were defined in terms of categories such as "experimental variables," or "social variables." Importantly, the term *variable* allowed for the investigation of psychological constructs that previously had been excluded from experimentation. For example, correlations among measures that were not experimentally expressible in stimulus–response terms (e.g., self-esteem and other "personality" variables) could now be scientifically investigated. The story of this "opening up" of scientific psychology to include measures of intraindividual personality variables such as self-concept is an especially important one for our purposes in this volume and will be addressed in much greater detail in Chapter 5. However, for now, it is sufficient to note that psychologists have continued to treat psychological phenomena primarily as attributes of individuals, with little consideration of the broader social contexts in which individuals live their lives.

Today, under the persistent sway of the scientific method (as psychologists have interpreted and adapted it), psychological studies are focused on a host of individual cognitive processes and mechanisms that were of little interest to earlier generations of behaviorists. For example, processes of informational input and output, cognitive operations and structures, and patterns of neurophysiological stimulation, activation, and inhibition are now much in vogue. However, empirical relationships among psychological phenomena are still commonly identified in terms of relationships between dependent and independent variables.

Traditional Histories of Psychology as an Applied Science

Psychology's scientific mode of inquiry, at least in principle, requires that explicit theories about psychological events and phenomena be corrected in light of new empirical evidence. Traditional histories of psychology, common in psychological textbooks and classic historical works in the discipline, assume this view of the history of psychology and its objects of study. Thus, traditional histories of psychology and applied psychology typically portray "a succession of progressively better theories, with development primarily attributed to cognitive factors: the analytic and experimental power of scientific procedure, that has allowed us to weed out misconceptions and bring us closer to the truth" (van Drunen & Jansz, 2004, p. 2).

For example, traditional historical works regarding the self are generally organized chronologically to reflect their contributions to the advancement of current conceptions and theories of the self. Thus, the historical works of James (1890), Erikson (1950), and Maslow (1943), among others (e.g., Bandura, 1977; Coopersmith, 1967; Freud, 1960/1923), are discussed in relation to their influence on the theoretical and research developments found in contemporary studies of self-constructs such as self-esteem, self-concept, self-efficacy, and self-regulation (e.g., Pajares & Schunk, 2002).

These historical analyses emphasize important theories, events, trends, studies, and researchers as contributing factors to a progressive understanding of individual behavior and the advancement of psychology as a discipline and profession. For example, Hock's (2002) *Forty Studies that Changed Psychology* discusses psychological studies that are "arguably the most famous, the most important, or the most influential in the history of psychology" (p. xii). Hock informs his readers that "the studies you are about to experience in this book have benefited all of humankind in many ways and to varying degrees. The history of psychological research is a relatively short one, but it is filled with the richness and excitement of discovering human nature" (2002, p. xviii).

This quotation makes it clear that scientific psychology is closely linked, in the minds of many psychologists and in the formal pronouncements of major psychological organizations, with professional applications of psychology for the good of both individuals and their communities. Indeed, from its founding as an independent discipline, psychology and psychologists have been interested in linking applications of scientifically based psychological knowledge to human improvement at both individual and collective levels through a wide range of professional interventions (Benjamin, 2007). As we shall see in Chapter 3, education has been a favored area for the application of psychological theories and research findings throughout the history of psychology. The close linkage between scientific and professional progress is one of the key features of psychology as a discipline and profession, one that has been maintained and broadened throughout its history. Today, the scientist-practitioner model of the American Psychological Association is assumed in a wide and expanding variety of psychological products and services marketed to the general public and to most social institutions, including educational systems and schools. In all of these instances, the basic "sales pitch" is the same—these products and services are scientifically tested and proven in ways that reflect the best contemporary scientific and professional practices of highly trained psychologists expert in psychological science and its applications.

The Idea of a Critical History of Psychology

In recent decades, the traditional approach to psychological science has been challenged (e.g., Danziger, 1990; Rose, 1998; Williams, 2005). The basis for this challenge is that the "natural science" view of psychology tends to ignore the social, cultural, historical, and political contexts of human experience. According to Fay (1996), psychology's attempt to apply natural laws to human experience demonstrates a commitment to methodological individualism, which explains social phenomena in terms of individual "behavior."

Underlying this individualism is an ontological atomism, which purports that "human needs, capacities and motivations arise in each individual without regard to any specific feature of social groups or social interactions" (Fay, 1996, p. 23). Thus, social context is explained by individual dispositions rather than the other way around. This interpretation of social phenomena, derived from the liberal ideology of the Enlightenment, understands the basic unit of social life as the individual. That is, we see ourselves as individuals, not as members of a group (Fay, 1996).

Although the scientific method may appear to make the study of the psychological properties of individuals more precise and potentially quantifiable and the entities themselves more clearly identifiable, the carefully controlled and relatively sterile contexts of the psychological laboratory frequently simplify and even prevent a proper study of persons in the contexts in which they live and act. For, properly understood, persons are social as well as biological beings whose psychological capabilities develop through interactions with others and objects in a world that is not only biophysical but also sociocultural. Kurt Danziger (1990, 1997a) explains how psychology has rejected the archival, textual methods of history and the real-life observational methods of anthropology in favor of the experimental methods of natural science. According to Danziger, the rejection of these and other venerable methods of social science is part of psychology's relentless campaign to be granted (and to benefit from) the status of a natural science. As such, scientific psychological research is assumed to be concerned with natural objects and processes, not historical or cultural objects and processes (Danziger, 1997a).

Psychology's adoption of seemingly neutral, asocial, and depersonalized terms—such as *behavior, stimulus–response*, and *variable*—has further reduced human social experience to proximate, external factors that can be separated from the core individual. The language of dependent and independent variables provides an aura of scientific neutrality and objectivity in descriptions of the social environment and the attributes and actions of individuals. Such language has a nonreflective quality, which has the effect of eliminating the 'subjective' meaning of a situation and replacing it with a new scientific explanation "in which 'persons' respond under the 'influence' of 'variables' that have the solidity of physical objects" (Danziger, 1997a, p. 171; also see Ash, 2005).

Psychology's goal of the progressive accumulation of scientifically derived knowledge about human nature also extends to historical inquiries within psychology. Traditional historical investigations, sometimes referred to as "Whig" histories, portray historical events as having direct relevance to contemporary concerns and research questions (what is called "presentism"), a rational and ameliorative evolution ("progressivism"), and an independence from social, political, and other contextual influences ("internalism") (Hilgard, Leary, & McGuire, 1991; Morawski, 1987).

> A Whig account of history sees history as a series of progressive steps leading up to our current state of enlightenment. A Whig history of science assumes that present-day science is essentially correct, or at least superior to that of the past, and tells the

story of science in terms of how brilliant scientists discovered the truth known to us today .... Whig histories of science are typically internal, seeing science as a self-contained discipline solving well-defined problems by rational use of the scientific method, unaffected by whatever social changes may be occurring at the same time. (Leahey, 1992, p. 35)

Some scholars (e.g., Taylor, 1995) have argued that the social sciences, including psychology, require methodologies that go beyond those common in the natural sciences. As early as the mid-nineteenth century, Dilthey (1989/1883) understood all science as sets of social and institutional practices, assumptions, and methodologies that have evolved both historically and culturally. Thus, science and its practices may be different in different times and places. Dilthey also recognized *meaning* as the central concept in the social sciences. Humans act intentionally and for reasons, and both intentions and reasons are infused with meaning. Based on such considerations, contemporary critical approaches to the history of psychology, including its objects and methods of inquiry, situate the scientific and professional practices of psychology within relevant sociocultural and historical contexts, contexts that help to clarify the social and personal meanings of these practices. Such an emphasis on context marks the works of historians of psychology such as Danziger (1990, 1997a), Herman (1995), Rose (1998, 1999), and others. According to the tenets of critical history, the past cannot be reconstructed, but we can construct perspectives on the past that can be tested by recourse to the various historical sources and traces that are available (see McCulloch & Richardson, 2000, and Megill, 2007, for introductions to contemporary critical history and its methods).

Moreover, such historical perspectives are relevant to concerns of the present *not* because they can yield prescriptions about what we ought to do and/or what will work. Instead, perspectives gleaned from critical historical inquiry are instructive because they demonstrate that things have not always been the way they are now and that what we currently take for granted and assume or presuppose uncritically is not the natural consequence of universal laws or edicts but the contingent consequence of particular patterns of sociocultural historical evolution and change. In other words, in human affairs, current conditions and practices could have been, have been, and might be once again different from what they are now. Thus, the entire purpose of critical historical inquiry, especially in the social and psychological sciences, is to increase our awareness of the ways in which social historical conditions and practices (including the assumptions, methods, findings, teachings, and interventions of social and psychological scientists) have entered into the history of our current societal institutions and practices (in areas such as politics and education) and even into our contemporary understandings of ourselves and others.

For example, Popkewitz, Pereyra, and Franklin (2001) illustrate how educators, educational theorists, and historians of education have interpreted education and schooling differently at different times. In the early part of the twentieth century, many educators and traditional historians saw the public school as an institution of democracy and progress. In contrast, revisionist historians in the 1960s and 1970s placed social regulation and control at the center of their inquiries, seeing school as an enterprise of power and control that middle/upper classes held over racial minorities and the urban poor. In their Foucaultian (named after French scholar, Michel Foucault) critical analysis, Popkewitz and colleagues (2001) contend that schools do not function simply to reproduce the existing culture. Rather, like other social institutions, schools are sites of contradictory and conflicting goals in which efforts of regulation and control are more implicit than explicit and may be resisted as much as they are embraced.

Popkewitz and associates (2001) define their critical perspective as "cultural history." Cultural history is a critical consideration of the present by making its manufacture of collective memories concerning the past available for examination and amendment. Cultural history examines the ways in which different systems of knowledge (available and used at different times and places) organize our sense of our selves through rules of reason, action, participation, and reflection. Popkewitz and colleagues understand their approach to be in stark contrast to an "empty history" that paints a picture of "a universal, boundless human progress associated with ideas of an infinite perfectibility, an additive viewpoint whose illusions are of a seemingly continuous movement from the past to the present, and whose methods have no theoretical armature" (Popkewitz et al., 2001, p. 4). This way of doing critical cultural history is particularly instructive for our aims in this book because it gives special emphasis to the ways in which the methods and practices of social and psychological science have contributed to our understanding of ourselves as distinctively psychological beings—that is, selves. In the general literature of critical historical studies in psychology, a salient hypothesis concerning the self-fashioning role of psychology and related disciplines, especially the practices associated with the research and professional arms of such disciplines, has been dubbed the "psy" hypothesis.

The "Psy" Hypothesis

The psy hypothesis was suggested initially by Michel Foucault (1965, 1986, 1988), but it has been elaborated and illustrated within psychology by Nikolas Rose (1998), Kurt Danziger (1997a, 1997b), Ian Hacking (1995, 1998, 2002), and Philip Cushman (1995) and within education by Thomas Popkewitz (1991), and Robin Usher and Richard Edwards (1994), among others. In both his early and later works, Foucault considered what Rose (1998) refers to as the "psy" disciplines (e.g., psychology, psychiatry, psychotherapy) as important social practices that shape our views of ourselves—as means through which we learn to examine aspects of ourselves in ways that make sense to ourselves and others. Where once we wrote letters, kept diaries, and went to confession, contemporary persons increasingly also take stock of themselves and attempt to manage themselves according to the psy discourses.

The psy hypothesis is the assertion that many of the disciplines and professions bearing the prefix *psy*, but especially psychology, are powerful technologies of the self that, especially in Western societies, have elevated and emphasized our everyday individuality in ways amenable to its management, both by individuals themselves and by others. By individualizing humans through measuring their capacities, classifying them on the basis of such calibrations, and inscribing and recording their attributes, deficiencies, individuality, and variability, disciplinary psychology has emerged as an influential technology of the self in Western societies. The effect of such psychological practices is to lend a visibility, stability, and seeming simplicity to aspects of persons that otherwise might remain hidden, shifting, and mired in complexities. And through these methods the phenomenal world also is normalized, so that individuals whose personal attributes and characteristics deviate from values deemed normal are made to stand out to themselves and others. Thus, we can now be aware of and concerned about this one's learning disabilities, that one's antisocial personality, and another's strongly positive or overly negative self-concept. And so can those thus afflicted. Moreover, with such categorizations come expert interventions and the promotion of professional services to society at large through its existing institutions, like schools, or through newly formed institutions, such as institutes for psychotherapy.

Consistent with and illustrative of such practices are psychological research and interventions focusing on self-concept. As Danziger (1997a) describes, such research became possible once psychologists had begun to explain everything from changing fashions to swings in public opinion and declines in traditional moral standards to the attitudes of individual citizens (e.g., Allport, 1937). For these psychologists, attitude went well beyond a disposition to act. In a move consistent with the increased individualism evident in American culture between the First and Second World Wars and since, psychologists gradually began to talk as if attitudes were real entities interior to and possessed by every functioning person. Once developed, the attitudes of a person were considered to be relatively permanent, inner possessions that exerted a causal influence on what a person believed, thought, and did.

The "natural reality" of psychologists' conception of attitudes was confirmed in the minds of most psychologists and many others when L. L. Thurstone and his student Rensis Likert developed various methods of measuring the attitudes of individuals (cf. Danziger, 1997a, pp. 146–152). The most popular of these consisted of simply asking people to rate the extent to which they agreed or disagreed with a variety of statements concerning whatever it was that was being measured. Such a method was related to methods then in use for purposes of public opinion polling and marketing research. Nonetheless, when it was coupled with psychologists' convictions that attitudes were "inferred entities that existed within the individual below the surface of observable behavior" (Danziger, 1997a, p. 148) and that these entities could be scaled and measured along a linear continuum know as "the attitude variable" (Danziger, 1997a, p. 150), many were convinced that the attitude measures of psychologists constituted an important scientific achievement. Psychology seemed to have succeeded in advancing itself in ways reminiscent of how increasingly sophisticated methods of physical measurement were associated with advances in the natural sciences, especially as portrayed in a new philosophy of science known as empirical realism, which at the time was eclipsing logical positivism as a basis for the practice of natural and social science.

With the practical use of psychological attitude research during and after the Second World War, the measurement of soldiers' and civilians' attitudes became widely accepted as a scientific practice in areas such as recruitment, personnel selection, and vocational and educational guidance. With popular use, the assumption that attitudes were natural possessions of individuals rather than discipline-enhancing creations of psychologists was reinforced. With attitudes measured and understood as inner psychological properties of individuals, different combinations of attitudes soon became associated with particular kinds of persons and understood as personality types or traits. Psychological research on attitudes and personality consisted of obtaining agree/disagree responses to a variety of questions (which could be interpreted psychologically) from a large number of individuals (typically and most conveniently, groups of students) and subjecting seemingly meticulous quantifications of these responses to a variety of statistical procedures. Of particular interest here is the way in which psychometric and statistical methods have been used in psychology to reduce the complexities of everyday human motivation, thought, and action to seemingly objective scores on psychological tests of attitudes and personality traits that serve the applied "scientific" interests of professional psychology. Whereas basic experimental psychology has employed biological, neurophysiological, and computational strategies of reduction in quasi-laboratory settings, professional psychology has made use of psychological measurement and statistics to extend the constructions of psychologists to the world outside the laboratory in ways that command the attention of the pubic and elevate the status of psychological science and practice in the popular mind.

Research on almost any attitude or personality trait proposed by psychologists as worthy of scientific or practical consideration now could be undertaken, including research on attitudes that individuals have about themselves. Within the historical tradition of psychological research on attitudes, aspects of selfhood—such as self-concept—are understood by psychologists to consist of causally efficacious properties of individuals that are implicated in a wide variety of personal actions and experiences and can be measured by individual responses to an appropriately constructed psychological measure. By creating numerous items on measures that claim to reveal a person's self-concept or self-esteem, generations of psychologists have operationalized the self. For many psychologists and others, an individual's ratings of the extent to which statements such as "I feel good about myself most of the time" are "more or less like me" not only describe but actually constitute the self.

The self understood as self-concept or self-esteem is thus made more accessible, but only at the obvious cost of reducing it to attitudinal variables that could be scaled and "measured" from sets of ratings on the questionnaires of psychologists. In effect, the entire exercise transforms an important set of metaphysical and ontological issues concerning the nature of human existence and agency to a grossly simplified exercise in methodology. For many scientific and practical purposes, the self has become a latent construct inferred from self-ratings on a particular instrument at a specific time and place. Psychologists have obtained what they consider to be a scientifically respectable method of measuring the self and have not been shy about advancing professional implications of their technical achievement. In Chapters 4 and 5, we will offer more detailed critical and conceptual histories of the psychology of self-esteem and self-concept and its incorporation into educational theories and classroom practices during the twentieth century. However, for the moment, it is instructive to consider another aspect of critical history, one initiated by Foucault and developed by contemporary neo-Foucaultians such as Nikolas Rose (1998).

Technologies/Practices of Selfhood

A technology is "any assembly [of practices and related conventions and artifacts] structured by a practical rationality governed by a more or less conscious goal" (Rose, 1998, p. 26). A critical analysis of the technologies that have evolved to shape human conduct in liberal democracies elucidates our contemporary experience of ourselves as certain types of persons—as free, self-governing, self-powering, and self-realized individuals. Through the critical examination of social-psychological technologies, one can examine how numerous institutional technologies (in settings such as schools, workplaces, governments, and disciplines, including the personal relations embedded therein) have helped to shape the self. For example, the school (through its structuring of time, space, subject matter and relations among teachers, students, parents, and staff) fosters students' incorporation of educational structures, processes, and content into their understanding and governance of their own conduct. Through their participation in schooling, they learn to understand, treat, motivate, and react to themselves and their actions in ways authorized by teachers and incorporated within educational activities and materials. Thus, given the values and practices evident in much contemporary public education in liberal democracies, schooling helps to constitute students as autonomous, self-governing individuals. To the extent that psychology enters into the determination of educational values and practices, it enters into the constitution of students as particular kinds of persons—that is, as psychologically concerned self-determining agents.

Modes of governing the self in nonpolitical domains (such as the technical knowledge and practices of experts, the organizational knowledge and practices of managers, or the interpersonal knowledge and relations within families) help to sanction political powers to govern individuals (selves) in particular ways (Rose, 1998). Rose argues that all of these technologies of the self can be understood in ways that foster and support particular political objectives. Thus, in liberal societies, practices and conventions in areas such as child rearing, personal relations, business, the military, and education produce ways of thinking, acting, and feeling in relation to autonomy, virtue, and harmony; yet at the same time they do not challenge or oppose the exercise of appropriate forms of social and political power. Rose (1998) contends that effective contemporary governance in liberal democracies is concerned with the ways that free individuals can be governed to use their freedom in appropriate ways. In this sense, power is not about domination and repression of subjectivity but about the ways in which influence can be exercised through subjectivity. It is here that disciplinary psychology has proven invaluable in contemporary liberal democracies. For it is in furnishing particular conceptions of selfhood and techniques for achieving and acting in accordance with these conceptions (within both institutional, public and personal life) that psychology has aided and abetted forms of subjectivity amenable to self-governance within liberal societies. Close affinity of psychology with liberal governance is afforded by the liberal argument to the effect that the collective good just is personal liberty. In other words, what is good for free individuals is necessarily good for their community.

Foucault describes all "technologies of the self," as techniques that

permit individuals to effect by their own means or with the help of others a certain number of operations on their own bodies and souls, thoughts, conduct and way of being, so as to transform themselves in order to attain a certain state of happiness, purity, wisdom, perfection, or immortality. (Foucault, 1988, p. 18)

In his early work, Foucault examined how the kinds of subjects that social institutions (such as schools, factories, hospitals, courts of law, and prisons) have constituted individuals to be have varied over time. In his later work, he turned to the study of technologies of the self that have their origins in social practices but function as tools through which we act on ourselves to create, reconstruct, and understand ourselves as subjects (e.g., confessions, letter writing, examinations/quizzes, clubs/cults, psychotherapy, psychology). When we utilize technologies of the self to shape and constitute ourselves, we are practicing freedom. However, this freedom and its practice may be linked to a variety of other interests, subservience to which may occasion more restriction than liberation. When the various technologies of the self that we employ are directed by scientific experts and others whose interests do not necessarily converge with our own, they may become oppressive and degenerate into techniques of domination. The concern of many neo-Foucaultians (e.g., Rose, 1998) is that too often in contemporary society the self has become a commodity for commercial and political interests. The irony is that in pursuing individual freedom we may adopt technologies of the self that actually reduce our freedom.

Whether focusing on discursive practices within disciplines like psychology or relations of power within social life in general, Foucault (1970, 1980, 1986, 1988) draws our attention to the contingent character of much of our knowledge about the world and ourselves. In psychology, our currently favored social scientific theories are not so much better, more true, or more functional than many other past and current systems of belief as they are different. Foucault suggests that the human social sciences aim at truth but deceptively understand and help to produce people in their own scientific and professional terms.

Of particular importance in psychology and education is the institution of schooling, which operates as a human technology and supports and educates or trains persons in various technologies of self. School is technological in that it seeks to organize the activities of persons under a "practical rationality directed toward certain goals" (Rose, 1998, p. 153). School attempts to maximize certain abilities of persons and constrain others in accordance with pedagogical knowledge inclined toward liberal objectives of autonomy, self-discipline, and self-development. However, the technology of school does not operate on its own. Psychological products or types of knowledge have been transported into contemporary Western schooling practices on various levels. For example, psychological procedures of authoritative observation and normalizing judgment have resulted in the individual's adoption of these practices to govern his or her own conduct (Rose, 1998). Thus, an individual's attributes and experiences can be compared to those of persons deemed to be psychologically normal and therefore desirable and can be adjusted accordingly. Psychology has become a technique for human management (Danziger, 1997a; Rose, 1998) that has expanded far beyond psychological laboratories and investigations to the management and education of selves.

For example, psychological and educational testing in schools encourages administrators and teachers to scrutinize students in ways consistent with particular conceptions of personal and social competence advanced in specific psychoeducational theories and practices. As a consequence of psychoeducational testing and interventions, teachers are able to recognize and treat students as gifted, having attention deficit hyperactivity disorder, suffering from test anxiety, being dyslexic, having been traumatized, being appropriately assertive, or possessing untapped leadership potential. But even more subtly and pervasively, students recognize and treat themselves according to these same categories, classifications, and associated ameliorative regimens. Disciplinary psychology has come to exert a powerful influence on the education of contemporary persons in that it gives us both language and practices for self-surveillance and self-intervention.

Of course, any field of human endeavor may exert important influences on the development of persons in educational contexts. Recent history is replete with examples of extramural influences on education and schooling, from the successful launch of the Sputnik 1 satellite in 1957 to the more recent tragedy of the Columbine massacre in 1999. Moreover, as Olson (2003) reminds us, schools as institutions have always provided and implemented norms, standards, and criteria for the assessment of student learning that have influenced our sense of what is and is not of value in ourselves and our activities. As such, the existing institutional structures and traditions of schools will continue to exert powerful influences on the education of persons, whatever disciplinary psychology brings to the school setting. Therefore, psychological practices and discourses in education must be considered alongside other sociocultural practices and discourses as these play out within the unfolding of historically established, institutional traditions of schooling.

Nonetheless, disciplinary psychology may warrant particular attention as a source of conceptions, categories, and practices of selfhood in educational contexts because it promises a harmonization of the sociocultural and personal aims of education. Educational aims such as preparing students for productive participation in the bureaucratic institutions of the larger society (as workers and citizens) may be seen as at odds with aims such as helping students to maximize their own talents and capabilities in ways that fulfill them as individuals. The former expectation assumes a level of engagement with systematic disciplinary knowledge adequate to the everyday demands of social, economic, and political functioning within a society. The latter assumes the cultivation and expression of understanding and action in accordance with personal interests and goals. Common educational purposes, such as intellectual development, may, of course, be viewed as in the service of any or all of the societal, institutional, or individual developmental goals of education. In this context, psychology may be perceived as a vehicle capable of delivering a broadly humanistic form of self-governance that permits desired levels of individual expression and fulfillment within an appropriately constrained and discipline-focused institutional framework that ensures both citizenship and social responsibility.

However, our position (one that we hope to support in the chapters to follow) is that the impact of psychological discourses and practices on the education of students in the United States and Canada has to date not been one of harmonizing the social and personal goals of schooling. During the period from 1950 to 2000 in particular, rather than helping to produce citizens and persons capable of contributing to the development and transformation of their communities and themselves in socially productive ways, psychological discourses, methods, and practices in schools have championed highly individualistic, inward-looking forms of selfhood that have helped make many students increasingly expressive, strategic, and entrepreneurial in pursuit of their own self-interest. As will become readily apparent in Chapter 3, this psychologized version of the self has both humanistic Romantic and scientific Enlightenment aspects but is primarily active in the service of its own instrumental gratification.

Preliminary Contentions and an Overview of What Is to Come

Since the self has been made readily accessible to psychological conceptualization, measurement, research, and intervention, it has become a tractable focus for the applications of professional psychology in education, psychotherapy, vocational counseling, and industrial-organizational psychology. In all of these areas, professional psychologists now routinely engage in and talk about how their interventions positively affect the self-esteem of students, clients, job seekers, and employees. The fact that at the dawn of the twenty-first century it was possible to walk into many elementary school classrooms in North America and find posters advertising all those things that students like about themselves and that make them special is but one example of the pervasive impact of psychologists' "self" research and practice. The obvious fact that one is not especially unique because one "can ride a bicycle" or "has a brother," is of little consequence in a world of facile descriptions masquerading as genuine self-consideration and reflection. In some psychological measures, human agency has been reduced to checking a "most of the time" box at the end of a written description of mostly uninteresting and uninspired dispositions and actions.

Of course many psychologists would regard such facile applications as unmitigated nonsense. Nonetheless it seems clear that this particular kind of nonsense would not exist were it not for psychology's mostly unwavering commitment to the idea that supposedly substantive agentic entities like self-concept can be measured successfully by the descriptions and rating scales employed in much psychological research and intervention. By reducing the question of selfhood or personhood to a mere description of how one currently is doing (as seen through the instruments of professional psychology), it becomes possible to achieve seemingly amazing results through rather straightforward psychological interventions purporting to enhance the self-esteem and self-worth of students, clients, and others. In the individualistic, self-concerned cultural context of America between 1950 and 2000, these interventions of professional psychology, aided and abetted by the ostensibly scientific foundation of psychology as a whole, were widely accepted as both efficacious and appropriate. Even now, professional psychological helpers appear on almost every horizon of human triumph or tragedy as these unfold within the North American landscape, typically armed with methods and techniques aimed at preserving the psychological functioning of those individuals who are celebrated or afflicted. And most often contemporary ideals of healthy selfhood developed during the latter part of the twentieth century form a general guide to overall psychological health and functioning.

In a simplified, naturalized psychological world, all the understanding or intervention that is required is one capable of measuring and altering individual responses to psychological measures and expert assessment. Since such understanding and change can be achieved relatively easily in the psychological laboratory, the classroom, or the psychologist's office, there is no need to deal directly with the everyday psychological and sociocultural world in which most complex human difficulties and challenges reside. In a simplified, reified psychological world where all that matters are the inner processes and experiences of individuals, nothing is too difficult to attempt and very few problems fail to yield to a psychological "fix." All that is required is that individuals understand themselves and change according to the ways and means that psychologists have fashioned through their research and clinical or educational practices. By the end of the twentieth century, as organized psychology gradually broadened its public venues and promoted its message with enhanced media "know-how," contemporary societies like the United

States and Canada had become more and more saturated with what might be regarded as some of the worst excesses of psychological scientism and professionalism. In concerned reaction, the first decade of the twenty-first century has witnessed a considerable backlash against some of the less desirable social consequences of psychological intervention in general (e.g., Baumeister, Campbell, Krueger, & Vohs, 2003; Dineen, 2000; Twenge, 2006; Twenge & Campbell, 2009) and of psychologically infused curricula in schools in particular (e.g., Stout, 2000). Correctly or incorrectly, such critics (including a growing number of psychologists) point to what they now regard as the runaway self-interest and entitlement of so many contemporary individuals both within and outside of schools.

In this book, we will argue that the self-conceptions adopted and promoted by psychologists during the latter part of the twentieth century may be described as broadly scientific and/or humanistic but that in either case the underlying idea was and remains that of a detached, masterful self that is focused on its own inner experience and its instrumental expression. As a result, these psychological conceptions of selfhood tend to be highly self-serving and focused away from our morally saturated concerns and practices as citizens engaged with others, some of whom might be quite different from ourselves.[3]

A further consequence of this sociocultural and political detachment from others is that such selves have relatively little educative value. For the goals of education must surely include the shaping of persons capable of engaging in the complex, layered life world with a critical awareness of that world, its practices, and their inextricable existence within them. Overly simplified linear strategies for managing one's inner psychological life—even if they can and do work to some limited extent on a straightforward, narrowly instrumental basis—must be seen as inadequate to the task of equipping citizens to interact intelligently and sensitively within a contemporary sociopolitical context informed by a variety of historical traditions and critical perspectives. To be tenable, conceptions of the educated person must go well beyond the detached, masterful, yet ultimately empty self that psychological theory, research, and practice have promoted and advanced (cf. Cushman, 1995).

In general we regard as healthy the fact that so much concern now is being expressed about the various matters that we have touched upon in this introductory chapter—matters that we will elaborate in the critical history and analysis of psychology and schooling that occupy the rest of this volume. However, it is our conviction, a conviction encapsulated in the aims of our book, that such concern, if it is to be directed in ways that promote education for the common good, will be more convincing and focused if it is

---

[3] This equation of "self-interest" or "self-serving" with "nonmoral," which we believe to be apt with respect to the kinds of psychological selves promoted in many American and Canadian schools during the second part of the twentieth century, is by no means necessary or axiomatic. In fact, as we will see in Chapter 2, some ancient accounts of personal flourishing (which included notions such as "self-serving") were understood to include concurrently what was good for one's community and others in it.

informed by a close examination of the relationship between psychology and education during the twentieth century, with particular focus on the education of psychological selves as enshrined in psychological theory, research, and practice. We do not contend that such a critical historical framing of relevant events in the recent past can possibly tell us how we ought to proceed with respect to the education of pupils as responsible adult persons. Rather, the aim of such a critical history is to understand our present situation better and to see how we got to this time and place, in which concerns about the purposes and goals of education and schooling with respect to personhood have once again attracted intensive scrutiny. How has it come to pass that the ever-present tension in liberal democracies between personal freedom and civic responsibility seems to have shifted so drastically in the former direction?

In the next chapter (Chapter 2), we provide a brief history of psychological selfhood in which we point to the relatively recent rise in conceptions of selfhood and personhood that celebrate the inner experiences, structures, and processes of individuals as sources of motivation, understanding, and identification. In Chapter 3, we recount a brief and somewhat selective history of educational psychology, that branch of contemporary psychology which has taken the study of what its practitioners regard as psychological aspects of education and schooling as its primary area of focus and expertise. Given the overall themes and aims of our book, it will not surprise the reader to discover that most of the ideas, persons, and events recounted in this chapter relate to psychological theories, research, and interventions concerned with educational policies and practices centered on the self-development of students in schools. However, broader social, cultural, political, and moral contexts within which psychology interacted with education in North America during the twentieth century will also be discussed, as will the interplay between psychology and education positioned within these contexts.

Chapters 4 through 7, then, are devoted to more focused, critical histories that examine ideas, events, persons, contexts, and difficulties/challenges specific to four major programs of self-related theory, research, and intervention in education—self-esteem (Chapter 4), self-concept (Chapter 5), self-efficacy (Chapter 6), and self-regulation (Chapter 7). In Chapter 8, we pull together various themes and patterns that have emerged in these more specific critical histories to develop a complex, multifaceted portrait of the kind of student produced by the various programs of psychological influence and intervention in education that we have discussed in previous chapters. This is an enterprising student, self-expressive and self-governing in the demonstration and pursuit of her or his self-interest. Our final chapter (Chapter 9) examines the recent reaction against what we are calling "the education of selves," and describes an alternative approach that is concerned with the education of communal agents. We conclude this final chapter with a consideration of what we think can be learned from the critical historical analyses we have attempted herein.

2 The Self Before and After Psychology
THE TRANSFORMATION BEGINS

OVER THE PAST few decades a number of philosophers, historians, and psychologists have attempted to trace and describe the sociocultural/historical evolution of the psychological self (Baumeister, 1986; Guignon, 2004; R. Martin & Barresi, 2006; Seigel, 2005, Sorabji, 2006). This is a conception of selfhood that envisions human experience and action as originating in *individual* human beings possessed of an *internal* structure or system that makes uniquely first-person experience, understanding, motivation, and action possible. This individualized and internalized self has been associated with a suite of apparently psychological capabilities, such as self-reflection, reason, two-way volitional control (to act or refrain from acting), first-person perspective, autobiography, psychological identity, self-understanding, and so forth. However, as indicated in the previous chapter, since the rise of disciplinary and professional psychology during the last part of the nineteenth century, such psychological capabilities and the self structures or systems that purportedly support them have most often been assumed to be reducible to more basic biological, behavioral, computational, and neurophysiological processes and structures. The history of psychology as a modern discipline and institution has been marked by a consistently strong commitment to an internalized individual self that renders the psychological makeup of each person unique in both experience and motivation yet is somehow said to be reducible to more basic biophysical mechanisms and entities that can be scientifically examined and illuminated.

As Martin, Sugarman, and Thompson (2003) point out, it is by no means obvious that the reducible selfhood required by scientific psychology is consistent with the agentic self-determination assumed and cultivated by professional psychology. After all, if selves really are nothing more than biological, behavioral, computational, and/or neurophysiological bits and pieces, how can they be thought to do the work that is assumed when psychological therapists, consultants, and practitioners encourage their clients to be more self-determined, self-assertive, and self-reflective? Does our biological neurophysiological makeup really make possible lives filled with meaning, self-concern, personal ambition, and reflection? For the most part, such difficult questions have gone unattended in the history of psychology. And despite a host of theoretical difficulties that seem to hover around the psychological self as an individual, internal, and reducible structure, this conception of selfhood has now become so widely endorsed in so much North American culture and institutional practice that it goes almost unremarked.

In this chapter, we attempt to trace a brief and selective history of the psychological self that we hope will position and clarify our critical history of educational psychology and its impact on the self conceptions of students in American and Canadian classrooms. In doing so, we draw both substance and inspiration from works in the history of psychology and selfhood by Roy Baumeister (1986), Charles Taylor (1989), Kurt Danziger (1990, 1997a,b, 2008), Philip Cushman (1995), Ellen Herman (1995), Charles Guignon (2004), Jeroen Jansz and Peter van Drunen (2004), Raymond Martin and John Barresi (2006), and Jerrold Seigel (2005). Although these various authors present historical accounts that differ in emphasis, theme, and particulars, they all converge on the conclusion that the psychological self as currently advocated by disciplinary, scientific, and professional psychology is a surprisingly recent invention. This conclusion does not imply that individuals have not had first-person experiences, motives, and interests throughout the history of evolved *Homo sapiens*. However, it is to say that only recently in human history have we begun to experience and understand ourselves as psychological beings concerned about such things as our personality traits, self-concepts and self-esteem, and unconscious motivations—beings who turn to psychological means and processes of personal inquiry, guidance, and therapy and often incorporate them into our everyday lives.

Historical Development of the Prepsychological Self

Our ability to read and understand historical, fictional, and autobiographical accounts dating from ancient Greece and Rome through the Middle Ages, Renaissance, Enlightenment, Romantic, and later periods of human history seems to support the idea that people in the past thought about and experienced life more or less as we do today. However, history is a very slippery beast in this regard, and it must never be forgotten that our sense of understanding past persons and events is as much a function of our current ways of conceiving and comprehending as it is of past ways of living and understanding. A good example is the interpretation and use we now make of Plato's ideas concerning ideal forms. Although many contemporary readers of Plato's dialogues understand that Plato thought our conceptions of truth and beauty, if drawn only from the world around us (the world of appearances), pale in comparison to understandings derived from the world of ideal forms, it is less clear that we today fully comprehend the cosmological and religious assumptions, including the belief in the transmigration of souls, implicit in Plato's texts. Nor are we likely to appreciate fully, even with appropriate instruction and assistance, what it was really like for a Roman soldier to endure the privations, hardships, and sacrifices of a legionnaire's life, buoyed by a sense of honor as an all-encompassing virtue. In other words, the understandings we have of the past (including people's experiences, motivations, and interests emanating from their sense of their lives and themselves) frequently relate to and say more about our understandings of our own lives and selves than they do about the understandings and experiences of past persons, societies, and ways of living.

Charles Guignon (2004), following Charles Taylor (1989), offers an instructive interpretation of past conceptions of authentic selfhood in comparison to our current conceptions of authenticity and selfhood. In doing so, Guignon makes a strong case that our conceptions and experiences of selfhood have varied considerably across historical time and place. Guignon begins by noting that it is tempting for people of today to interpret the ancient Socratic dictum "Know thyself" as an injunction to follow the currently popular psychological strategy of "turning inward in order to get clear about our own most personal feelings and desires" (2004, p. 13). However, Guignon goes on to argue that it is very unlikely that Socrates or his popularizer, the great classic philosopher Plato, had any such psychological advice in mind. Rather, according to the Platonic reading of Socrates, individual humans were considered to be parts of a wider cosmic context or ordering of the world and to play particular roles within it. In this context, the best that individual human beings could do was to know their place within the cosmic order.

Far from encouraging a focus on a person's inner feelings and desires, knowing oneself was thought to be a matter of understanding and assessing how one measured up to ideal types and standards that defined one as a particular instance of humanity. In this sense, self-knowledge was not aimed at "being yourself" but rather at coming to understand how to live appropriately according to your nature within the cosmic order. In the case of individual human beings, this meant that they should conduct themselves according to standards of what was right and good as defined by universal ideals for humankind. Thus, in Plato's (1980/360 bce) *Laws*, we read,

> You do not seem to be aware that this and every other creation is for the sake of the whole, and in order that the life of the whole may be blessed; and that you are created for the sake of the whole, and not the whole for the sake of you. (903c)

This is a very far cry from our current psychologically informed conception of authentic self-understanding as emanating from reflection on an inner core of personal experience and recollection. Nonetheless, Plato's philosophy did revolve around a distinction between the world of appearances or quotidian existence and an ideal cosmos of perfect forms and functions for all things (including human beings) that could be *recollected* (remember that Plato and most Greeks of his day believed in the transmigration of souls) through contemplative reason—a distinction that was to have a powerful effect on subsequent thinkers, some of whom eventually formulated more psychological notions of inner reflection and recollection.

Plato's student Aristotle developed a still highly regarded system of ethics in which individual flourishing was linked intimately to the good of the community (more of this in Chapter 9). In contrast to the tensions that we currently experience between individual and collective interest, Plato, Aristotle, and the Greek and Roman Stoics (including Cicero and Seneca) endorsed early forms of what might be regarded as psychological selfhood or perhaps even psychological self-analysis. However, what was striking about these early "psychologies" (although they included many variations on this theme) and remarkably different from those of today was the extent to which the earlier versions tended to a view of self and self-knowledge as relational. Not only did these ancient philosophies caution that the self could be understood only in relation to the cosmos but they also held, more specifically, that relations within a community of social others were fundamental to any notion of selfhood (cf. Nussbaum, 1994; Sorabji, 2006). In consequence, the severing of self-interest from social interest and the good of communities (which is so palpable in the focal events discussed in this book) was neither theoretically nor practically feasible in much ancient thought.

It was Christianity, especially as developed in the influential writings of St. Augustine, including his groundbreaking autobiography (*Confessions*), that first promoted a type of genuinely modern "inwardness" in processes of self-understanding. In many ways, the Christian story, organized around eternal salvation, provided a narrative structure for the self and its transformation. Nonetheless, Augustine's *Confessions* does not treat the self in a modern, secular, psychological way. Augustine does propose a duality of an outer self that is false in contrast to an inner self that is true; however, his inner self is not self-encapsulated but inextricably bound to God. Individual humans are not bound to themselves but are God-directed. The inward turning advocated by Augustine is thus a turning away from worldly things toward God, with the aim of being in the right relation to God—a relation that best guides our worldly comportment. The goal of self-understanding advocated by Augustine is not to get in touch with one's own true inner self but rather to release oneself from egotism, to lose oneself by giving oneself over to the direction of God as the source of one's existence.

Thus, for ancient Greeks and medieval Christians, the self was tethered to—and understandable within—a wider context of organized being (cosmological and theistic); that is, self-understanding connoted an awareness of the interconnectedness and interdependence of all things. Self-knowledge flowed from a recognition of human limitations in the face of forces beyond human control—forces greater than oneself to which one must yield.

Indeed, as Danziger (1997b) has noted, the earliest uses of the word *selfe* in the English language (around 1300) carried strong connotations of a sacrilegious egotism, something to be condemned as a vice rather than celebrated as a virtue. However, from the sixteenth to the eighteenth centuries in western Europe, what we now regard as the modern worldview unfolded gradually in ways that eventually permitted the emergence of more contemporary psychological conceptions of selfhood. One of the best-known lines of English literature, "to thine own self be true," from Shakespeare's *Hamlet*, written toward the end of the sixteenth century, heralds a sea change in the landscape of the self and speaks evocatively across subsequent centuries.

Nonetheless, Shakespeare's intended meaning, around 1590, was probably a long way from our current conceptions of authentic selfhood. In the context of the play, it is quite clear that the injunction to be true to oneself is intended as advice to be true to self in order to be true to others. As Guigon (2004), points out, "there is no suggestion that being true to oneself is valuable in its own right ... what is at stake here is not yet authenticity as we [contemporaries] now understand it, but rather the virtue of sincerity" (p. 26), which is a social, not a personal virtue. Nonetheless, during the sixteenth century there occurred three events that proved crucial to the formation of the modern worldview, including a new sense of a more interior, personal, and private self.

The first of these events was the Protestant Reformation. The reformers aimed to bypass the rigid and authoritarian practices of the Roman Catholic Church (such as the sale of indulgences and other rituals of intercession) by stressing the importance of each individual's devotional relation to God through such practices as individualized confessions focused directly on each person's inner intentions rather than on her or his public actions. Such "practices of inwardness," to adopt Michel Foucault's (1984) apt phrase, encouraged a preoccupation with what was going on within individuals (their intentions, feelings, motives, and desires) and lent credence to a distinction between an inner personal reality that was more true (especially when expressed honestly to God) than an outer personal reality consisting of one's bodily and active presence in the world.

A second event in the sixteenth century, propelled by the work and writings of early scientists like Galileo, was the advent of modern science. The relevance of modern science to the prepsychology of selfhood is to be found in the methodological objectivism through which these early investigators approached and understood the world and their works. The role of the scientist as a detached, masterful observer and discoverer of the physical laws of the universe created an anthropocentric conception of the inquiring person as a knowing subject who objectifies, understands, and controls objects and events. It is only in relation to such a knowing subject that the universe and its secrets unfold. This new, scientifically equipped individual sought power and mastery over nature with mathematical precision and elegance. No longer were persons and their selves content to find a limited place in the cosmos in compliance with the grand scheme of things and in accordance with the will of God.

Somewhat later, when René Descartes talked about making ourselves masters of nature, he implied not only that, through science, we could remake the world according to a rational plan but that we could also remake ourselves, for we too are natural beings subject to the laws of science and their strategic application. It was Descartes' thought and writings, in particular, that introduced an enduring duality between subjectivity or mind on the one hand versus body and world on the other. In his famous *cogito ergo sum* ("I think, therefore I am"), Descartes (1960/1641) claimed that the only thing that was beyond doubt, established a convincing proof of his own personal existence, and could be depended upon as a reliable foundation for knowledge of the world and himself was his own thinking. With the beginnings of modern science, the knowing subject and the knowledge garnered by human scientific technologies became powers with which to reckon.

The third event—initiated during the sixteenth century (but more fully realized in the centuries that followed)—that exerted a significant impact on the emergence of the prepsychological self concerned a new understanding of the relation between individuals and societies. Whereas people in ancient and medieval times had thought of the universe as a single cosmological order within which both nature and society were structured, this new understanding—probably encouraged by the greater social mobility that followed the dissolution of feudalism—viewed societies as human-made through various processes of social contracting among individuals. Philosophers like Thomas Hobbes (1962/1651) began to talk about society as a contractual arrangement agreed to by individuals as a desirable alternative to an imagined natural condition characterized as a war of all against all. For Hobbes, society was merely a collection of isolated self-concerned individuals whose motives he reduced to their own appetites, the most fundamental of which he considered to be the lust for power. Nonetheless, despite their basic asociality, such individuals contracted together for their mutual benefit so as to avoid their own destruction. Consistent with his reductive individualism, Hobbes thought that the causes of society were to be found in individuals. He did not place any importance on the possibility of reciprocal influence of societies on their individual members. In fact, he regarded men as fully developed in the absence of social relations—"The causes of the social compound reside in men as if but even now sprung out of the earth and suddenly, like mushrooms, come to full maturity without all kinds of engagement to each other" (Hobbes, 1962, Vol. 1, p. 109).

Together, the Protestant Reformation, the rise of modern science, and the view of individuals as society makers greatly enhanced a sense of persons as individual subjects possessed of significant capabilities and powers that enabled them to know and construct nature, society, and themselves. However, all of this, as undeniably important as it is for understanding the prepsychological self, stops short of any idea of the self as an inner psychological structure that can be employed instrumentally for the attainment of individual ends in ways signifying personal health. To trace the beginnings of more truly psychological ways of thinking about ourselves, both Charles Taylor (1989) and Kurt

Danziger (1997b) draw our attention to the ideas and works of John Locke, whom they regard as pivotal in the history of the psychological self.

Locke's approach to selfhood was both empirical and psychological in that he rejected the extreme reductionism of Hobbes and the dualism of Descartes. Locke understood selfhood to equate to a psychological form of personal identity that consisted of a continuity of consciousness enabled by memory and imagination. Locke held that individuals, by remembering past experiences and imagining future actions, experience themselves as retaining the same identity over time. "Since consciousness always accompanies thinking, and it is that which makes every one to be what he calls self, and thereby distinguishes himself from all other thinking things, in this alone consists personal identity" (Locke, 1959/1693, I, p. 450). Locke's emphasis on the continuity of consciousness and remembrance as constitutive of identity or selfhood was directly related to a form of self-examination that, in many ways, anticipated more contemporary forms of psychological self-examination. The self thus conceptualized appropriates actions undertaken in the past and contemplated in the future, for which an individual accepts responsibility.

It is these aspects of Locke's thought that Taylor (1989) and Danziger (1997b) stress in recognizing Locke's ideas as harbingers of contemporary psychological selfhood. Both Taylor and Danziger understand the Lockean self as differentiated from an individual's experiences and actions in a way that allows the self (as a continuing consciousness that somehow lies behind both experiences and acts) to monitor, reflect upon, understand, and determine its conduct. As the owner and collector of its actions, this is a self that is engaged in a relentless process of self-objectification. Therefore, both Taylor and Danziger stress that the Lockean self is a punctual self that may be understood as "composed of empirical phenomena that can be observed, analyzed, and known, just like other worldly phenomena" (Danziger, 1997b, p. 142). Although for Locke the appropriate vantage point for relevant observations of the consequences of selfhood was both private and introspective, his emphasis on *observation* left a powerful legacy for a wide variety of more contemporary, empirically minded psychologists. The idea that the self and its experiences and actions could be observed and studied in ways that could illuminate individuals' motives, tendencies, and actions has been a core assumption of almost all subsequent systems of psychological thought. In recognizing this historical legacy, Taylor and Danziger have identified John Locke as the father of the psychological self and its empirical study.

However, at least some recent scholars have argued that such interpretations of Locke's writings on identity and selfhood have tended to ignore important social aspects of Locke's thought. For example, Jerrold Seigel (2005) has taken Taylor (1989) to task for tending to gloss over the extent to which Locke regarded the self as tethered to both the body and society. Seigel argues convincingly that the personal identity that Locke established as a continuity of consciousness "existed together with the organic identity every individual possessed as a 'man'; however reflective the first became it never substituted for the corporeal identity of the second" (2005, p. 99). The Lockean self was always embodied. Consequently, "what memory tied together was not merely a series of states of consciousness, but a range of actions carried out by bodily means" (2005, p. 99). Moreover, not only is the Lockean self not isolated from the body and its worldly commerce, Locke also recognized that "our first person viewpoint grounds a selfhood that is incomplete and imperfect, given all the ways in which we may fail to recognize aspects of ourselves, through forgetting, willful denial, or mental weakness" (Seigel, 2005, p. 102). Finally, as interpreted by Seigel, Locke did not neglect a strong relational dimension in his discussions of personal identity. For in stressing the moral responsibility each individual had for personal actions, Locke recognized that individuals do not exist entirely on their own terms. Indeed, some of Locke's followers (e.g., Edmund Law, 1769, as cited by Seigel, p. 104) argued that Locke, by "making personhood a matter of responsibility for one's acts ... [recognized] that personal identity was essentially a social matter."

However Locke's treatment of selfhood is interpreted with respect to the extent of its embodiment and sociality, there can be no question that, by taking the self as a set of consciously continuous and accessible experiences and actions, Locke paved the way for subsequent programs of self-examination and self-study that eventually contributed to those programs of psychological research and intervention with which we are concerned in this book. Several eighteenth-century European scholars built upon Locke's ideas in diverse ways that both agreed and disagreed with positions taken by Locke himself. Some, such as David Hume, were highly skeptical of Locke's claim that the self was an agent capable of choosing and determining experiences and actions and thus taking responsibility for personal conduct. In fact, Hume went so far as to question the very existence of the self and denied that our experiences, memories, imaginings, and personal identifications required any kind of inner psychological self at all. However, against Hume, many British moralists (e.g., Bishop Butler and Thomas Reid) strongly supported the idea of a morally responsible self that could be enlisted as a reflective monitoring agent to assist individuals in policing their conduct for the longer-term interests of both themselves and society.

As discussed by Seigel (2005), Locke's ideas concerning conscious self-reflection and moral agency as prominent features of selfhood were developed in a particularly interesting and innovative way by Adam Smith. Smith (1976/1759) interpreted moral agency as a form of self-control necessary to govern oneself according to ethical and social imperatives, which he referred to as *self-command*. What was perhaps most novel about Smith's approach was that he attributed the development of self-command (and the self more generally) to a sympathetic openness to others and their concerns. For Smith, social interaction with others encouraged self-development in that it is through engaging with others that we come to see ourselves and to understand our responsibility for gaining control (self-command) over our feelings and behavior as well as our ability to do so. Although Smith's ideas concerning the genesis of selfhood in our social, interpersonal engagement with others pointed to a possibly productive way of theorizing relations between social engagement and personal development, they proved to be no match for the much more adversarial relationship between self and society advanced by Jean-Jacques Rousseau.

Perhaps no eighteenth-century thinker was to be as influential in the history of prepsychological and psychological selfhood as Rousseau. As Seigel (2005) notes, "Jean-Jacques Rousseau occupies the most prominent place in the history of self-awareness and self-examination" (p. 210). Rousseau not only theorized a highly contradictory self forged from the conflicting forces of nature and society but also formulated, in his text *Émile*, the first and one of the most influential articulations of psychological development and its educational implications. But he did not stop there. Equally importantly, he helped to create the foundation for contemporary ideas of self-understanding, self-expression, and authenticity, which motivated both nineteenth-century Romantics and twentieth-century psychologists. Thus, the centrality of Rousseau's ideas to a critical history of educational psychology with respect to the educational consequences of psychological conceptions of selfhood is undeniable. Rousseau's understanding of selfhood shared with Smith (and also with some interpreters of Locke) the idea that social experience was necessary for self-understanding. However, Rousseau also maintained that the social life and relations that selfhood required carried the seeds of self-destruction because of their oppressiveness—an oppressiveness born of invidious and inequitable social opportunities and comparisons that robbed individuals of their naturally good and transparent self-love (*amour de soi-même*) and replaced it with an inauthentic and self-destructive self-regard (*amour propre*).

In contrast to Hobbes' portrayal of natural human existence as "a war of all against all," Rousseau imagined an idealized pastoral place and time in which natural humans enjoyed simple, uncomplicated existences mostly unencumbered by enforced social routines, regulations, and fashions. In such a state, all individuals would enjoy nonreflective natural pleasure in their free movement and unfiltered, unspoiled experiences while also feeling a natural sympathy (*pitié*) with others. However, as people began to live together in stable communities that provided a sense of persistence and particularity in the identities of individuals, they begin to depend on others not only for their daily subsistence but also for their sense of self-acceptance and self-regard. They began to compare themselves to others and against the views of others. As social arrangements became increasingly entrenched and hierarchical, the innocent love of their own existence (which included compassion for others) dissolved into a kind of self-regard that finds and seeks both satisfaction and discontent in relation to others; eventually it issues in desires to dominate, use, and/ or succumb to others. In this way formerly free beings are subjected to the inevitable consequences of social life. On the one hand, they are able to identify and experience themselves as individual beings, related to yet separate from others. On the other hand, they fall prey to a host of social comparisons and artificialities that prevent them from forming idealized and authentic attachments to themselves and others. Of particular importance here is Rousseau's understanding of reason as a socially enabled form of reflection that supplants more basic and authentic modes of existence ruled by unsullied passion for life and experience.

Rousseau's own life (as related in his autobiography—which, like Augustine's, was also entitled *Confessions*—and in numerous biographies) testified dramatically to the inescapable tensions created by our inevitably conflicted social existence. In his great political work *The Social Contract*, Rousseau attempted to envision ways to overcome these tensions between society and self and between different forms of selfhood; however, it is clear that he never really succeeded in doing so, either in his scholarship or his life. In the words of Seigel (2005),

> By his last decade, he [Rousseau] had concluded that it was just … [these tensions] that made him unable to live in society, because interaction with others imposes an expectation of continuity and stability on his behavior that he found both oppressive and destructive of his best impulses. (p. 219)

Many scholars devoted to Rousseau's life and works have noted the ways in which his ideas concerning the complex relations between society and selfhood heralded a new age of authenticity and self-expression in human experience. Starobinski (1988) explains that with Rousseau, "We have moved from the realm of truth to that of authenticity" (p. 198). To which Guignon (2004) adds, "What comes to light as authentic truth (i.e., subjective truth) is the activity of self-fashioning or self-making itself. We just are what we make of ourselves in the course of our quest for self-definition." And further, "Once we have the image of self-discovery formulated by Rousseau, the task of self-knowledge and self-realization can be thought of not merely as similar to artistic creation, but as the ultimate form of artistic creation, the form to which all the other arts, as self-expressions, are subordinate" (p. 69).

What Rousseau bequeathed to the Romantics and some of the founders of disciplinary psychology in the nineteenth century was the idea that to be yourself is to accept the task of self making in a way that grants authenticity to your own genuine feelings of the moment. Needless to say, this was a message that found resonance in Romantic poetry, music, and art—for example,

> To let each impression and each germ of a feeling come to completion wholly in itself, in the dark, in the inexpressible, the unconscious, beyond the reach of one's own intelligence, and await with deep humility and patience the birth-hour of a new clarity: that alone is living the artist's life: in understanding and creating. (Rilke, 1954/1903–1908, pp. 29–30)

In the words of Wordsworth (1966), "The mind of man becomes a thousand times more beautiful than the earth on which he dwells" (xiv, 450). With Rousseau and the Romantics, all of the prepsychological ingredients are in place for a new psychological view of selfhood that is related to objective truth and science on the one hand (the Lockean legacy) and to subjective authenticity and artistic creativity on the other (the Rousseauian legacy). The former tradition of selfhood values and privileges methods of objective self-monitoring and rational consideration. The latter tradition of selfhood values and privileges methods of subjective experience and affective expression.

The abbreviated history of prepsychological conceptions of selfhood that has been presented here is necessarily highly selective and restricted to only a handful of relevant historical figures, ideas, and sociocultural transformations. However, it hopefully serves to demonstrate that the ways in which human beings have understood themselves have varied considerably over the course of our history and sociocultural evolution. Our contemporary understanding of ourselves as deeply psychological beings is not a consequence of some sort of natural endowment, impervious to time and place, but rather bears the marks of a long and complex history of changing traditions and ways of life both active and reflective. We now turn to a brief historical consideration of modern conceptions of selfhood that have informed the discipline of psychology from its inception in the late nineteenth century and, most particularly for our purposes, influenced the ways in which psychology interacted with education in the last half of the twentieth century with respect to promoting particular forms of selfhood in school settings.

Historical Development of the Psychological Self Proper

Both Lockean and Rousseauian conceptions of selfhood have exerted considerable influence on the ways in which disciplinary, scientific, and professional psychology has understood psychological personhood. In what follows we hope to clarify the ways in which the theories, research, and interventions of psychologists regarding the self have incorporated and attempted to integrate both objective/rational and subjective/affective conceptions of selfhood using rhetoric and methods that celebrate structured self-examination and self-regulation on the one hand and creative self-discovery and self-expression on the other.

Attempts to integrate such seemingly incompatible self-conceptions are evident in the work of two of the founding fathers of modern psychology, William James and Sigmund Freud. For a brief period in the late nineteenth and early twentieth centuries, integrative theorizing about the self dominated the work of a first generation of psychologists who focused on relations between society and selfhood, relations that continuously transform our ways of being in the world and experiencing it. However, as we shall see, this systematic, complex undertaking soon gave way to distinctively modern psychological ways of reframing the self as a highly individuated, internal, and reductively simplified set of psychological processes and structures that could be located within the immediate surroundings and inner experiences of individual persons with little concern for broader historical, sociocultural, and contextual considerations. In what follows, we will emphasize how this dramatic reframing of selfhood served the purposes of disciplinary psychology as a newly emergent independent field of social scientific study in ways increasingly consistent with (1) the idea that psychology should be developed as a science analogous to physics and (2) the rise of a new, radical form of political and social individualism in American and Canadian society during the twentieth century.

But first, to position the emergence of psychology as an independent social science of mind and selfhood around 1879, a brief consideration of social and political conditions during the nineteenth century will be helpful. It was during this century that many of the tendencies toward individualism that have been discussed thus far achieved fruition. By the early 1800s, traditional rural societies grounded in the collective life of extended families and villages were being supplanted by expanding urban centers in which anonymous individuals interacted for short-term purposes of trade, commerce, and industry. This shifting demographic was fueled by improved means of agriculture and sanitation that increased production and health to the point where large numbers of people could be fed and accommodated in large cities, with fewer dying of hunger and disease. Through industrial expansion, many people acquired significant wealth, resulting in greater social inequalities. Economic booms for some existed alongside crises of poverty for others. Nonetheless an emerging middle class, especially in the United States, clamored for greater political influence, especially at civic levels, where they endorsed a bourgeois politics of liberal individualism that increasingly attributed political rights and responsibilities to individuals rather than to village councils or urban corporations.

At the same time, organized religion was increasingly challenged by secular and scientific orientations to private and public life. Many politicians, in particular, now looked to secular, scientific means of organizing social life, including methods of quantification that could be employed to chart urban populations in order to provide necessary services and infrastructure (Rose, 1998). In these and other ways, the idea of a scientific analysis of social life, focused on individual rights and duties, strengthened the appeal of liberal individualism as both a public and personal creed. New discourses and practices concerning one's social position emerged that emphasized individual achievements and personal characteristics. Such individualism freed many from more long-standing traditional attachments to communities and churches, even if it also courted instability and insecurity in everyday life. In the face of increased social competition and pressures, individual members of urban communities championed their rights and freedoms as well as their own opinions and lifestyles, especially in the privacy of their own homes. This separation of private from public life was accompanied by more rigid divisions of labor between the sexes and greater concern for individual well-being versus the common good of communities.

At the same time and in the wake of Darwin's publication of his theory of evolution, some social Darwinists began to advocate social and political views that increasingly emphasized the relative success of individuals by attributing it to differences in character and ability. In cases where economic and demographic circumstances seemed insufficient to account for differences in relative success, new forms of explanation focusing on the mental characteristics of individuals began to flourish (van Drunen & Jansz, 2004). During the mid- to late 1800s, especially in Europe and the United States, practices such as phrenology (inferring mental characteristics from the shape of the skull), eugenics, and early forms of psychometric (mental) measurement (e.g., Galton, 1973/1883) were much in vogue. A focus on the material success and well-being of individuals was particularly pronounced in the United States.

The new emphasis on personal character, ability, and success was also accompanied by an interest in individuality of a quite different kind. Freed from the daily exigencies of ensuring their immediate survival, many members of the middle and upper classes embraced Romantic ideas concerning the centrality and importance of feelings and superior sensibilities that originated in a deeply interior aspect of one's person, a source of intuition and "gut instinct" that could be relied upon, sometimes even more so than reason and calculation. Self-scrutiny of an authentic inner self was evident in much of the popular literature and poetry of the day, and diaries and autobiographies flourished.

In some quarters, the idea of deeply interior forms and sources of selfhood was further burnished by a newly available belief in unconscious processes and structures of personality that were understood to lie behind one's conscious experience and conduct. As Baumeister (1986) has argued, English Victorians were especially concerned that their innermost motives and desires might be inadvertently displayed through involuntary public acts of self-disclosure, leading to greater efforts to self-monitor a complex psychological interior. Supported by reports of hypnotic and dissociative states (e.g., Hacking, 1995), attempts at deeply interior forms of self-surveillance became increasingly common. All in all, by the final quarter of the nineteenth century, many urban dwellers, and those charged with their political administration, had embraced forms of self-understanding that were increasingly individualistic, inwardly focused, and removed from the hurly burly of public life involving others. For these individuals, private life was paramount as a refuge from the travails of a competitive, challenging society, and as a source of self-fulfillment through acts of self-reliance. The best that might be expected under such circumstances was to be left alone to conduct one's personal life in relative separation from others—an ambition that could be fostered by a rugged individualism, competitively poised in public and reflectively contemplated in private.

Not surprisingly, such an inner individualism provided a rich grounding for the emergence of disciplinary psychology in the last two decades of the nineteenth century. The focus on individual abilities, characteristics, and inner processes by individual members of society, and the concern with counting and assessing individuals as a prerequisite to more efficient means of governance of urban communities (Rose, 1998), combined to create a fertile soil in which newly emergent psychological theories of mind, self, and conduct could find nurturance. Such theories, as developed by the founding fathers of scientific and professional psychology during the last part of the nineteenth century, and as embellished and refined throughout the twentieth century, significantly augmented and transformed ideas concerning the reductively individualized and internalized forms of selfhood just discussed.

However, it is important to emphasize that the full impact of the trinity of individualism, internalism, and reductionism on psychological theories of selfhood did not manifest until the mid-twentieth century. In what remains of this chapter we offer a general sketch of the history of the psychological self proper (i.e., as developed by scientific and professional psychologists), from the late 1800s to the end of the twentieth century. In subsequent chapters, especially in Chapters 3 to 7, we provide much more detailed and critical historical accounts of the conceptions of selfhood favored by educational psychologists (Chapter 3), and promoted in programs of psychological theory, research, and practice in the areas of self-esteem (Chapter 4), self-concept (Chapter 4), self-efficacy (Chapter 5), and self-regulation (Chapter 6). But for now a much more general historical overview of the period from 1880 to 2000 will suffice.

In the late 1800s in the United States and Canada, psychological ideas concerning the self were influenced greatly by the writings of William James and Sigmund Freud. Although Freud's ideas have subsequently exerted a pervasive influence on many areas of contemporary life from the arts to the economy, it was the ideas of William James that captured the attention of many disciplinary psychologists during the 1890s and early 1900s. Although sympathetic to empirical research in psychology and certainly not unaffected by the nascent individualism in American society just described, James authored a comprehensive and balanced theory of the self.

In his *Principles of Psychology*, James (1890) observed that the self, or more precisely our experience or consciousness of ourselves, has both subjective and objective aspects. In other words, we are conscious of ourselves as both subjects and objects of our experience. James referred to the subjective self (the "I") as pure ego, and although suggesting that such a self seems necessary as a "knower" and "experiencer," struggled with Humean skepticism concerning whether or not we could know and say anything about this self, which seems to be responsible for our experience and consciousness but itself seems to lie beyond our experience and consciousness. According to James, the self as knower cannot know itself other than as an empirical objective self. Consequently it was James's conception of the empirical self (the self as object) that occupied most of his theorizing. In fact, James discussed at least three different, yet related and integrated empirical selves. The *material self* is made up of all of those things that we understand as ours—one's body, possessions, and those others with whom one interacts. The *social self* consists of the reactions of others toward us and consequently is known to us as a somewhat incongruent set of others' reactions, conveying impressions of ourselves that may differ quite considerably across different others and different interactions and relations with them. Finally, the last aspect of the empirical ("Me") self is the *spiritual self*, which includes a person's "inner or subjective being" (James, 1890 p. 296). For James, the spiritual self did not equate with a soul or necessarily connote religious beliefs. It consisted of that constant stream of experiential consciousness which attends our lives and which we recognize as ours. Of all our experiences, it is our feelings that seem to relate to and reveal the most about our private selves.

Although James's self is both multiple and comprehensive, recognizing social as well as psychological constituents of our selfhood, he nonetheless stays within the emerging tradition of a distinctively psychological approach to the question of the self (its existence, nature, and functions). He holds that a major life task for all of us is to find a defining character and role, one that gives a sense of unity and purpose to our lives. For James, being fully human is a matter of embracing some sense of core selfhood above and beyond all others. "So the seeker of his truest, strongest, deepest self must review the list carefully, and pick out the one on which to stake his salvation. All other selves thereupon become unreal" (James, 1890, p. 294). Thus, when all is said and done, William James, widely recognized as the founder of American psychology, comes down in favor of an inner psychological self for which individuals themselves are responsible. Although not a reductionist in the manner of many members of subsequent generations of American behavioral, cognitive, and biological psychologists, James clearly privileged the inner individual—a hallmark of mainstream psychology throughout the twentieth century.

The idea of a deeply interior psychological self accessible to psychological expertise was much more fully developed in the contributions of Sigmund Freud. When set against James's "stream of consciousness" as the defining character of the inner self, Freud's most enduring contribution to psychology is the idea that we are mostly unaware ("unconscious") of the true psychological mechanisms and processes that determine our experiences and actions. As both an "internalist" and a "determinist," Freud believed in deeply interior psychological causes of our experience and conduct. However, unlike James and most other academic psychologists of his day, Freud held that the most powerful genesis of our experiences and actions are internal forces about which we have little conscious awareness and even less knowledge, and over which we have little or limited agentic control: "We are lived by unknown and uncontrollable forces" (Freud, 1960/1923, p. 17). The Freudian psychic mechanism operates at a mostly unconscious level and is the real cause of our doing the things we do, with the conscious ego or self little more than a surface appendage. According to Freud, when excitation or pressure of any sort is introduced into the psychic apparatus, we experience such pressure as physical and psychological upset, which we expunge by behaving in ways into which we frequently have little insight. This being so, the ultimate quest of all living things is to reach "a complete and final quiescence" (Guignon, 2004, p. 99).

Freud's ideas concerning the psychosexual origins of psychological pressures and their behavioral symptomatic release have become part of contemporary popular culture. So much so, in fact, that (perhaps somewhat mimicking Freud's patients' ignorance of the sources of their symptoms) we are seldom conscious of their origination in the unique theoretical synthesis crafted by Freud and his followers over 100 years ago. For Freud's ideas not only introduced a purportedly real and highly influential causal force to our psychological interiors but also helped to pave the way for a view of psychology as a domain of expertise with theories and practices capable of exorcizing our inner psychological demons.

Like Rousseau, Freud held "that what we call civilization is largely responsible for our misery, and that we should be much happier if we gave it up and returned to primitive conditions" (Freud, 1961/1930, p. 12). However, unlike Rousseau, Freud admonished us to "get over it." Since we now cannot live without civilization, we are doomed to a life of suffering and coping as best we can with its costs, some of which are manifest in the sexual and aggressive interpersonal relations bred within our evolved and "civilized" existence—an existence within which we are, by nature, far from good. In consequence, it is only by learning to tame our wilder and more destructive impulses under the sway of social regulations and inhibitions that we are of any use to ourselves and others. As Guignon (2004) puts it,

> From this standpoint, the distrust of the social circumstances of life in the older conception of authenticity [Rousseau's] now seems highly problematic. Society may inhibit and repress us, it seems, but it is also the only thing standing between us and "The Horror" Kurtz saw in Joseph Conrad's *Heart of Darkness*. (p. 104)

Whatever mysteries of selfhood James and Freud entertained through their respective metaphors of "the stream of consciousness" and "the death instinct," the early days of disciplinary psychology were populated by a wide variety of psychological theories positing forms of psychological selfhood that were not only highly individual and interior but also thought to relate in various ways to the social conditions and events of our lives. James, Freud, and other early psychologists were not interested in cutting us off entirely from our social lives with others; they found a place within their theories for the inevitable tensions their psychological theorizing created with respect to self–other relations—for example, James's social self as part of his empirical "Me" and Freud's emphasis on society as both fueling and assuaging our antisocial tendencies. Still others, during the early days of psychology, offered more harmonious and formative theories that related selfhood to its social conditions.

As Valsiner and van der Veer (2000) point out, a few early psychologists developed social, relational theories of human development that understood selfhood as actually constituted in our relations with others within social interactions and practices. In the United States and Canada, these socially attuned psychologists included James Mark Baldwin, John Dewey, and George Herbert Mead, all of whom understood selfhood as requiring interactivity with others as a means of differentiating oneself from others and taking and understanding positions, actions, and attitudes from first-, second-, and third-person perspectives. Mead (1934), in particular, held that we are not born with self-consciousness and a first-person perspective but rather develop these and other aspects of ourselves by interacting with others, thus gradually coming to react to ourselves as others have reacted to us. When such self-responding occurs, we become aware of ourselves as both objects that can be known and subjects that are capable of such knowing. Although this aspect of Mead's thought bears some similarity to James's understanding of the self as both an "I" and a "Me," Mead explicitly theorized the self as remaining in constant lifelong interaction with the perspectives of others and the society at large in ways that constituted selfhood in increasingly abstracted and multifaceted ways. Such ongoing interactivity was essential for the self as an agentic source of novelty, creativity, and problem solving. Thus, unlike many later twentieth-century theories and programs of research concerned with selfhood, Mead and other early sociogenetic psychologists understood self-development in highly social terms. For them, the best way in which to develop and refine our sense and understanding of ourselves was to look around to the reactions, perspectives, and possibilities for self-development resident in our interpersonal, social, and cultural contexts. Such an interactive, relational strategy stands in stark contrast to the search for an authentic inner core of psychological wisdom and direction that is somehow built into our psychobiological being.

Eventually, however, theories such as Mead's—with its emphases on social and cultural traditions and practices together with its complex social-psychological dynamics—proved difficult to test empirically, at least according to what many psychologists understood to be the methods of physical science, which they assumed also ought to apply to psychological phenomena such as the self and mind. Moreover, the valuing of communal attachments and collective enterprises ran counter to newly emergent North American values of individualism and entrepreneurship. Public demand and economic support flowed in the direction of individual self making and success, not in the direction of social, communal, and collective life in cooperation with others. In consequence, after a promising start during the early days of disciplinary psychology, the first generation of psychologists committed to the study of persons interacting holistically with others within the social and cultural world was eclipsed during the first half of the twentieth century (especially in North America), and much of the time since then, by other programs of inquiry in psychology.

During the early and middle twentieth century in North America, behavioral approaches to psychology that studied the activity of a variety of animals (including humans), under highly controlled and restricted conditions, fitted well with then popular doctrines of experimental manipulation and design (Winston, 1990). These approaches were joined, during the 1930s, by newly formulated approaches to the study of personality that made extensive use of self-report questionnaires and statistical psychometric techniques. By abandoning sociocultural context altogether in favor of standardized assessments employing mostly paper-and-pencil measures, the new personality psychology promised greater mathematical/scientific precision and generality (Nicholson, 2003).

During the last half of the twentieth century (the period of particular relevance to our examination of the influence of psychology on education with respect to changing conceptions of students as psychological selves), psychologists of different orientations working in the various subdisciplines of psychology conducted a variety of "self" studies. Humanistic psychologists contributed a new, even more radical form of individualism and interiorism by insisting on the uniqueness of each and every individual person and advancing doctrines of self-actualization, self-assertion, and self-reflection that, despite occasional testimonials to the importance of communal life with others, mostly facilitated levels of self-concern and self-searching previously unknown in the annals of Western civilization.[1] At roughly the same time, cognitive psychology came into prominence and eventually replaced behavioral psychology as the mainstream orientation of psychologists after 1960. Buoyed by powerful metaphors of information and computer processing, cognitive psychology soon morphed into cognitive science and cognitive neuroscience, understood as rigorous sciences capable of exhuming the true inner sources (computational by analogy and neurophysiological in actuality) of one's mind and selfhood. Thus, major programs of psychological research during the last half of the twentieth century (programs concerned with self-concept, self-esteem, self-efficacy, and self-regulation) focused primarily on the inner psychological functioning of private selves and displayed little concern with aspects of personhood such as character, moral agency, biographical detail, or social relations (Martin, 2007).

Complementing and furthering psychology's late-twentieth-century unprecedented focus on interior selfhood was a long-standing tradition of experimentation in social and developmental psychology that effectively restricted social influences on psychological subjects (such as sociocultural traditions, artifacts, rituals, conventions, and practices) to independent variables that exert proximal, local, short-term, and decomposable effects on the actions of individuals acting in highly constrained laboratory situations (Danziger, 2000). In effect, such experimental manipulations effectively reduced culture and society to a small number of contextually detached, here-and-now interactions between researchers or their confederates and research subjects (typically university undergraduates). Thus, the mainstream psychology of the late twentieth century succeeded in reducing both persons and their historical, sociocultural contexts through a combination of humanistic and cognitive emphases that directed the theoretical and empirical activities of most psychologists to our innermost experiences and feelings on the one hand and to our neurophysiological and cognitive processes, structures, and mechanisms on the other. In these ways, psychology during the later twentieth century achieved an unparalleled focus on the interiors of individuals, celebrating inwardly tuned individuals who search for the true sources and most basic elements of their psychological lives.

---

[1] It is often said that radical individualism is a typically American sociocultural phenomenon that dates to at least the American Constitution and the Revolution of 1776. However, this claim has been convincingly refuted by historians like Barry Alan Shain (1994), who argues that for the vast majority of its existence, American society emphasized "a good political life that is enduring, democratic, and communal" (p. xviii). Such an assessment is consistent with our conviction that the impact of twentieth century psychology on the individualism clearly evident in many quarters of contemporary American and Canadian societies should not be underestimated.

Of course there were occasional exceptions to the foregoing attempts of mainstream psychology and psychologists to reduce persons to selves that purportedly could be measured through the personality and self-report measures and procedures of psychologists or could be equated to the functioning of cats, dogs, and rats in mazes and puzzle boxes, or to information-processing flowcharts, or to the running of computational software. By 1980, a new generation of sociocultural psychologists began once again to advocate more truly relational, contextualized approaches to psychology. These psychologists drew not only on the earlier sociogenetic labors of Baldwin, Dewey, and Mead in North America but also on the cultural historical psychology of Lev Vygotsky in Russia and the works of a wide variety of European psychologists who had adopted more critical poststructuralist and postmodern perspectives on contemporary forms of radical individualism, reductionism, and scientism. At the same time, a minority of psychoanalytically oriented psychologists (building on the work of pioneers like Alfred Adler, Harry Stack Sullivan, and Ian Suttie) began to exert a small but consistent influence in more applied areas of psychology. However, such efforts to reform the strong individualism and reductive internalism of mainstream cognitive science made few significant inroads prior to the twenty-first century.

As we shall see in the chapters to follow, the unfortunate fate of most alternative, more socially oriented psychological theories during the twentieth century was to be marginalized by highly popular and powerful forms of behavioral and cognitive psychology that championed highly individualistic and reductive approaches. It was these mainstream approaches that enabled the emergence of a variety of self studies in psychology and applied psychology that supported and extended an increasingly narcissistic, decontextualized individualism in American and Canadian society during the 1960s to the end of the twentieth century—much of which remains with us today, despite many recent and strong reactions against such self-absorption.

Conclusions and Implications for a Critical History of Educational Psychology

Our primary purpose in this chapter has been to provide a brief and selective history of the psychological self, understood as a highly individualistic and internalized source of our experiences and actions that is removed from particular social and cultural contexts, circumstances, and interactions with others. It is clear that certain aspects of such a self have an ancient history. Nonetheless, the combination of individualism and internalism that mark the psychological self has only recently become associated with a scientific worldview that understands such a self as reducible to our cognitive and neurophysiological processes and structures. The result is a self that is highly amenable to the research and interventional practices of disciplinary psychology, especially as it has developed in American and Canadian societies.

Specific attention to many of the details concerning the history of the psychological self during the twentieth century is deferred to Chapters 3 to 7, which contain critical histories of educational psychology in general, and of psychological theory, research, and intervention in the areas of self-esteem, self-concept, self-efficacy, and self-regulation in particular, especially as applied to the education of pupils in American and Canadian schools from 1950 to 2000. Before approaching these topics, it is important to emphasize that the conception of the psychological self as an interior possession of individuals—one that issues from, and may be reduced to our cognitive neurophysiological makeup—is a very recent understanding. It is easy for contemporaries to overlook this key historical fact because this conception of the psychological self has become so pervasive in North America that it is now more or less taken for granted in the popular media and our every-day lives.

Many ancients and medievalists attributed their inner thoughts and feelings to their gods in ways that reflected a natural ordering of the cosmos and their limited places within it. Most citizens of the Enlightenment and Romantic eras retained a compara-tively limited sense of themselves and their duties and responsibilities—a sense that was tied to their social locations, customs, and positions. However, during the last half of the twentieth century, many people began to understand their selves as powerful sources of experiences and actions that they could come to know and control so as to achieve their life goals and free themselves of circumstances that they were anxious to discard. This deep sense of creative expression and agentic control of ourselves and our destinies was aided and abetted in no small measure by the ideas, methods, and ministrations of scien-tific and professional psychology.

Disciplinary psychology has not only promoted particular understandings of our-selves as sole proprietors and masters of our life experiences and accomplishments and helped us to adopt them but has also has created new ways for us to develop, act, and be particular kinds of persons. In Chapter 1, we discussed some of the ways in which critical historians of psychology like Nikolas Rose (1998) have used the ideas of Michel Foucault to examine the ways in which psychology has helped to institute particular practices of self-governance in Western liberal democracies—practices that somewhat deceptively encourage each of us to practice means of self-regulation consistent with the comport-ment of ouselves as freely choosing, satisfied, and responsible citizens and consumers. For Rose and other critical psychologists, psychology is a set of scientific and professional practices of self-understanding and self-regulation that makes available highly effective institutional technologies through which people can actualize themselves in ways that fit easily and comfortably within the expectations of modern industrialized democracies and their governments. In consequence, our deeply psychological ways of understanding ourselves and acting on our self-assessments and desires tend, for the most part, to be good for the societal status quo. To put it most bluntly, as long as we are mostly concerned with our inner individual selves, we tend to seek contentment in ways that discourage concern with our social, political, and economic circumstances and systems and their careful examination. Whereas medieval serfs were oppressed by force, many of us today willingly participate in our own oppression under the guise of optimizing our individual psychological health and well-being without significant involvement in social or political activities aimed at improving the broader contexts of our communal lives.

In fairness, it is also clearly the case that our current, psychologically enabled conceptions of ourselves, our interests, our rights, and our perceived needs also have an undeniable "up side." For when we do manage to direct our attention and concerns to matters outside of ourselves, our enhanced capacities for reflection and concern and awareness of our rights and responsibilities sometimes can help us to act individually and collectively in organized and sophisticated ways that obviously would be impossible in the absence of a sense of ourselves as individuals who have the right to our concerns and feel some degree of confidence in our abilities to make things happen. Thus, as we shall also see in the chapters to come, our contemporary psychological selfhood is both bane and boon, ally and traitor. Consequently, although what we offer in this book is a critical history of the psychological self in relation to education and schooling, it is important not to ignore or dismiss the fact that possibilities for positive, desired forms of personal and communal life require some aspects of what we refer to as the psychological self (or selves). Our primary targets in the pages to follow are what we regard as several particularly pernicious aspects of the influences of self psychology on American and Canadian education from 1950 to 2000. Nonetheless, before we conclude, we hope to make it clear that we are not advocating a wholesale or total abandonment of everything associated with these conceptions of selfhood.

A good way to prepare readers for what follows is briefly to describe some of the ideas of Canadian philosopher of science and historian of psychology Ian Hacking (1995, 1998, 2002, 2006) concerning the ways in which psychology has contributed to the making up of new ways of being persons. Hacking's approach, what he refers to as *historical ontology*, is based on the claim that new kinds of things have emerged and continue to emerge throughout human history. Some of these things are concrete cultural artifacts, such as different styles and kinds of housing, tools, machines, and clothing. Some of them are less concrete but nonetheless influential technologies, such as printing, computing, and digital imagery. Still others are even more abstracted but still influential, such as systems of mathematics, languages, currencies and the economic systems that accompany them, trade agreements, and academic disciplines such as physics and psychology. All of these things—as they are developed, refined, and employed by human beings—transform both the biophysical (think of pollution) and sociocultural (think of inner cities) world.

What Hacking wants to add to this eclectic and far-reaching set of emergent entities and processes is the idea that as human inventions, technologies, domains of knowledge, and institutional arrangements emerge and are modified over time, they are incorporated into our language and social practices in ways that make possible different ways of being persons. For example, with airplanes and air travel came the professional occupation of airline pilot, which, when inhabited by individual human beings, morphed into an entire lifestyle (a way of being a person), complete with expectations and actualities of layovers in exotic locales, physical requirements and examinations, and responsibilities for cabin/craft crews and passengers. Very little of this way of being a person could have been imagined, let alone experienced, before the historical emergence of aircraft and the international flight industry. Moreover, what has just been said about airline pilots also holds for radio DJs, wedding planners, computer engineers, personal coaches, and a host of other occupation-centered ways of being persons. Even more generally, the language we use, and the conventions and practices that grow up around this primary tool of social interaction and organization, picks out and recognizes different possibilities for our personal being and development. For example, not only the lives of professional detectives but also our everyday tendencies to inquire into mysterious happenings and the ways in which we do so owe much to the modern genre of detective fiction, which developed as recently as the mid-1800s, with initial texts by Charles Dickens, his friend Wilkie Collins, and others.

Within his framework of historical ontology, Hacking (1995, 1998, 2002) has a particular interest in examining the ways in which the theories, research, and interventional practices of psychologists have made possible new ways of being persons. Like Foucault (see Chapter 1), Hacking believes that psychology provides a powerful set of perceptual and conceptual lenses through which many of us—who act under the various descriptive possibilities afforded by the ideas, methods, and procedures of psychologists—come to understand and present ourselves. In his 1995 book *Rewriting the Soul: Multiple Personality and the Sciences of Memory*, Hacking provides a detailed historical analysis of how psychological research on memory came to be combined with particular kinds of psychotherapeutic interventions—and with cultural fixations on dissociated personality and celebrity in the literature and media—especially during the 1980s in the United States and Europe. According to Hacking, these and other relevant sociocultural and psychological ideas and practices made it possible for certain individuals to experience and act out their lives as "multiples," individuals with several distinct personalities that may be subjected to therapeutic methods (such as encouraging a "multiple" to engage in conversations between her different personalities) to effect greater psychological health. To the extent that the theories, research, and professional practices of psychologists furnish us with new ways to classify and act, they provide us with new ways of being persons, with self-understandings, identities, actions, and lifestyles that were not previously available and inhabited.

> A new way or modified mode of classification may systematically affect the people who are so classified, or the people themselves may rebel against the knowers, the classifiers, the science that classifies them. Such interactions may lead to changes in the people who are classified, and hence in what is known about them.... Inventing or molding a new kind, a new classification, of people or of behavior may create new ways to be a person, new choices to make, for good or evil. There are new descriptions, and hence new actions under a description. It is not that people change, substantively, but that as a point of logic new opportunities for action are open to them. (Hacking, 1995, p. 239)

Hacking (2006) currently cautions against adopting the overgeneralized language of natural versus human kinds and prefers to examine each instance or case of "person making" in its own historical terms and context. With such cautions in place, Hacking's historical ontology is very useful for our current purposes. By adding historical ontology to the critical historical and conceptual orientations and methods we discussed in Chapter 1, we can now turn to a more detailed and particular historical, theoretical, and practical examination of that branch of psychology (i.e., educational psychology) which interacted with the education and schooling of American and Canadian children and adolescents throughout the twentieth century but especially and with much greater focus and organization during the last half of that century.

3   Educational Psychology's Role in the Education of Selves

IN MOST SOCIETIES and under most forms of government, education has an explicit sociopolitical mandate to produce particular kinds of persons, citizens who participate in the maintenance and development of their communities and themselves. Psychology has no such explicit mandate. And yet, in Western liberal democracies, there can be little question that psychology has become extremely influential in determining how we understand and evaluate ourselves and our lives in general and how we think and go about education and schooling. As we have seen in the first two chapters, psychology (as a social science, profession, and academic discipline) focuses on individuals and their psychological lives, usually understood as private and internal to each person. Most psychological conceptions of self and self-governance are instrumentally ordered around the enhancement and empowerment of individuals' abilities to achieve their own ends.

Education, on the other hand, is socially organized and sponsored to shape the young to the norms and conventions of adult society and to teach them what is real and true in the world. While not necessarily or entirely consistent, such goals of education attempt to ensure that the additional educational goal of facilitating the development of individual potentials is pursued in a manner broadly consistent with the collective good of contributing to and perhaps advancing the interests of state and community. To overlook this crucial difference between education and psychology is to risk confusing the psychological growth and development of the individual with the education of individuals as active participants in and contributors to their communities. It is to forget that individual freedom and ability ideally should be balanced by civic virtue, which entails a joint commitment to an always difficult amalgam of freedom and collective social well-being.

Most contemporary statements of educational goals include some combination of the intellectual, social, and personal development of persons and citizens. As just noted, in Western liberal democracies, a central tension in such formulations is that between civic virtue and individual freedom, where the former emphasizes the good of the community and the latter emphasizes the rights of the individual. This tension has been central to liberal thought from the Enlightenment to this day. The more or less consistent standard liberal line has been that when push comes to shove, basic rights of individuals—such as freedom of speech and association (usually qualified in an attempt to ensure that their exercise by some individuals does not impede similarly free exercise by others in the society)—should trump collective goods such as social equality. Most importantly, in the liberal state, collective goods must never be forced upon citizens but must be chosen more or less freely by them; when consensual agreement is impossible because of communal diversity, the rights of individuals and groups to covenant to different goods should be respected and tolerated, subject once again to the qualification that their pursuit does not impede similar rights of others with different visions of the good.

In consequence of such views, liberal theorists in education have sought to balance civic virtue and individual freedom. For example, Gutmann (1990) suggests a form of democratic education that "empowers citizens to make their own decisions on how best to combine [individual] freedom with [civic] virtue" (p. 19). Such an approach addresses the classic liberal tension between individual rights and collective goods in an equally classical liberal manner—that is, by giving individuals the tools to engage with others in the open and free debate and determination of decisions and courses of action. What this means for education is that preparation of the kind of citizen promoted in statements such as those by Gutmann (1990) might best be served by helping students to acquire the attitudes, skills, and abilities that will allow them to analyze and critically consider both their own perspectives and those of others and to express their views and concerns as clearly as possible in public contexts with due respect for the rights of all concerned. Such an education might emphasize the historical formation of liberal states; formats, contexts, and strategies of democratic debate; and knowledge and methods conducive to critical thinking, among many other relevant contents. It also might focus on the encouragement of such personal virtues as honesty, integrity, and benevolence and aim to equip all students with strong communicative competencies.

There are many examples of liberal democratic theorizing in education that could be examined with a view to considering similar kinds of links between educational goals and the preparation of particular kinds of citizens and persons. However, the important point is that education in most contemporary Western states has an explicit mandate to produce particular kinds of citizens and persons capable of living productively and cooperatively within liberal democratic communities.

The Public Institution of School and the Professional Practice of Psychology

Education is a public trust, and schools are public institutions devoted to delivering on that trust. In contemporary liberal democratic states, schools operate under explicit laws, charters, and constitutions that detail their roles, jurisdictions, obligations, and entitlements to their communities, administrative and teaching staff, parents and children, and the larger society. Psychology, as a social scientific discipline and professional service, has no similarly pervasive institutional arm. Psychology is concerned with the study of the action and experience of human individuals. Although it is reasonable to view the mental health systems in many contemporary societies as institutions, these are not typically set up to be universally accessible, and their mandates are ordered primarily around the provision of services to individuals who meet particular diagnostic criteria that single them out from their fellow citizens.[1]

Clearly the distinction being drawn between schools as public institutions with explicitly universal social mandates versus psychological clinics as less formal institutions without such mandates can be drawn too starkly and is perhaps somewhat overly simplified. However, there should be no doubt that schools are the major vehicles of initiation into the expectations and practices of the larger society with respect to roles, rules, norms, and standards of functioning. As Olson (2003) has noted so succinctly, schools are "successful only to the extent that [they] succeed in helping persons to see themselves as the institution sees them" (p. 294). Schools are a meeting ground where the pupils' subjective and localized experiences are reconfigured within a broader sociocultural context of relevant norms, practices, and structures of knowing and being. In schools within liberal democratic states, students have the right to their own beliefs, but the institution of schooling (as representative of the educational interests of the broader society) "retains the right to judge whether or not [a] belief is valid, true, or worthwhile" (Olson, 2003, pp. 294–295).

The relevance of the foregoing distinction to what follows is that it is precisely this distinction that is often forgotten or otherwise obscured when psychologists and disciplinary psychology have actively promoted their disciplinary knowledge and professional interventions in schools. In what follows, it will be demonstrated and argued that psychology's increasing involvement in education and schooling carries significant implications for the education of persons in contemporary societies. This claim is perhaps best illustrated by an examination of the work of educational psychologists who have focused on the "selves" of learners and insisted that pupils' self-development, self-esteem, self-concept, self-efficacy, and self-regulation should be of central importance to education.

---

[1] None of this is to suggest that psychology does not function as a set of institutionalized professional and scientific practices. The point is that psychology does not function explicitly as a central social institution in the manner of schools and educational systems.

Educational Psychology in Historical Context

By the end of the nineteenth century, extended, public schooling had come to coincide with the widespread prohibition of child labor. Where previously children had been treated as small adults and workers, an extended period of childhood now became situated, at least for much of the day, in schools. Institutionalized systems of formal education were now responsible for the educational development of children in ways that respected the child's status as a child yet would promote a transition from the perspectives and abilities of children to the understandings and competencies of adults. In time, adolescence, a previously nonexistent concept, came to mark this transition.

Whereas in earlier times religious and medical perspectives and practices had dominated popular approaches to child rearing and education, a new set of interventionist practices, informed by the newly minted discipline of psychology, emerged at the dawn of the twentieth century. Psychologists like Granville Stanley Hall (1970/1893, 1896, 1906), who were committed to the scientific study of children and their development, forged close working relationships with teachers and other educators in what became known as the child study movement, dedicated to the collection of data about normal developmental trajectories. Large-scale surveys were conducted over several years throughout the 1890s that asked parents, teachers, and other professionals in education to observe and record data on everything from children's emotions and food preferences to their self-images.

At the same time, various efforts at educational reform emerged both in America and Europe based on joint concerns with respect to the perceived inadequacy of existing schools to prepare students for a new and evolving set of societal demands and the perceived inability of traditional pedagogical methods to meet students' needs. These efforts at amelioration were targeted at replacing rote learning and coercive discipline with more progressive emphases on students' own experiences and developmental and educational needs. In the wake of the child study movement and various early efforts at educational reform, educational psychology emerged as a powerful force in teachers colleges and departments of education in the early 1900s. Although courses in educational psychology had existed in a few such quarters for much of the latter part of the nineteenth century (Charles, 1987), the new educational psychology, championed by psychologists like Edward Lee Thorndike (1903), promised a decidedly scientific resolution to educational concerns of the day. Thorndike's quantitative approach to learning and education, with its emphases on repetition and reinforcement, actually did little to address concerns over rote learning as a pedagogical method, but it did pave the way for a wave of contemporary and future educational psychologists to bring their tools of psychological assessment, measurement, and experimentation to schools.

Other psychologists, such as Lightner Witmer—who in 1896 established the first diagnostic and treatment center for children with learning difficulties at the University of Pennsylvania—adopted a more clinical approach to concerns surrounding children and education. Witmer also pioneered a variety of psychoeducational diagnoses and interventions intended to contribute to the psychological welfare of individual schoolchildren (Fagan, 1996). The development of new forms of psychological testing, especially intelligence tests (developed initially by French psychologist Alfred Binet), greatly enhanced the perceived expertise of a growing number of psychometrically inclined psychologists in the field of education. With such expertise, the definition and assessment of difficulties such as mental retardation were transferred from the province of medicine to that of psychology. By the 1920s, educational psychologists working in schools and in school-related clinics could claim expertise in educational research and educational testing in ways that linked these enterprises to both individuals and groups of children and adolescents. By this time, parents and teachers had come to rely increasingly on educational psychologists for information on how the educational development of children should be determined, measured, assessed, and improved. For the rest of the twentieth century, educational psychologists were able to employ their now widely acknowledged expertise in educational research, assessment/measurement, and psychoeducational intervention in an ever-expanding variety and number of psychological applications in schools.

By the early 1920s in the United States, the mental hygiene movement, based on the pioneering work of Witmer and others, had mostly replaced the earlier child study movement associated with Hall and his collaborators. By 1932, the National Committee for Mental Hygiene was operating 232 child guidance clinics nationwide, which provided preventive, assessment, and treatment services to the nation's children and families— initially with an emphasis on discipline but increasingly with a focus on the empathic understanding of children's perspectives (van Drunen & Jansz, 2004). Child guidance clinics also appeared in England and Holland in the late 1920s. Although these clinics advocated a team approach to child assessment and treatment that included psychologists, most leadership roles were occupied by physicians. Nonetheless, as treatment orientations became more focused on empathic understanding, the methods employed for diagnosis and intervention were almost entirely psychological.

In the meantime, psychologists, especially as experts on the assessment of intelligence and a growing array of related mental abilities, continued to make enormous inroads into schools. During the 1920s and 1930s, tests of intelligence and ability fitted easily with themes of progressive education stressing a combination of efficiency and the adaptation of curricula and instructional methods to individual learners. Throughout the 1940s, 1950s, and 1960s, behavioral psychology drew the attention of educators to patterns of reinforcement and methods of graduated learning and behavioral control that were quickly adopted in both mainstream and special education. The understanding of teaching as an applied behavioral technology was strongly advocated by psychologists like B. F. Skinner (1968). At the same time, humanistic psychologists like Carl Rogers (1969) promoted a very different approach to education that focused on the natural tendencies of children to learn and develop themselves in positive ways in the relative absence of pedagogical authority and techniques. This joint focus on behavioral technology and scientifically aided efficiency and accountability on the one hand and child-centered, humanistic caring and concern on the other was to become fertile soil for the development and use of psychological expertise.

Following the Second World War, psychology in the schools proliferated through the introduction of school psychology as a new profession, the development and introduction of new forms of psychoeducation, and the continued growth of testing. After the war, the mental hygiene movement expanded its reach beyond the child guidance clinics by arguing that schools had a major role to play in the promotion of good mental health. By aligning themselves with this movement, school psychologists established themselves as essential contributors to educational systems and programs throughout North America and Europe. Soon, most teachers and parents were familiar with terms such as *school readiness, fear of failure*, and *low self-esteem*.

At the same time, educational research, especially with the U.S. reaction to the Soviet Union's launching of *Sputnik I* in 1957, received increased funding that saw many newly minted cognitive psychologists follow their behavioral brethren into the burgeoning fields of research on teaching and instructional design. The Cold War also motivated large-scale testing and guidance programs in the United States to ensure that human potential and talent could be recognized and utilized in the interests of both individuals and the nation. By assessing and theorizing aptitude and individual differences and urging that instruction be adapted to them, a new generation of educational psychologists contributed in significant ways to what van Drunen and Jansz (2004) have referred to as a "psychocracy: a social structure in which psychology played a decisive role in the distribution of educational chances and social position—and therefore in the legitimization of social difference" (p. 82). Increasingly, in large part due to psychological testing and intervention in schools, teachers, parents, and students themselves became sensitized to previously unremarked differences among pupils with respect to such things as "aptitude for learning," "learning difficulties and disabilities," "troubled children," and "gifted learners."

In the 1960s and 1970s, educational and school psychologists also devoted their attention to the problem of disadvantaged children, but with a new emphasis on emancipation, educational opportunity, and social amelioration versus the focus on discipline and control that had marked the early days of the child guidance centers. Child development centers and educational programs such as Head Start began to operate in urban areas marked by poverty and social difficulty. However, the 1980s and 1990s witnessed a retrenchment of psychosocial funding and programming in schools and communities in both North America and Europe. Some of this cutting back can clearly be linked to a generally conservative turn in Western politics and culture. However, it also reflected a trend toward the medicalization of developmental issues and a biophysical turn within psychology itself; witness, for example, the treatment of attention deficit hyperactivity disorder with the drug Ritalin (DeGrandpre, 2000). At the same time there can be little doubt that the psychologizing of education was here to stay.

Western societies are now oriented to children and their psychological development and well-being in ways that would have been inconceivable to people living in the nineteenth century. Indeed, it is within this larger context that measures, studies, and psycho-educational interventions related to students' self-esteem, self-concept, self-regulation, and self-efficacy have come to play an increasingly influential role in the education of children and adolescents as both citizens and persons. Given that our purpose in this book is to examine in considerable historical and critical detail the impact of psychology on education and schooling as it relates directly to these programs of self study and intervention, we devote the rest of this chapter to an analysis and organization of conceptions of selfhood in the work and writings of educational psychologists during the last half of the twentieth century.

Conceptions of Self in Educational Psychology

As a means of understanding the conceptions and practices of selfhood constructed and promoted by psychologists, it is instructive to consider the kinds of work evident in that enormous body of literature comprising studies of the psychological self. A search of the PsychInfo database (Martin, 2004a) reveals that the total number of entries in psychology published during the 100 years from 1901 to 2001 that contained the word *self* in their titles was 45,594. Of these, 18,774 appeared between 1990 and 2001 and more than 10,000 appeared in the 1970s and again in the 1980s. The total number of these writings appearing before 1950 was a comparatively meager 1,434. The 1960s, as might be expected, ushered in the accelerating growth in "self" publications (with 2,904 such articles), which has continued ever since.

The 1960s also marked a significant growth in psychologically oriented studies of the self within educational contexts. A more detailed look at the kinds of studies conducted since 1960 that appear to be of direct relevance to education can be obtained from an analysis of entries in the ERIC database containing the word *self* in their titles (Martin, 2004a). Of the 14,686 such publications that appeared from 1960 to 2000, the top four areas of more specific study were self-concept (1,540 entries), self-esteem (1,379 entries), self-efficacy (503 entries), and self-regulation (235 entries). When trends of growth are examined for each of these four types of self studies, self-esteem, self-efficacy, and self-regulation show a continuing pattern of significant growth over this period of time, with work in the areas of self-efficacy and self-regulation more than doubling during the 1990s. By comparison, work in the area of self-concept peaked in the 1970s and has shown a steady decline ever since. For example, the number of entries for self-concept during the 1970s was more than double that of the 1990s. Clearly, the currently emerging areas of popular self study in educational psychology and education in general are self-esteem, self-efficacy, and self-regulation. Nonetheless, in terms of total number of publications, work in the area of self-concept continues apace with publications in these other related areas of self study.

What conceptions of the self are contained in psychological research and writing about self-esteem, self-concept, self-efficacy, and self-regulation? A close reading of a representative sampling of entries in these areas since 1960 reveals two underlying conceptions of selfhood. One is a somewhat reductively scientific conception of the self as a compilation of self-descriptions, appraisals, judgments, and strategies documented in the quantitative measures of educational psychologists. The other is a broadly humanistic, even somewhat romantic conception of the self that at first glance appears to resist these same formulations, and to reflect some sort of unique inner core of phenomenal, experiential life within each learner.

Although we will argue that these two conceptions of the self are really not as different as they might initially appear to be, it is nonetheless instructive to examine descriptions drawn from the work of prominent educational psychologists that seem to support an interpretation of two apparently conflicting self-conceptions—one scientific and one humanistic. In what follows and for reasons that will quickly become apparent (but have already been hinted at in Chapter 2), we refer to the humanistic self as the *expressive* self and the scientific self as the *managerial* self. By way of contrast with these forms of psychological selfhood, which dominated the last half of the twentieth century in American and Canadian schools, we will also consider briefly a third kind of self that was just starting to be advocated by a small minority of educational psychologists toward the end of the twentieth century, in part as a reaction to the expressive and managerial selves advocated by mainstream educational psychology, especially during the latter half of that century.

Thus, for much of the rest of this chapter, we examine three conceptions of selfhood evident in the twentieth-century publications of educational psychologists: (1) the *expressive self* (mostly but not only evident in studies of self-esteem and self-concept); (2) the *managerial self* (mostly but not only evident in studies of self-regulation and self-efficacy); and (3) the *communal self* (evident in certain formulations of selfhood contained in some work in the areas of situated learning, social cognition, learning communities, sociocultural psychology, hermeneutics, pragmatism, and critical theory but rarely encountered in the self-related studies of traditional or mainstream educational psychologists, especially prior to 1990).

The Expressive Self

In the 1950s and 1960s, humanistic psychologists like Abraham Maslow (1954) and Carl Rogers (1957) reacted against the prevailing behaviorism of the day and spearheaded a renewed focus on internal processes, with an emphasis on individually unique and affectively laden experiences. In educational psychology, numerous studies began to focus attention on the self-esteem and self-concept of schoolchildren, often in terms of congruency between self-descriptions and self-ideals (e.g., Long, Henderson, & Ziller, 1967; Soares & Soares, 1969). Others focused on relationships between measures of self-concept/self-esteem and academic achievement and motivation—a focus that continues into the present day (for reviews, see Kohn, 1994; Wigfield & Karpathian, 1991). What is perhaps most interesting about the vast literature concerning self-concept and self-esteem in school contexts is that although it was initiated by humanistic impulses to recognize the uniqueness and emotional experience of children in school settings, it quickly broadened its empirical and theoretical footing through mergers with more traditionally scientific forms of psychology and educational psychology.

One such merger was with psychometricians who developed numerous scales and subscales for the measurement of self-esteem and self-concept during the 1950s, 1960s, and 1970s (e.g., Piers & Harris, 1964). A second merger occurred once the cognitive revolution in psychology and applied psychology had taken a firm hold in education by the late 1960s; it involved a new breed of cognitive psychologists interested in structures and operations of cognition in classroom settings, including motivational and affective components (e.g., Shavelson & Bolus, 1982).

By the dawn of the twenty-first century, approximately 3,000 studies of self-esteem and/or self-concept were listed in the ERIC database. Many of these examined the factor structure and psychometric properties of an expanding array of measures and scales (e.g., Byrne & Shavelson, 1986; Winne & Walsh, 1980). Many also examined relationships among measures of self-esteem/self-concept, academic achievement and motivation, and a number of other personality variables (e.g., Ames & Felkner, 1979; Jordan, 1981). The self-experiences of learners were described and rated in measures of self-esteem and self-concept, such as The Rosenberg Self-Esteem Scale, the Coopersmith Self-Esteem Inventory, and the Piers-Harris Self-Concept Scale for Children, which contained items such as: "I feel that I do not have much to be proud of," "All in all, I'm inclined to feel that I'm a failure," and "I am good in my schoolwork."

In consideration of why many educational psychologists and others were and continue to be concerned about students' self-concept and self-esteem, it is surely insufficient to answer that these self-related beliefs, thoughts, and feelings seem to be connected in a positive manner to students' academic achievement. Indeed, a recent comprehensive review of empirical evidence concerning self-esteem and performance (Baumeister, Campbell, Krueger, & Vohs, 2003) concluded that "The results do not support the view that self-esteem has a strong causal effect on school achievement. Indeed, most of the evidence suggests that self-esteem has no impact on subsequent academic achievement" (p. 13). Clearly, something more fundamental and powerful seems to propel the conviction that high levels of self-esteem and self-concept are worthy educational goals in themselves. What this something else might be is clearly indicated in the following quotation from Arthur Combs (1961), one of the leaders of the self-concept and self-esteem movement in educational psychology in the 1960s:

> It is a basic principle of democracy that "when men are free, they can find their own best ways" .... The kind of openness we seek in the free personality requires a trust

in self, and this means, to me, we need to change the situations we sometimes find in our teaching where the impression is given the student that all the answers worth having lie "out there." I believe it is necessary to recognize that the only important answers are those which the individual has within himself, for these are the only ones that will ever show up in his behavior. (Combs, 1961, pp. 22–23)

Or consider the following comments by contemporary educational psychologists working in the still popular area of self-concept:

Self-concept is valued as having a powerful mediating influence on human behavior. A positive self-concept is widely considered fundamental for psychological health, personal achievement, and positive relationships. Self-concept is thought to make such a difference, that people who think positively about themselves are healthier, happier, and more productive. Hence, enhancing self-concept is considered necessary to maximizing human potential, from early development and school achievement, to physical/mental health and well being, to gainful employment and other contributions to society. (Craven, Marsh, & Burnett, 2003, p. 96)

What the remarks of Combs (1961) and Craven and colleagues (2003) make clear is that our sense of the importance of self-related phenomena like self-concept and self-esteem stems from our deep attachment to the importance of *self-expression* as a basic right and obligation of individual members of society, who bear a unique and potentially valuable first-person perspective on the world and themselves. Feeling good about and having positive conceptions of ourselves allow us to express our individuality in ways that benefit both ourselves and society. More recently, the view that students' rights and opportunities for self-expression should be protected has figured prominently in the writings of educational psychologists concerned with issues of gender, ethnicity, race, and class. "Thus, efforts to encourage [all] adolescents … to express themselves in ways that will be respectfully heard is a challenge that educators must face if we genuinely want to support the development of students' authentic selves" (Harter, Waters, & Whitesell, 1997, p. 171).

The expressive self that underlies much writing and research by educational psychologists, especially in areas such as self-esteem and self-concept, is a highly sensitive, reactive inner core of the person. This deep interior is fueled by a general and powerful tendency toward self-development in relation to a natural and social desire for expression. At the same time, children and adolescents often experience fragility in their legitimate efforts to locate, understand, and express their authentic inner selves to such an extent that teachers and parents must remain ever vigilant against experiences that might interact with such natural and socially desirable self-expressivity in anything less than optimally positive and encouraging ways. "Self-actualizing people see themselves in positive ways, and you do not get this from having failures" (Combs, 1961, p. 19).

The Managerial Self

Whereas measures of self-esteem and self-concept employed by educational psychologists broadly reflect humanistic concerns for unique individual expression and self-understanding, more recent research in educational psychology reflects a much more cognitive, rational, and instrumental perspective on selfhood. In the 1980s and 1990s, studies of self-efficacy and self-regulation in educational psychology increased dramatically in both number and prominence to the point where they became as prevalent as research and intervention studies in the areas of self-esteem and self-concept (Martin, 2004a). Whereas measures and research on self-esteem and self-concept focused on self-worth and self-understanding with a general sense of encouraging student self-expression and fulfillment as uniquely worthy human individuals, the new measures and research on self-efficacy and self-regulation focused primarily on the self's ability to monitor, manage, motivate, strategize, and reinforce itself with respect to the successful completion of specific academic tasks. Self-regulation is defined as a "learner's intentional monitoring and managing of cognitive and motivational strategies and the learning environment to advance toward goals of instructional tasks" (Winne & Perry, 1994, p. 213). Self-efficacy concerns "people's beliefs about their capabilities to exercise control over their own level of functioning and over events that affect their lives" (Bandura, 1993, p. 118).

Much research on self-regulation in school contexts examines the effects of interventions intended to enhance students' abilities to self-regulate (Boekaerts & Corno, 2005). For example, Butler (1998) examined the effectiveness of an instructional approach intended to improve the self-regulatory capabilities of university students who were experiencing learning difficulties, and Zimmerman (1997) examined the effects of goal-setting and self-monitoring on female adolescents' performance of a motor task. Popular measures of self-regulation are the Motivated Strategies for Learning Questionnaire (Pintrich & DeGroot, 1990) and the Learning and Study Strategies Inventory (Weinstein, Goetz, & Alexander, 1988). Examples of items on each of these scales respectively include "When I study I put important ideas into my own words" and "I make sample charts, diagrams, or tables to summarize material in my courses." Most measures of self-regulation contain several subscales intended to measure components of self-regulation, such as the use of cognitive strategies, motivation, information processing, and self-efficacy (e.g., "I expect to do very well in this class").

Measures and studies of self-efficacy and self-regulation are devoted almost exclusively to goal-related activities within classroom learning tasks. In this work, the self is conceptualized as highly rational and strategic, making use of cognitive processes and operations to process information so that it can be meaningfully stored, recalled, and assembled when the learner is confronted with specific academic tasks. So popular has research on self-regulation and self-efficacy become that several edited volumes have appeared that summarize and promote the burgeoning numbers of research studies along with theoretical and practice-oriented articles, devoted to these topics (e.g., Bandura, 1995; Boekaerts,

Pintrich, & Zeidner, 2000; Schunk & Pajares, 2004; Schunk & Zimmerman, 1994, 1998; Zimmerman & Schunk, 1989). Recently there have also been explicit suggestions that research in the areas of self-regulation and self-efficacy can not only benefit learners in classrooms but will also have more general applicability to lifelong learning and social improvement.

> Teachers who consider their students' self-efficacy beliefs, goal setting, strategy use, and other forms of self-regulation in their instructional plans not only enhance students' academic knowledge, but they also increase their students' capability for self-directed learning throughout their life span. (Zimmerman & Schunk, 2003, p. 452)

The conception of selfhood that underlies the work of educational psychologists in the areas of self-efficacy and self-regulation is that of the self as strategic manager. Students in classrooms and people in everyday life are pictured as highly rational and deliberate processors of information. The self of the self-regulated learner and person is constituted of specifically focused sets of executive skills and strategies attuned instrumentally to the accomplishment of specific academic and life tasks. The central concern is the development and promotion of a self-confident individual agent capable of simultaneous action and reflection on this action, much like a stereotypical scientist in close scrutiny and judgment of experimental phenomena of interest, albeit with a decidedly social conscience and concern for others. Having said this, it is by no means always clear that the highly scripted and externally imposed sequences of strategic activity and instruction evident in many studies and interventions in the area of students' self-regulated learning leave adequate room for the fostering of what might be regarded as freely chosen self-determination with respect to students' selection and enactment of their learning and study practices (Martin, 2004b; see also Chapter 7).

What the Expressive and Managerial Selves Have in Common

Despite their obvious differences, both the expressive and the managerial selves of educational psychology are united in being constituted predominately of individuals' interior processes and functions. Whether engaged in unique creative expression or strategic goal-oriented action, these selves operate from a highly personal inner core of being. Both expressive and managerial selves are Cartesian selves isolated from—though highly interactive with—their surrounds. Both embrace Enlightenment and/or modern forms of dualism marked by strong divides between inner and outer, mind and world, and personal and social. The self that lies behind research on self-esteem/self-concept and self-regulation/self-efficacy is an inner bastion of individual experience and existence that surveys the exterior landscape for signs of affirmation and possibilities for expression on the one hand, and clues to strategic action on the other. Its most vital resources are located within itself as it acts as final arbiter over whether or not its strategies are effective or its appraisals self-sustaining. Academic tasks and social experience can both be accomplished and controlled by this masterful self's attention to its own basic organismic tendencies and potentials and/or its metacognitive strategic ruminations. This is a self that already possesses and is in command of its own internal resources for managing itself and requires only a facilitative grooming from teachers and others to become more fully socialized and intellectually engaged.

Toward a More Communal Self

The historical development of psychology as the social scientific study of predominately *individual* behavior and experience undoubtedly is heavily implicated in the kind of self-hood just described (see Chapter 2). Nonetheless, toward the end of the twentieth century several educational psychologists expressed dissatisfaction with their discipline's continuing embrace of a highly individualistic conception of selfhood. In particular, they voiced concerns about the relative exclusion of more social and cultural aspects of self constitution and functioning. "Our main ... focus needs to change from the study of isolated and decontextualized individuals, processes, states of mind, or interventions to their study within wider psychological, disciplinary, social, and cultural contexts" (Salomon, 1995, p. 106). Such calls for a more sociocultural conception of selfhood had been predated by studies of social and linguistic mediation of learning conducted by a small number of educational psychologists in the 1970s and 1980s, influenced by then newly available English translations of the works of Lev Vygotsky (1978, 1986/1934) (see Martin, 2006a, for a review). Nonetheless, for present purposes, it is instructive to note that most such work was not concerned primarily with selfhood per se. On the other hand, Bandura's (1986) social cognitive theory attended explicitly to questions of selfhood and agency in a way that emphasized the immediate social context of the learner. However, Bandura and his followers, although highlighting the importance of social and contextual factors, stopped well short of theorizing the kind of historical sociocultural constitution of selves and learners that typified Vygotsky's thought (cf. Rohrkemper, 1989).

At any rate, Salomon's (1995) and others' (e.g., Goodenow, 1992) calls for a more communal, less individual conception of selfhood soon were answered by a growing body of work in educational psychology in general that was based not only on Vygotsky's sociocultural historical activity theory (e.g., Das & Gindis, 1995; John-Steiner & Mahn, 1996; Tappan, 1998) but also on Deweyan and Meadian pragmatism and symbolic interactionism (Bredo, 1994; Prawat, 1995), culminating in a variety of socially oriented research studies employing methods such as discourse analysis, microethnography, sociometry, group interviews, cultural ecology, and design experiments (see Anderman & Anderman, 2000; Sandoval & Bell, 2004; Wentzel & Berndt, 1999). The view of the learner evident in these undertakings clearly shifted away from that of the detached, inner-focused agent common to both the expressive and managerial selves discussed above. In particular, the underlying conception of selfhood evident in some relatively recent sociocultural theory and research in educational psychology (Martin, 2006a) is that of a communal self formed through interaction with others in families, classrooms, and elsewhere. This communal self is always embedded in a co-constitutive self–other, self–societal dialectic. It is a self that is cut from the fabric of those sociocultural conventions and ways of life into which we are born as biophysical human beings and come to exist and understand ourselves as particular kinds of persons.

Nonetheless, there are considerable differences in the extent to which the various communal selves advanced in recent theory and research in educational psychology might be said to converge on a socially constituted, deeply engaged idea of personhood. For example, many researchers in areas such as situated cognition (e.g., Kirshner & Whitson, 1997) and design-based research (e.g., Sandoval & Bell, 2004) retain a conception of the individual learner in which reflective cognition might still be said to have primacy over interpersonal activity and in which classrooms are still seen primarily as collections of individuals.

For the most part, the kinds of communal selves assumed in most extant work in educational psychology stop short of the more thoroughly collective conceptions of agency and selfhood found in much contemporary educational philosophy, sociology, and policy studies (e.g., Schutz, 2000) and in several other areas of psychology (e.g., Harré, 1998; Martin, Sugarman, & Thompson, 2003). In particular, the vast majority of self-related research and theory advanced by contemporary educational psychologists in the areas of self-esteem, self-concept, self-regulation, and self-efficacy retains a decidedly individualistic tone—for example, "Self-determination theory … highlights people's inner motivational resources in explaining healthy personality, development, and autonomous self-regulation" (Reeve, Deci, & Ryan, 2004, p. 33). As Jackson, Mackenzie, and Hobfoll (2000) note, even when "some theories of self-regulation, in particular social cognitive models … do recognize social context as a component of self-directed behavior … the impact of socially mediated factors often assumes a status that is far inferior to individually based components" (p. 280).

Recognizing this state of affairs should not be interpreted as advocating a strong form of social determinism in which human agency is reduced to social structures and processes. Clearly, any viable educational theory, psychological or otherwise, must contain resources capable of supporting human innovation and change at both collective and individual levels. Nonetheless, the tendency of many educational psychologists— even those who claim adherence to more social, communal forms of selfhood—to elevate individual cognitive activity over interdependency and interactivity should not go unremarked. At this writing, educational psychology has not endorsed a consistently communal form of selfhood to rival the consistency with which it continues to promote more individualistic expressive and managerial conceptions of the self. Moreover, although some sociocultural work in educational psychology that has adopted Vygotskian cultural historical (e.g., John-Steiner & Mahn, 1996) or American pragmatic (e.g., Bredo, 1994) thought has endorsed promising versions of communal selfhood, for the most part these have yet to be incorporated into research in areas such as self-concept and self-regulated learning (see Hickey & Granade, 2004; McCaslin, 2004; and Rohrkemper, 1989, for some notable exceptions). It is thus reasonable to consider the communal self as a promissory note, at least in self-related programs of psychological research in education.

Sociocultural and Institutional Context

With the foregoing conceptions of selfhood in place, it now is possible to attempt to situate those conceptions within the broader sociocultural context in which they have been developed, especially in the United States and Canada but also in other Western nations. As recorded in Chapter 2, by the early years of the twentieth century the industrial revolution and the urbanization and social mobility that it fostered had created new bureaucratic demands for the counting, organization, and governance of individuals through newly formed scientific and social scientific techniques of surveying, recording, and statistical aggregation. Such methods and the attitudes and conceptions that accompanied them were not only of great value to officials and employers but also suggested rigorous means of self-scrutiny, efficiency, and management to aspiring, ambitious workers and people in general (Rose, 1998). At the same time, the impact of Romantic, Victorian, and psychoanalytic conceptions of selfhood—which converged on the idea of a deeply interior, private individual center of personal experience and perspective—had become part of the Western social fabric and were widely reflected in popular literature, cinema, advertising, and everyday life (Baumeister, 1987). By the early 1900s, conformity and individuality thus sat side by side in social and personal understandings and attitudes about the self (e.g., Pfister, 1997).

Not surprisingly, for much of the twentieth century, social institutions in Western societies were hard pressed to accommodate the inevitable tensions between social requirements and individual demands emanating from this joint commitment to society and selfhood. Of course, as mentioned previously in this and the two preceding chapters, ever since the Enlightenment, liberal democratic societies have experienced a basic tension between individual rights/freedoms and civic virtues/responsibilities (Fairfield, 2000). For the most part, the response of liberal democratic institutions to this tension was to emphasize personal rights and freedoms in the private lives of citizens (i.e., in the home and during leisure hours) and social, communal responsibilities and regulations in public life (outside the home, during work, and in those dealings with others governed by law and convention). However, when more psychological ideas concerning the self as an inner bastion of creative expression, self-actualization, and self-governance began to proliferate in the first half of the twentieth century, public social institutions like legal, economic, political, and educational systems were assailed by demands for greater recognition and facilitation of these "new" forms of selfhood. As already suggested in Chapters 1 and 2, when these same institutions began to appreciate the potential benefits of harnessing psychological forms of self-expression and self-management to public institutional policies (Rose, 1998) and practices, psychological ways of understanding selfhood found their place in both public institutional and private life.

By the middle of the twentieth century, the social and psychological demands on schools and broader educational systems (together with the strategic responses of such institutions to these demands) were such as to place the goals and practices of student personal development alongside more traditional goals and practices of socialization and preparation for citizenship. Moreover, demands for attending to and fostering the personal development of students no longer stopped at the idea of intellectual learning and development but began to include strongly felt concerns for the positive emotional, experiential, and psychological development of students as persons capable of recognizing and actualizing their common and unique potentials through enhanced forms of self-understanding and strategic self-management (Olson, 2003).

Figure 1 is a schematic depiction of a sociocultural psychological landscape demarcated by the bipolar sociopsychological dimensions of individual freedom versus civic virtue, self-control versus self-fulfillment, and institutional socialization versus personal development. In the top right-hand portion of the diagram is a multidimensional cluster (self-control, institutional socialization, and civic virtue) representing a sociopsychological niche conducive to a form of self-governance that respects and furthers existing sociocultural organizations and values. In the bottom left-hand portion of the diagram is a multidimensional cluster (self-fulfillment, personal development, and individual freedom) representing a sociopsychological niche conducive to a form of self-assertion that respects and furthers the actualization of free and self-determining individuals.

To see more precisely how the expressive and managerial selves of educational psychology combined to appeal to educational systems struggling with the conflicting demands just described, imagine the managerial self of educational psychology superimposed on the upper right-hand portion of Figure 1 (as indicated by the higher of the two dotted ovals) and the expressive self of educational psychology superimposed on the lower left-hand portion of the figure (as indicated by the lower of the two dotted ovals). By effectively positioning its two main conceptions of selfhood in this way within the sociocultural, institutional, and psychological tensions depicted in Figure 1, disciplinary psychology effectively offered schools and the broader society a scientifically credible yet individually sensitive way of reconciling conflicting demands for the institutional socialization and personal development of children and adolescents through education. Of course much ultimately would depend on how successfully the hybrid managerial-expressive self (constituted by a shuttling back and forth between the upper-right and bottom-left sociopsychological niches in Figure 1) could accomplish its mission of reconciliation. In what follows, it is argued that the hybrid managerial-expressive self, referred to earlier as a masterful self, is ultimately unable to integrate personal and societal demands of schooling with respect to the formation of selves as communal agents.

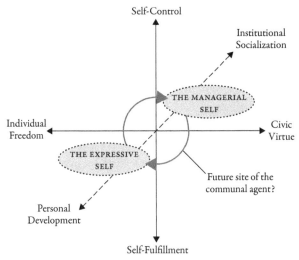

FIGURE 1 A sociocultural, psychological landscape of the selves of educational psychology.

An Initial Critical Consideration and Preview of Things to Come

Both the expressive and managerial selves underlying the research and intervention practices of educational psychologists in the areas of self-esteem/self-concept and self-regulation/self-efficacy share a common emphasis on individuals' inner processes and functions. In fact, it is precisely their claim to have specific expertise with respect to understanding, probing, and improving such processes and functions that warrants the professional involvement of educational psychologists in schools: "The scientifically sound research methods of psychology constitute one of the greatest inventions of the 20th century and hold great promise for improving educational practice" (Mayer, 2001, p. 84). What distinguishes psychology from other social sciences of potential and actual relevance to education is nothing more or less than psychology's focus on individual experiences, thoughts, and actions. But can such expertise concerning individuals' inner psychological processes and functions speak adequately to the kinds of concerns and tensions discussed immediately above?

In a recent discussion of our contemporary commitment to authenticity as a desired personal characteristic and goal, Charles Guignon (2004) argues that a purely psychological approach to authenticity, in which it is understood as a description of a person who understands her own feelings and expresses them transparently in her actions, is inadequate. The personal and social value currently placed on authenticity cannot emanate only from its characterization in terms of emotional psychological experience and expression. Authenticity also requires a commitment backed by reason, and such a reasoned commitment can arise only in the context of shared practices and values, for reason itself is based inevitably on the conventions and norms of social groups. This is not to deny that the material world imposes constraints on what is reasonable but to say that sociocultural and linguistic practices are indispensable to our rational functioning.

Democratic systems work best when they comprise persons who exercise discernment and judgment with respect to at least some common goals and beliefs. When someone fails to stand behind his reason-backed beliefs, he imperils a democratic social system that is predicated on exactly that which he now fails to do. A free and democratic society requires that its members be committed to the unrestricted exchange of reasoned views. Furthermore, such an exchange assumes that citizens are persons guided by moral commitments and reasons and knowledgeable about matters that confront them and their society. The role of education in such a society is to ensure minimally functional levels of knowing and understanding that go beyond our own inner selves and to attend to the world in which we live with others and what we currently know about it (even if such knowledge is always being revised and is never certain). Authentic selfhood or personhood is possible only in the context of shared traditions, practices, and ways of life with others. Psychological conceptions and models of self-esteem and self-regulation focused mostly on the feelings and strategies of individuals provide too narrow a venue for robust personal development or effective citizenship.

Many theorists (e.g., Mead, 1934; Vygotsky, 1986/1934; Wittgenstein, 1953) have concluded that self-understanding would be impossible without a recognition and understanding of others gained by participating with them in joint social interactions. Historically established social practices and the conventions and norms that accompany them provide criteria, concepts, and roles defining us as persons with first-person experiences and moral obligations. The self-understanding and self-control of a twentieth-century American congressman differ from the self-understanding and presentation of a senator of the early Roman republic or the comportment of a contemporary politician in the Middle East. The selfhood experienced by an affluent urban feminist differs from that of an impoverished rural traditionalist. We comprehend ourselves as the authors of actions that are praiseworthy or not because of our participation in social interactions with others, which takes place within ways and traditions of living permeated by values, goods, and injunctions. It is because we are first and foremost active in sociocultural contexts with others that we come to recognize and understand ourselves (Mead, 1934).

Therefore, when educational psychologists encourage us to esteem and express ourselves on the one hand and to engage in strategic planning in pursuit of personal goals on the other, it is important to understand that such valuing, expression, and instrumental strategizing are available to us because we understand ourselves as persons in ways made possible by our communal relations with others. It is against criteria and conventions available within our communal lives and joint understandings that we can discern and judge our own efforts at creative accomplishment. This was the reason why both Rousseau (1979/1762) and Locke (1959/1693), albeit in very different ways, emphasized moral and political considerations in their famous treatises on education—emphases that are mostly ignored in contemporary psychological conceptualizations of self-esteem and self-regulation that otherwise bear an unmistakably Rousseauian and Lockean imprint respectively.

Turning to a deep inner psychological core is not the answer to the search for self and other understanding. The ability to engage actively and thoughtfully with a diversity of perspectives would be impossible outside of a careful examination and consideration of the various perspectives in question, and these certainly do not all reside within us. Yet it is precisely such abilities that are so highly valued by many educational philosophers (Gutmann, 1990) as desired educational attainments of students who might become productive persons and citizens. It is through sustained, serious engagement with perspectives that differ from our own that we can function effectively in the sociopolitical arena and coincidentally expand our self-understanding (cf. Mead, 1934). Education is about expanding our horizons, not narrowing them by focusing primarily on ourselves.

The hybrid expressive-managerial self (portrayed in Figure 1 as attempting to shuttle between the personal/individual and social/institutional aims of education), although certainly not devoid of important qualities of selfhood and agency, is too focused on its own interior experience and motives to support the kind of ongoing integrative, conciliatory work of striking an appropriate balance between the personal/ individual and social/institutional aims of education. Such a self is both too individualistic and too instrumentally attuned to serve as a theoretical anchor for the education of communal agents, understood as learners capable of participating gladly and consistently in socially meaningful activities with others to achieve ends that are communally valued.

Recapitulation and Transition

Thus far, we have outlined our project as an attempt to examine, interpret, and evaluate the educational consequences of psychological theories, research, and intervention practices focused on students' self-understanding, self-worth, and self-governance. In Chapter 1, we provided information concerning the nature of psychology as an applied social science and described our undertaking as a critical history of psychology in education focused on the impact of psychological conceptions of selfhood in American and Canadian education during the last half of the twentieth century. In Chapter 2, we sketched a selective history of psychological conceptions of selfhood as reducible to internal processes and structures of individuals removed from worldly contexts of sociocultural traditions, practices, and interactions with others. In this chapter, we have focused more specifically on a critical history of educational psychology, culminating in an examination and evaluation of conceptions of selfhood that we interpreted as the expressive and managerial selves of educational psychology. We also introduced the idea of an alternative kind of selfhood—a more communal self, assumed in the work of a small minority of psychologists and educational psychologists by the end of the twentieth century.

In the next four chapters, we take detailed critical looks at each of the four major programs of self theory, research, and intervention pursued by educational psychologists in the twentieth century, especially during the last half of that century—self-esteem (Chapter 4), self-concept (Chapter 5), self-efficacy (Chapter 6), and self-regulation

(Chapter 7). It is our hope that these more intensive examinations of major programs of self study in educational psychology will enable an increasingly clear idea of the many difficulties that we believe attend the educational applications of expressive (self-esteem and self-concept) and managerial (self-efficacy and self-regulation) conceptions of psychological selfhood. We then consider (in Chapter 8) ways in which psychological conceptions of selfhood, and the psychoeducational practices they encourage, seem to have changed many American and Canadian students during the second half of the twentieth century. Here, we employ Ian Hacking's (2002) "historical ontology" (see the final section of Chapter 2) to explore how "the selves of educational psychology" created and made available new ways of being students that placed new demands on teachers and schools. Finally, in our last chapter (Chapter 9), we consider the possibility of encouraging more communal forms of social and psychological selfhood in American and Canadian classrooms in an attempt to achieve a more balanced and sustainable intertwining of personal and social virtues in the educational development of students as persons and citizens.

4   Feeling Good About Yourself
SELF-ESTEEM AS AN EDUCATIONAL GOAL

DURING THE LAST half of the twentieth-century and into the twenty-first century, American and Canadian educational systems placed a high value on heightened self-esteem as an important aim of education. After all, who of us would want our children not to feel as good about themselves as possible, especially when leading educational researchers proclaim that self-esteem provides a crucial building block on which all our actions and experiences are based. "People who think positively about themselves are healthier, happier, and more productive...self-concept is fundamental to enhancing human potential, from early development and school achievement, to physical/mental health and wellbeing, to cultural identity and social justice" (Shavelson, 2003, p. xiii).[1] The corollary is that low self-esteem is responsible for almost all individual and social difficulties. So pervasive is this phenomenon that many contemporaries "cannot think of a single psychological problem—from anxiety and depression, to fear of intimacy or of success, to spouse battery or child molestation—that is not traceable to the problem of low self-esteem" (Branden, 1984, p. 12). Given that self-esteem has such profound consequences for every aspect of our existence, it would be unpardonable for schools, educators, and educational researchers to neglect the cultivation of this core human resource.

---

[1] Although the term *self-concept* appears in this quotation, to "think positively" about oneself is more a matter of self-worth than self-understanding and is therefore better interpreted as self-esteem.

Thus, it is not surprising to find a dramatic and steady increase in research reports and writings about self-esteem cited in major databases such as ERIC, PsycINFO, and Web of Science from 1960 to 2005.[2]

Nonetheless, an important attitude of free inquiry is a willingness to put even our most trusted bromides to conceptual, theoretical, and empirical analysis and evaluation. When self-esteem has been examined in this way, the results and interpretations forthcoming have been much less conclusive than the foregoing statements and sentiments proclaim. In what is perhaps the most comprehensive evaluative review of research and theory concerning the educational and social effects of high self-esteem, Baumeister, Campbell, Krueger, and Vohs (2003) reach the following general conclusions:

> The benefits of high self-esteem fall into two categories: enhanced initiative and pleasant feelings. We have not found evidence that boosting self-esteem (by therapeutic interventions or school programs) causes benefits. Our findings do not support continued widespread efforts to boost self-esteem in the hope that it will by itself foster improved outcomes. (p. 1)

Of added relevance to education and schooling is their further conclusion that "the modest correlations between self-esteem and school performance do not indicate that high self-esteem leads to good performance. Instead, high self-esteem is partly the result of good school performance" (p. 1) (also see Kohn, 1994).

Although these observations are extremely helpful, there is a tendency in such evaluations to give priority to empirical issues and data as if these alone might resolve the complex social and educational issues at stake. However, questions of educational aims cannot be decided on empirical bases alone, as vital as such information obviously is. For example, given evidence that "self-esteem does lead to greater happiness" (Baumeister et al., 2003, p. 1), should it be promoted actively in schools despite evidence that "efforts to boost the self-esteem of pupils have not been shown to improve academic performance and may sometimes be counterproductive" (Baumeister et al., 2003, p. 1)? Any possible resolution of questions such as this requires a turn to educational argument that involves conceptual, theoretical, and critical considerations. As a prelude to such considerations at the end of this chapter, it will be helpful to (1) place our contemporary focus on the self-esteem of students within a historical context that makes connections to the cultural evolution of both educational aims and conceptions of selfhood and (2) examine in some detail specific examples of contemporary psychological and educational attempts

---

[2] The only exception to this steady increase in writings about self-esteem in any of these major databases is a slight decrease in ERIC citations for self-esteem from 1996 to 2005. However, even here the number of articles on self-esteem for these 10 years is greater than for any previous period other than 1986 to 1995. When figures for all three databases are combined, with allowance for possible duplication, a conservative estimate is that by 2005 there were over 30,000 publications on self-esteem, mostly celebrating its educational, psychological, and social merits. At least one third of these appeared after 1995.

to measure this quality and intervene so as to improve the self-esteem of children and adolescents in American and Canadian schools. Such contextualizing and exemplification enable a critical reinterpretation of reasons and arguments for advancing heightened self-esteem as an educational aim, which, in turn, suggests alternative possibilities to safeguard the personal and social development of pupils.

Self-Esteem in Historical Context

As discussed in Chapter 2, it is difficult for most contemporaries to imagine that selfhood and self-esteem, understood as aspects of personhood that are central to our existence as individuals in society, are relatively recent arrivals on the cultural historical landscape. In English, the word *self*, used as a noun, first appeared around 1300, and from then until near the end of the seventeenth century had primarily negative connotations as a kind of blasphemous arrogance that improperly challenged religious and social orders of the day (Danziger, 1997a). However, by 1694, John Locke, in the second edition of his famous *Essay Concerning Human Understanding*, was able to discuss the self (or personal identity) in predominately secular terms as an internal focus or point from which individuals could witness and monitor their experiences (Taylor, 1989). Since Locke, the notion of human consciousness has become imbued with a self-consciousness that accompanies many or most of our experiences and actions. As a consequence, we do not as selves *live* in our actions and experiences so much as we possess or *own* them. By the early eighteenth century, the core idea of the self as an experiencer (an owner and evaluator of experience) had become secularized and carried positive connotations in everyday speech and activity (Toulmin, 1977).

The inner psychological self had been invented (Lyons, 1978), and from this time onward the flow of approval and disapproval that attended the social activities of individuals could be understood as directed at their "selves" rather than at their specific actions. One important consequence of this linguistic, conceptual, and experiential revolution was that the language of self-evaluation shifted away from conceptions of guilt and sin toward ideas of blameworthiness and self-esteem. Today, the

> objectified self that persons now harbor within them is above all an object of approval and disapproval, both by others and by the person herself. This self is always conceived as an object of variable worth, and therefore the desire to raise or maintain its worth comes to be regarded as an identifiable human motive. (Danziger, 1997a, p. 145)

By the early eighteenth century, even some religious leaders, like Bishop Butler (1950/1726), had concluded that the main trouble with humanity was not that people had an overabundance of self-love but that they had too little of the right kind of self-regard. The idea of "the right kind of self-love" received a highly unique rendering in the writings of Jean-Jacques Rousseau, regarded by many as the father of modern progressive education and developmental psychology (Mayer, 1966). Rousseau believed that human beings are naturally inclined toward a form of self-love (*amour de soi-même*) that is centered around caring for oneself in a manner that blends easily with a genuine concern and sympathy for others, but that this natural self-love is corrupted by societal demands and expectations for individuals to compete with one another for resources and prestige. Society thus breeds a kind of vanity and self-importance (*amour propre*) that diminishes and twists authentic self-love and compassion for others. Rousseau produced highly original and influential writings in political and educational theory that advanced possible ways of limiting the corrupting influences of society on its members.

The primary purpose of his educational theorizing was "to prevent *amour de soi* [*même*] from turning into *amour propre*, for this is the true source of man's dividedness" (Bloom, 1979, p. 10). To this end, Rousseau (1979/1762) proposed a developmentally graduated form of education that promotes the self-satisfaction of persons of equality in a way consistent with their natural tendencies toward *amour de soi-même*. To avoid premature confrontation with others' wills in a way that would lead to overly strong forms of *amour propre*, Rousseau insisted that the early education of the child should be structured in such a manner that the child will always do what she wants, but that what she wants to do will be what is educationally appropriate. The teacher's role is to choose the child's activities judiciously to ensure that she will not be required to make social comparisons with others before she is satisfied with herself and truly concerned with others. Since the publication of *Émile* (or *On Education*) in 1762, Rousseau's emphasis on the interests and self-love of the child has influenced more than two centuries of "progressive education," earlier forms of which tended to retain his emphasis on moral and political education but later forms of which often have taken more decidedly psychological directions.

Although there is considerable debate concerning the precise nature of agreements and disagreements among various educational doctrines that might be included under the banner of progressive education (e.g., Adelman, 2000), it is most often held that Rousseau's ideas initiated and in many ways sustained the movement. "Pestalozzi, Herbart, Froebel, the Macmillans, Montessori, Caldwell, Cook, Dewey are his [Rousseau's] successors; and such devices as the Nursery School [Kindergarten], the Dalton Plan, the Play Way, and the Project Method are the practical results of what they taught" (Jacks, 1950, p. 116). In particular, Rousseau's emphasis on the interests, activities, and development of pupils gradually became enshrined in a general form of education that focused on the whole person, individual differences in interests and abilities, and learning by doing, especially through play and concrete problem-solving situations. Even more influential was his overarching concern for the authentic self-esteem of the learner as a buffer against the potentially invidious comparisons with others that are encouraged by traditional modes of education and society in general.

Well-known educators like Pestalozzi, Herbart, and Froebel established the first non-traditional schools and kindergartens in Switzerland and Germany in the late 1700s and early 1800s, developing a variety of neo-Rousseauian educational theories and methods. In different ways and with different emphases, all grappled with the tensions between nature and society, self and others, and personal freedom and civic duty/virtue. Many of their educational concerns were highly moral and political—so much so that several of their followers (especially those of Froebel), around 1868, fled to the United States as refugees from political ferments in Europe, where their ideas were interpreted as threats to church and state (Adelman, 2000).

The moral and political tenor of the early European progressives received an influential rendering in the educational writings of the American philosopher and psychologist John Dewey, who—together with his wife, Alice, daughter Evelyn, and colleagues like George Herbert Mead—became immersed in a variety of educational experiments, including the establishment and running of the famous Laboratory School sponsored by the University of Chicago. The educational plan adopted in the Chicago Laboratory School was based initially on Froebel's kindergarten, albeit with a more explicitly social and pragmatic rendering, and consisted largely of following and responding to the child's nature (Deegan, 1999). Although Dewey's emphasis on children's play and interests was frequently interpreted as a misplaced abandonment of more traditional educational aims and methods, Dewey was primarily concerned with achieving a social democratic *via media* between what too frequently are cast as oppositional polarities, such as curriculum content versus learner interest and self versus community. For example, in a succinct response to his critics, Dewey (1938) made it clear that starting with the life experience and interests of the child in no way precludes ending with the organized subject matter of the established disciplines.

> The utilization of subject-matter found in the present life-experience of the learner…is perhaps the best illustration that can be found of the basic principle of using existing experience as the means of carrying learners on to a wider, more refined, and better organized environing world, physical and human, than is found in the experiences from which educative growth sets out. (p. 82)

In a similar manner, starting by safeguarding the self-interest and self-esteem of the learner in no way precludes ending with community involvement and interest in others. Most of Dewey's educational writings are concerned with describing in theoretical detail the conditions and processes involved in such educational transformations.

Progressive emphases on the nature, development, and self-esteem of the child also held considerable attraction to the developing discipline of psychology. By the early twentieth century, the ideas not only of Rousseau but also of Darwin, Freud, and others had created a theoretical and practical niche within which psychology could develop rapidly as a social science and profession claiming unique expertise in matters relating to the self (cf. Baumeister, 1987; Cushman, 1995; Herman, 1995). The burgeoning presence of psychology in educational and other social institutions received enormous support from the opening up of the new field of personality psychology, which quickly became joined to social, developmental, and educational branches of the discipline. Perhaps no single psychologist was more directly responsible for establishing a psychological science of personality and selfhood than Gordon Allport (1937), an individual who directly and indirectly influenced subsequent generations of psychologists and educational psychologists concerned with both self-expression and self-management.

> Allport mapped out a self that reflected the new realities of industrial, urban America. This was a self that could be known, governed, managed; it was a self that could be embraced by employers and officialdom and one to which upwardly mobile individuals could aspire. Paradoxically, this was also a self that promised liberation from standardization and a heightened level of individuality. Individual measurement would transform an intangible value—individuality—into an empirical reality and in the process would free Americans from the sociological straitjacket of group-based categories. (Nicholson, 2003, pp. 100–101)

Allport's central contribution was to advance an approach to selfhood that combined concern for scientific rigor and control with humanistic impulses for self-development and fulfillment.

The Measurement of Self-Esteem

As noted in Chapter 3, the 1950s, 1960s, and 1970s witnessed a humanistic reaction against the behaviorism that had dominated American psychology during the first half of the twentieth century. Humanistic psychology encouraged a renewed focus on inner processes in psychology, with an emphasis on individually unique affective experiences. Consistent with Allport's endorsement of a joint commitment to humanistic impulses and social scientific methods, many educational psychologists in this period employed measures of self-esteem and/or self-concept to investigate relations of these constructs with intelligence and academic achievement (Bledsoe, 1964; Engel & Raine, 1963; Phillips, 1964). Piers and Harris (1964) developed a popular and influential measure of children's self-concept in 1964, which was subsequently revised and expanded and is still widely utilized. Results of early correlational studies often indicated a moderately strong relationship between self-concept and academic achievement (e.g., Ozehosky & Clark, 1970; Sears, 1970; Williams & Cole, 1968). Although some researchers distinguished between self-esteem and self-concept by emphasizing that the former referred to self-worth while the latter referenced self-understanding or self-belief, measures like the Piers-Harris Self-Concept Scale tended to blur this distinction and included items that probed both of these aspects of selfhood.

Throughout the later part of the twentieth century, many North American educational psychologists took a more interventionist approach, focusing on the diagnosis and enhancement of children's self-esteem and self-concepts. Research in these areas usually involved comparisons of pre- and post-intervention student responses to paper-and-pencil measures, such as the Tennessee Self-Concept Scale (Roid & Fitts, 1988) or the Piers-Harris Self-Concept Scale (Piers & Harris, 1964), in which the respondent places a mark beside the statement that is most like him or her. Scores on such inventories were also correlated with student scores in various areas of academic achievement (Marsh, 1986). Results from much of this research were interpreted to demonstrate that increases in self-esteem and/or self-concept result in increases in academic achievement. For example, self-esteem in preschool children contributes "significantly to predictions of third grade academic performance" (Bridgeman & Shipman, 1978, p. 17), while global and academic self-concept scores contribute significantly to variance in academic achievement (Jordan, 1981), and children with high rather than low self-concepts attribute their academic success to their own skills (Ames & Felkner, 1979).

Once again, the blurred distinction between the constructs of self-esteem and self-concept is indicated in the interchangeability of esteem and concept scales during this period. For example, studies by Kelly (1970), Trowbridge (1974), and Zirkel and Moses (1971) examined self-concept using Coopersmith's Self-Esteem Inventory. Alternatively, Harris and Braun (1971) examined self-esteem using the Piers-Harris Children's Self-Concept Scale. Several other studies reported on definitional and statistical issues related to the self, including dimensions of the self (e.g., Guardo & Bohan, 1971; Richmond & White, 1971), semiprojective measures of self-concept (Cicirelli, 1971), and the application of self scales to different populations (White & Bashaw, 1971). Trowbridge (1972) examined socioeconomic status and self-concept and contended that "the search for an adequate, meaningful tool to measure a child's self-concept was the most difficult and crucial part of the study" (p. 532).

Several other studies focused on the reliability and validity of self-esteem and self-concept scales. For example, Michael, Smith, and Michael (1975) examined the factorial validity of the Piers-Harris Children's Self-Concept Scale for different age populations, while Battle (1976) conducted a test-retest reliability study of the Canadian Self-Esteem Inventory for Children and Drummond and McIntire (1977) examined the factor structure of the Self-Esteem Inventory and the Self-Concept and Motivation Inventory. The perceived need for the development of more accurate assessments of self-esteem was indicative of the continuing dominance of the scientific, or at least psychometric, method in psychology.

A number of other studies and projects focused on ways to promote a positive, independent, and responsible sense of self in children. For example, Wang and Stiles (1976) examined a program called the Self-Schedule System and concluded that this program was effective in the development of children's concept of self-responsibility, including their beliefs that they could control and be responsible for their classroom behaviors and learning outcomes (notice that *self-responsibility* here refers to responsibility for oneself and not responsibility to others). Mattocks and Jew (1974) discussed ways in which teachers could contribute to the development of children's self-concepts. They contended "that the teacher's role in shaping the self-concept of the child has not been sufficiently emphasized. The general goal of education should include encouragement of the child's dependence upon his efforts, decisions, and self-control" (p. 204). Hauserman, Miller, and Bond (1976) presented a procedure designed to raise the self-concepts of four children with negative self-concepts; they reported a large gain in self-concept score by every child exposed to the procedure.

Of course it should not be too surprising to discover an improvement in the self-esteem scores of students who received a psychoeducational intervention intended to improve self-esteem, especially when measured in ways consistent with the content of that intervention. Indeed, it would seem odd if students exposed to specific curricular content and activities intended to improve their self-esteem did not demonstrate higher levels of self-esteem than students who were not exposed to this content and these activities. Whether or not such results indicate a genuine increase in a persistent and reasonable sense of self-worth grounded in students' actual abilities and goals is unknown but seems debatable.

Alongside investigative applications of self-enhancement programs was the publication of books on self-esteem and self-concept. Many works were directed to parents and teachers, providing guidance and recommendations on ways to enhance children's self-esteem and self-concepts. Exemplary titles included *Your Child's Self-Esteem: The Key to His Life* (Briggs, 1970) and *Self Concept and School Achievement* (Purkey, 1970). Other books were written for students of educational psychology; they included titles such as *Self-Worth and School Learning* (Covington & Beery, 1976) and *Enhancing Self-Concept in Early Childhood: Theory and Practice* (Samuels, 1977). Some authors and researchers used Maslow's theory of self-actualization as a framework for discussions of self-esteem in children (e.g., Farmer, 1982; Parish & Philip, 1982; Nystul, 1984), while still others focused not only on self-esteem but also on self-control (e.g., Humphrey, 1984; Mischel & Mischel, 1983).

As we shall explore more extensively in Chapter 5, several investigators concentrated on definitional and statistical issues related to self-esteem and self-concept (e.g., Shavelson, Hubner, & Stanton, 1976; Winne & Walsh, 1980). For example, Shavelson and Bolus (1982) examined subject-specific and general self-concept among adolescents using the Tennessee Self-Concept Scale and the Piers-Harris Self-Concept Scale. They concluded that self-concept is multifaceted and hierarchical and that there is a "causal predominance for self-concept over achievement" (p. 15). Byrne and Shavelson (1986) examined the multifaceted structure of self-concept to determine whether academic self-concept could be discriminated from academic grades; they concluded that general self-concept could be distinct from but related to academic self-concept. More recently, Marsh, Hey, Roche, and Perry (1997) developed and tested the Physical Self-Description Questionnaire with elite and nonelite adolescent athletes, concluding that discriminating among different kinds of self-concept broadens our understanding of how the self-concept functions in school contexts.

The measurement of self-esteem and self-concept continued to the end of the twentieth century and beyond, with many attempts to obtain more complete and accurate measures of self-esteem and self-concept by revising and expanding existing instruments and measures and creating new ones. The development, testing, and subsequent revisions of self measures have mostly focused on improving the statistical reliability and validity of the instruments and enhancing discriminations among various aspects and dimensions of the measured self. For example, the Self Description Questionnaire (SDQI) originally examined self-concept variables across academic and nonacademic domains (Marsh, Smith, & Barnes, 1983) but subsequently has been expanded to include the SDQII and SDQIII for measuring general or global self-concept across age groups and the ASDQI, ASDQII, and ASDQIII for measuring academic self-concept across age groups. However, as elaborated in Chapter 5, such statistical and psychometric work is not the same as detailed conceptual analysis of what we mean by self-concept and self-esteem. As scholars like Wittgenstein (1953) and Smedslund (1988) have consistently pointed out, it is impossible to resolve or clarify conceptual matters through empirical research, psychometric or otherwise. Such clarification requires careful examination of the assumptions and conceptions evident in our uses of relevant everyday and professional language.

In this regard, an examination of items on self-esteem and self-concept scales reveals a focus on an emotional, personally valued self. For example, The Rosenberg Self-Esteem Scale (RSES) is almost exclusively directed at the respondents' feelings about themselves without specific reference to others. Items on this scale reflect a general judgment of one's worth as evident in items such as "I feel I do not have much to be proud of," "I feel that I have a number of good qualities," and "I wish I could have more respect for myself." The Coopersmith Self-Esteem Inventory (CSEI) contains items similar to those in the RSES, such as "I'm pretty happy," "I can usually take care of myself," "All in all, I'm inclined to feel that I'm a failure," "I often feel ashamed of myself," and "I have a low opinion of myself." The self-concept scales also ask respondents to describe and judge themselves on similar items. For example, the 80-item Piers-Harris Self-Concept Scale for Children (PHSCS) contains statements such as "I am unhappy," "I am good-looking, and "I am good in my school work." Similarly, the SDQI has items such as "I am good-looking", and "I like all school subjects" (Marsh, Smith, & Barnes, 1983).

These measures of self-esteem and self-concept seem to assume a sensitive, self-striving, purposeful, self-concerned, and humanistic self. Such a conception of personhood is devoid of any consideration of the self as historically and socioculturally situated. Indeed, any meaningful connections between the self and others are almost nonexistent in the items that constitute such scales and subscales. There are, of course, statements regarding one's relationship to others, particularly peers and parents. But, the degree to which one feels that others like him or her certainly does not constitute a genuine social or moral connection to others. Further, statements such as "I am as sociable as I want to be," "I get along with others," "I'm easy to like" (CSEI), and "I am able to do things as well as most other people" (RSES) are more reflective of a radically isolated individual who acts dispassionately and instrumentally within the social world. There is little here that reflects a socially committed person who acts dutifully and/or virtuously in a communal context. Greer's (2003) genealogy of self research and measures in psychology reveals a similar theme—a general lack of integration of the measured self with meaningful moral and social commitment. "Questions of agency, intentionality, reflexivity, and moral judgment are gaps left behind in the wake of the disciplinary [i.e., disciplinary psychology's] transformation of the self" (Greer, 2003, p. 101).

Interventions to Enhance Self-Esteem (A Brief Case Study)

As already noted, attempts to measure self-esteem have been closely linked to attempts to demonstrate improvements to self-esteem as a consequence of psychoeducational interventions. Stout (2000) points out that the appeal of self-esteem interventions in American schools (and probably in Canadian schools as well) is closely connected to strong strands of individual accomplishment in the larger society, especially assumed connections between life success and self-reliance.

> The very strong individualism that characterizes much of American culture no doubt explains why the self-esteem movement has become more popular here than anywhere else in the world.... The idea of self-esteem also appeals to Americans because it refers to the concept of self-reliance, which is the underlying principle of the American Dream: study hard, pull yourself up by your bootstraps and you too can be a success. It is the perfect expression of "life, liberty, and the pursuit of happiness." (p. 15)

Stout goes on to lament the widespread and uncritical adoption of self-esteem as an educational goal in itself—a goal that she believes is responsible for dysfunctional levels of narcissism, student labeling and victimization, excessive emotionalism, feelings of entitlement, and cynicism. To support her views, Stout presents evidence of high levels of intellectual self-confidence and self-esteem in the absence of adequate levels of substantive knowledge and ability.

> For example, according to a recent study by the Higher Education Research Institute at UCLA, 53.6 percent of college students reported a strong sense of intellectual self-confidence (compared to 34.8 percent in 1971) and 69 percent of freshmen expect to earn a bachelor's degree, compared to 58.7 percent in 1974. Unfortunately, the reality for most of these young people falls short of their expectations. In 1995 just

28 percent of high school graduates between the ages of 25 and 34 had completed four or more years of college. Instead of ensuring that kids have a strong foundation of knowledge, today we ensure that they have very high self-esteem. We have traded substance for image....According to the U.S. Department of Education, nationally about 30 percent of all college students take at least one remedial course, and at my university, for example, over half the students require remedial help. The self-esteem movement has given false expectations to our children and has thereby deprived them of real hope. Realizing that they have been cheated, is it any wonder they become cynics? (p. 41)

At this writing, views like those of Stout (2000) are familiar to anyone who has attended to either the relevant professional and scholarly literature or to popular media coverage concerning the educational and societal effects of inflated levels of self-esteem. Given this familiarity, it is not our intention here to attend further to such views. Our overall purpose is to examine critically the influence of psychological conceptions of self-hood on students, education, and schooling during the last half of the twentieth century in the United States and Canada. The fact that by the end of that century Stout and others had begun to remark and document a negative impact of self-esteem and other psychological conceptions of selfhood on pupils and their education is obviously relevant to our project. However, to obtain a more concrete sense of exactly how daily life in classrooms was affected by a widespread promotion of self-esteem and self-concept in American and Canadian schools during the final decades of the twentieth century, we have selected representative materials from the recommended learning resources of the British Columbia Ministry of Education (BCME) regarding the development and enhancement of students as "selves" (for a comprehensive examination see McLellan, 2008). What follows in this section may best be thought of as a brief case study of educational policy and practice with respect to the promotion of psychological forms of selfhood in one North American jurisdiction (the Province of British Columbia, Canada).

In the Province of British Columbia, recommended learning resources are instructional materials that have been approved by the Ministry of Education for use in the province's schools. These materials come in various forms, including print, games, manipulatives, videos, and software "that support BC curriculum, and that will be used by teachers and/or students for instructional and assessment purposes" (British Columbia Ministry of Education, 2005, p. 299). Although teachers have choice in selecting materials for use in the classroom, they must use provincially recommended resources or learning resources that have been approved at a local school board level. Learning resources are aligned with grade, subject area, and curricular goals and range from classroom kits and programs to schoolwide programs and broader school-community partnership initiatives.

Many learning resources that address the personal development of students are packaged as psychoeducational kits, and offered to improve students' personal competencies and skills, such as self-esteem and self-discipline. These kits, often self-contained modules aimed at individual success within specific programs, include titles such as *100 Ways to Enhance Self-Concept in the Classroom: A Handbook for Teachers and Parents* (Canfield & Wells, 1976) and *Especially You*, an 18-minute video that helps students develop coping skills "by emphasizing the importance of feeling good about oneself, developing strong decision-making and problem-solving abilities and respecting differences" (National Film Board of Canada, 1989, p. 1).

Other programs are geared at enhancing personal management and career-building competencies. For example, the *Destination 2020* resource for grades six and seven "is designed to help students recognize the many skills they are acquiring now and how these skills will be useful in their future careers" (National Life Work Centre, 2005, p. 1). Personal decision making is a common component of learning resources. For example, a video and activities package entitled *Making Decisions* is designed to prevent drug and alcohol abuse. Lessons within the package (entitled "The Whole You," "The Importance of Needs and Wants," "Our Personal Goals," "Decisions, Decisions, Decisions," and "The Choice is Mine") emphasize making decisions that promote individual skills such as assertiveness, self-confidence, thinking for oneself, and considering how choices affect one's own life (Mangham, 1999, as cited in British Columbia Ministry of Education, 1999b, p. 1).

The BCME also recommends the Healthy Buddies program as a suitable classroom program that meets prescribed learning outcomes across a number of subject areas from English language arts to physical education. Healthy Buddies empowers elementary schoolchildren to live healthier lives by providing them with knowledge about the three components of health—physical activity, healthy eating, and feeling good about oneself—as well as encouraging positive attitudes toward them (British Columbia Children's Hospital, 2010). The program is a "school-based healthy living program providing direct instruction to intermediate students in the areas of nutrition, physical activity, and emotional health and self-esteem" (British Columbia Children's Hospital, 2010, p. 2). The program has three themes that are

> based on the understanding that the health of an individual depends upon three equally important components [identified as] moving your body, nutrition, [and] feeling good about yourself .... [Students learn] to value who they and others are on the inside [and] about being "positive buddies." This role can help kids feel good about themselves as productive, valuable people. (British Columbia Children's Hospital, 2010, p. 3)

Here, we see a merging of the managed and expressive selves of educational psychology (Chapter 3)—the acquisition of skills, whether in the shape of physical coordination skills or verbal skills such as kind comments, makes students feel good. Whether or not such skills are indicative of a social commitment to the well-being of others is less clear. The inclusion of the word *buddies* in the title of the program is testimony to an altruism that is much less obvious in the program itself. The program materials seem much more concerned with how one's buddies can assist one's positive self-development than with how individual children can become good buddies to others.

The Healthy Buddies program is marketed to teachers and school administrators as a scientifically valid, appealing, easy-to-use package that targets student development while also addressing practical and administrative concerns. For example, the program is "comprehensive and multi-factorial," referring to the fact that the program is based on a study that employed a number of self-report measures, including Harter's Perceived Competence Scale. The "learning aids include fun card games, skits, poster design challenges, and cooperative in-class activities" (British Columbia Children's Hospital, 2007, p. 4) and the "fitness activities are incredibly easy for teachers to facilitate" (British Columbia Children's Hospital, 2010, p. 4). Also, the matching of older and younger students from intact classes as "buddy classes…in the gym helps address the shortage of gym time and space that exists in many elementary schools" (British Columbia Children's Hospital, 2010, p. 4). The implication is that students' well-being can be enhanced in a timely and efficient manner to conserve limited educational resources.

Friends for Life is another psychological program designed for classroom application that purports to teach "cognitive and emotional skills in a simple and well-structured format" (Barrett, 2001, p. 1). The Ministry of Education partnered with the Ministry of Children and Family Development in 2004 to implement the program "as a classroom-based universal prevention program or as an early intervention risk reduction strategy for anxiety" (Barrett, 2001, p. 1). The Friends for Life teacher kit is described as a "scientifically validated cognitive behavioral program…designed for ease-of-use in a day-to-day Canadian classroom setting…to prevent anxiety and depression and encourage resilience and self-esteem" (Barrett, 2001, p. 1). The program "promotes important self-development and educational concepts such as self-esteem, problem-solving, self-expression, and building positive relationships with peers and adults" (Barrett, 2001, p. 1). The Friends for Life website advertises program snippets in the form of "free downloads," as well as an online shopping service to purchase a range of materials. Also included on the website is an advertisement by the BCME stating that "The No. 1 goal of our education system is to help B.C. students achieve their best. FRIENDS provides the early support some children need to reduce their anxiety and make their school years healthier and more successful" (Friends for Life, 2008, p. 1).

Action Schools! B.C. is yet another prevention program designed to assist schools in the promotion of healthy living, with an aim to "achieve long-term, measurable and sustainable health benefits…based on four health targets that incorporate health and academic outcomes" (British Columbia Ministry of Health Services, 2005, p. 11). One of the program modules, designed for classroom application, is entitled the "healthy self," and claims that "self-esteem and specific competencies [identified as athletic, social, and academic, once again derived from Susan Harter's Perceived Competence Scale] are key indicators of a healthy self in children" (Harter, 1982, as cited in British Columbia Ministry of Health Services, 2005, p. 32). Action Schools! B.C. promotes the use of "programs and activities aimed at improving self-concept in children" (British Columbia Ministry of Health Services, 2005, p. 62), such as "Self-Esteem BINGO," the "Self-Confidence Quiz," "Things I Do Well," and "Hero in You," an "online education program designed to motivate, inspire, and encourage youth to set and achieve meaningful personal goals" (British Columbia Ministry of Health Services, 2005, p. 11).

Another example is the Esteem Team—a goal-setting program designed "to inspire and educate Canadian youth…[in] life skills, values, and goal-setting strategies that apply to all young people, no matter what they hope to achieve" (Esteem Team, 2005, p. 41). The program consists of seven lesson activities and worksheets that are "flexible, user-friendly and specifically designed to meet the needs of busy teachers" (Esteem Team, 2005, p. 2). According to this program, "students will learn responsibility, accountability, self-assessment and above all, empowerment" (Esteem Team, 2005, p. 1).

The BCME also endorses programs designed to enhance students' personal and social responsibility. These often involve partnerships between schools, school districts, and provincial and federal institutions that utilize "guiding legislation," such as human rights policies and laws, in the development of school policies and initiatives. For example, the B.C. Safe Schools Centre is a partnership between the BCME, British Columbia solicitor general, and local school districts that provides a centralized resource program for educators, parents, and students regarding issues such as bullying. The center provides information and access to manuals, kits, and programs for personal development, such as self-esteem, self-concept, and self-efficacy enhancement. Manuals and kits include titles such as *Building a Positive Self-Concept: 113 Activities for Adolescents*, and *Building Self-Esteem in the Classroom*; these are "grade-leveled workbooks designed to help students appreciate their uniqueness" (British Columbia Ministry of Education, 2004c, p. 4).

A remarkable claim of many of these programs is that students will reap personal and social benefits simply by completing the required steps, sessions, and activities. The Friends for Life program "ensures [that] even children whose distress has gone undetected by parents, carers and teachers will be helped" (2008, p. 2). The implication is that nonspecialized teachers can deliver the user-friendly lessons during normal class times and that the educational power of such a psychoeducational intervention lies in the structure, content, and method of the program itself. Further support for the educational authority of such programs, kits, and activities (beyond the fact that they are ministry-approved) is in their claims that they are evidence-based, user-friendly, fit well within and across existing curricula, include well-scripted lesson plans with ready-made activities and assessments, and are applicable to a wide range of students. It is not difficult to understand the appeal of these psychoeducational products, particularly for teachers who must consider issues such as time, students' abilities, and personal expertise on the one hand and achievement of curricular goals on the other.

The emphasis on the personal growth and achievement of students in such kits and programs reflects psychological theorizing and research on the development of children as individuals. By promoting individual achievement, the attainment of personal skills and abilities (identified both in terms of self skills and scholastic skills), and assessment at the individual level, all will be well for both learners and teachers. For example, the Making Decisions program is designed to promote skill development in making major decisions through learning activities such as role playing, vocabulary, and paragraph writing; it is recommended for the B.C. Grade 6 Personal Planning curriculum, which aims to promote "skills such as time-management, self-assessment, [and] goal-setting...that can enhance their personal well-being" (British Columbia Ministry of Education, 1999a, p. 1), and to "maintain an appropriate sense of personal worth, potential, and individuality" (British Columbia Ministry of Education 1999a, p. 3).

The BCME also provides a list of achievement indicators that teachers may use for assessing students' success in meeting learning outcomes associated with particular curricula. In the Health and Career Education Curriculum for grade 4, Career Exploration, success in the program is indicated by students' abilities to "develop an inventory of their personal attributes (e.g., skills, interests, accomplishments; things they're good at, things they've learned to do, things they like to do, things they don't like to do), and modify this inventory periodically" (British Columbia Ministry of Education 2004a, p. 25). Note the focus on individual interests and likes/dislikes, with little consideration of the possible relevance of such attributes or interests in relation to those of others. For the grade 5 Healthy Relationships program, students receive further instruction said to relate to their relationships with others. However, once again, success is indicated by a student's ability to "create a self-inventory of their interpersonal skills (e.g., listening, honesty, sharing, co-operation, respect, empathy, inclusion, refusal skills, assertiveness, seeking help, anger management)" (2004b, p. 33) and by the student's own personal assessment of skills, such as setting "goals for improving selected interpersonal skills (e.g., identify skills they want to improve, identify strategies for improvement)" (2004b, p. 33). In these programs, individual students determine what relationship skills they need to improve. Teachers are directed to evaluate the self-development of students via objective markers but also in consideration of the individual students' personal goals and interests.

In summary, in the province of British Columbia, Canada, a wide variety of provincially and locally approved teaching and learning resources in the form of classroom programs, guidelines, technical supports, and suggested classroom and school initiatives are offered to teachers, school administrators, and other educators (e.g., school counselors), many of which focus directly on the personal, psychological, and self-development of students. Teachers and school administrators have implemented many of these resources in their classrooms and schools. For instance, several dozen B.C. schools have participated in the Healthy Buddies program since 2006, and since the initiation of the Action Schools! B.C. program, an estimated 595,170 students have registered!

Not surprisingly, classroom teachers struggle with meeting the demands of such programs while also ensuring that students achieve substantive knowledge and understanding in various core areas of study (e.g., language arts, mathematics, science, social studies) appropriate to their grades and abilities. As noted by Olson (2003), the teacher tries, often unsuccessfully, to balance the needs of the curriculum with the personal development of the student. This tension frequently materializes in the context of student assessment. For example, Katz (2001, as cited in Olson, 2003, p. 221) asked teachers to describe their approaches to teaching a mandated curriculum. Teachers reported that they were conflicted between honoring the mandated standards and recognizing the growth of individual students. One teacher reported that

> The Ministry documents say "the student will independently…" [write a report on Louis Riel]. [One child] might only be a level 2 but I'll give him a 3 plus because he has come so far. The guy next to him who has all the grey matter upstairs and is just lazy, he gets a 2. So sometimes I just toss what the Ministry says aside; I'm working with this kid's self-esteem and he has put in hours on it. (Katz, 2001, as cited in Olson, 2003, p. 221)

Another teacher said "Oh, I'll go through [the assignment] the first time and see where he stands according to everybody else [the norms]. Then I'll go back and look at where he is himself [relative to] what I know he has done in the past" (Katz, 2001, as cited in Olson, 2003, p. 221).

Such teacher reports with respect to "balancing" curricular goals and student assessment illustrate teachers' concerns for students' selves and self-development at the classroom level. In the first instance, the teacher noted the child's efforts and interpreted them as representing achievement, while the academic performance of "the guy next to him" was deemed less worthy on the basis of the teacher's sense of the relative academic abilities and work habits of the students. In the case of the second teacher, we see the evaluation of a student compared to other students and compared to his own abilities and past performance, suggesting that this teacher values personal progress and development as equal to (or more important than) level of academic achievement per se.

It is not surprising that teachers and other educators value and promote the personal development of students. Many educational policies and practices champion individual development. The personal development of students is advanced in broad educational aims and goals; in specific curriculum areas, achievement is sometimes explicitly defined in terms of personal skill development (e.g., British Columbia Ministry of Education, 1999a). Enhancement of individual students' self-esteem and self-management is often tied to academic achievement. In particular, many classroom practices are designed to achieve subject-specific learning objectives through the attainment and refinement of self-regulatory skills and the enhancement of students' self-esteem. Thus, many programs (including some that have been highlighted here) focus on developing students' selves as a method for improving their academic performance. In the United States, the National Board for Professional Teaching Standards (2002) has five core propositions that identify the skills and aptitudes of effective teachers. Under the first proposition, titled "Teachers are committed to students and their learning," accomplished teachers are identified as those who "develop students' cognitive capacities and respect for learning. Equally important they foster students' self-esteem" (National Board for Professional Teaching Standards, 2002, p. 3).

Americans and Canadians live in a social world that emphasizes the right to pursue personal goals and interests and advocates individual responsibility for personal decisions and actions. In the education system, these values permeate most pedagogical practices, including those intended to enhance communal ideals such as social responsibility and to help students master curriculum content. In this regard it is important to recognize explicitly a core assumption discernible in the foregoing descriptions of curricular materials available in the Province of British Columbia. This assumption is that the development of children and adolescents as social beings with commitments to others can be achieved by helping students to develop specific social skills that make them feel good about themselves in relation to others. Behind this assumption is the psychoeducational idea that life with others can be reduced to a set of individual skills that can be employed instrumentally to achieve social relations that effectively enhance one's sense of self as a social being. In other words, the classic tension in liberal democratic societies between individual and social ends is resolved by effectively treating others as means to one's social satisfaction and success.

Yet despite such psychoeducational programming, conflicting demands of individual goals of self-enhancement and social goals of harmonious relations with others continue to be much in evidence within contemporary educational contexts. In British Columbia, *The Report of the Royal Commission on Education, A Legacy for Learners 1988,* states that:

> Our expectations for schools are high. We have, in fact, an ambitious social as well as an educational agenda for them, as we seek to support our social structure in various ways. In the broadest sense, we have long expected schools to serve as agencies for civic and democratic development and as places where our culture and values can be sustained and transmitted to the young. (Montmarquette, 1990, p. 91)

Nonetheless, as acknowledged by the *Social Responsibility Performance Standards*—a recently developed handbook for assessing the civic/social engagement of students—social/civic engagement more often than not "is a secondary focus of other school activities" (British Columbia Ministry of Education, 2001, p. 7). In British Columbia, social responsibility is an educational objective that falls under the educational goal of human and social development, which is one of three broad goals of the general K–12 B.C. curriculum (the other goals are intellectual development and career development). It is important to note that the ministry emphasizes that "intellectual development of all students is the primary goal of education in British Columbia," (British Columbia Ministry of Education, 2001, p. 1), yet programs promoting individual and social development, such as Realizing Individual Potential and Becoming Responsible Citizens, "are grounded in the recognition that emotional and social development are as important to healthy, educated citizens as academic achievement" (British Columbia Ministry of Education, 2001, p. 1). Presumably, social aims of schooling, such as the inculcation of civic responsibility and cultural transmission, can issue from an education that enshrines a wide range of human knowledge and accomplishment in core curricula delivered in ways that encourage respectful participation and open dialogue with teachers and other students. However, it is less clear how educational materials and practices that focus on the acquisition and refinement of individual skills and strategies related to self-esteem might contribute to either social or intellectual development, given that development in these areas requires that students acquire concern and competence in areas outside of their individual perspectives and sense of well-being.

Critical Considerations and Alternatives in the Education of Persons

Is the educational cultivation of enhanced self-esteem really capable of contributing to personal and social betterment in the manner envisioned by so many contemporary educators and policy makers? As mentioned earlier, several scholars have recently challenged the empirical basis for such an assertion (e.g., Baumeister et al., 2003; Kohn, 1994). However, as we just have indicated, there are important conceptual, theoretical, and critical considerations that also challenge such a sweeping conclusion.

Clearly, the now voluminous literature in educational psychology that has accumulated around the promotion of the self-esteem of schoolchildren and adolescents generally places a high premium on self-discovery, self-expression, and self-fulfillment without much explicit discussion of broader educational aims or the social, cultural, moral, and political contexts of education. Take, for example, Canfield and Wells's (1994) book, which offers educators a multitude of ways to enhance students' self-esteem and self-concept in the classroom. In a chapter on academic strategy (in which the authors assert that self-esteem and academic competence are reciprocal in nature), a "class applause" activity is described to the teacher as:

a simple technique for cheering up a fellow class member.... When a candidate for class applause has been identified, have everyone jump to their feet, clap their hands, and shout words of encouragement and affection for the "down" person. Tell students that they can also ask for a standing ovation when they feel like they want or need one. They simply have to raise their hand and say "I would like a standing ovation." Then give it to them. (Canfield & Wells, 1994, p. 251)

The authors also dedicate twenty-seven pages of the book to an "annotated bibliography of the best available resources" (pp. 263–290) on self-concept and self-esteem, such as books, videotapes, programs, curriculum materials, and other instruments (e.g., self measurement tools). This is just one of many examples among others (e.g., McDaniel & Bielen, 1990; cf Kohn, 1994) of the ever-expanding panoply of psychoeducational interventions now in place in most North American school systems that target enhanced self-esteem as a primary goal quite independently of any other educational aims.

With the widespread acceptance of these products by educators and the general public in Western societies, self-expression and individual fulfillment now stand as educational aims in their own right, separated from and sometimes seemingly in competition with institutional aims of schooling that have traditionally emphasized intellectual development in the service of productive citizenship, understood as active, effective participation in the political, economic, sociocultural, and moral practices that constitute life with others within communities and nations (Olson, 2003). Even when these latter aims of education are mentioned by proponents of self-concept and self-esteem, they are likely to be treated as derivative from apparently more important inner psychological resources. To emphasize the extent to which this conclusion is warranted, we once again quote from Craven, Marsh, and Burnett (2003):

> A positive self-concept is widely considered fundamental for psychological health, personal achievement, and positive relationships. Self-concept is thought to make such a difference, that people who think positively about themselves are healthier, happier, and more productive. Hence, enhancing self-concept is considered necessary to maximizing human potential, from early development and school achievement, to physical/mental health and well being, to gainful employment and other contributions to society. (p. 96)

As discussed in Chapter 3, Guignon (2004) challenges the idea that authenticity is only a matter of inner emotional experience and expression. He points out that authenticity also requires a commitment backed by reason and goes on to argue that any such reasoned commitment can arise only in the context of shared practices and values within a social context. Charles Taylor (1991) makes a similar point in recognizing that any human agent who seeks significance and meaning in life must exist within a horizon of important questions, and that such a horizon is available only within a historically established sociocultural way of life. The upshot of such reasoning is that personally and socially productive forms of self-expression and self-fulfillment—of the sort envisioned by Branden (1984, 1995), Canfield and Wells (1994), Craven and colleagues (2003), McDaniel and Bielen (1990), and so many others—cannot issue from the activities of an isolated, detached psychological self attentive primarily to its own internal experiences and feelings.

Democratic organizations (classrooms, schools, communities, and nations) work only when their members exercise discernment and judgment with respect to at least some shared goals and beliefs. But standing behind one's beliefs, in a manner conducive to full participation in democratic exchanges and institutions, is not primarily a matter of having elevated self-esteem. A free and democratic society is possible only if its members are committed to the unrestricted exchange of views, and such exchange assumes that citizens are persons, with moral commitments and reasons, who are knowledgeable about the issues that confront them and their society. When conceptions and models of self-esteem and self-concept focus only on the feelings and experiences of individuals, they provide much too narrow a venue for the education of persons and citizens.[3,4]

The fact that so many proponents of self-esteem in the classroom and school have little to say about moral and political matters is indicative of the pervasive individualism that afflicts this area of contemporary educational theory, research, and practice and its relative neglect of the sociocultural (including the moral and political) constitution and concerns of fully functioning citizens and persons. It is simply educationally unsound to hold that the fostering of self-esteem and self-concept in classrooms is an adequate basis for the preparation of students as full participants in the sociocultural contexts in which they are embedded.

Instead of encouraging students in schools to "turn inward" in ways that privilege their own experiences, feelings, and perspectives, Philippe Meirieu (2005) maintains that school is a place where children must learn to disengage from their own experiences, situations, and preoccupations through ongoing interaction with other children and the curriculum. "*L'École doit aider l'enfant à renoncer à être au centre du monde*" (School must help the child to reject being at the center of the world) (p. 68). Children must learn that there are conventions and practices of correctness and truth that resist or may go against their own desires, and that they must participate in such practices and judge themselves and others accordingly. For Meirieu, a critical aspect of this escape from their immediate desires is learning to respect and consider other perspectives. "*À l'École, on apprend à*

---

[3] In fairness it should be noted that even the most vocal advocates of self-esteem in schools and society at large do not recommend the kinds of psychoeducational interventions adopted by some psychologists, teachers, and others. For example, Nathaniel Branden (1995), sometimes recognized as the father of the self-esteem movement, writes,

> If one examines the proposals offered to teachers on how to raise students' self-esteem, many are the kind of trivial nonsense that gives self-esteem a bad name, such as praising and applauding a child for virtually everything he or she does, dismissing the importance of objective accomplishments, handing out gold stars on every possible occasion, and propounding an "entitlement" idea of self-esteem that leaves it divorced from both behavior and character. (p. 203)

[4] It should also be pointed out that several prominent research psychologists have discussed the possible dangers of attempting to elevate self-esteem through facile methods of psychoeducational intervention. For example, Carol Dweck and her colleagues (e.g., Kamins & Dweck, 1999) have consistently demonstrated and warned that positive feedback that is intended to be self-enhancing can actually increase feelings of insecurity and vulnerability, especially if used to refer to or evaluate individual children rather than their actions. Nonetheless, Branden and other advocates and more neutral researchers such as Dweck, continue to cling to a radical individualism that understands educational success and life accomplishment as relatively independent of social, cultural, political, and moral considerations and contexts.

passer progressivement de son point de vue et de ses intérêts personnels à la recherche du bien commun" (At school, one learns to move beyond one's own point of view and personal interests to search for the common good) (p. 72). Indeed, a major goal of education is to help children take and evaluate different perspectives in cooperation with others within problem situations. For Meirieu, such perspective taking is an indispensable part of the development of students as persons and citizens.

Schooling provides many excellent venues for the study and facilitation of personal development as an expansion of the perspectives available to students. Taking and evaluating different perspectives encountered in formal curricula and informal classroom activities is an important part of the educational process in any society but is especially critical for the preparation of citizens in democratic societies. The self-development of persons and citizens is not primarily a matter of turning inward to discover one's authentic self or of carefully cultivating a positive self-image, self-concept, or repertoire of self-regulatory strategies. As possibly useful as any of these might be, they are of limited educational value unless they make contact with perspectives available in interpersonal and community activity, including those perspectives that constitute a representative sampling of what currently are considered to be our best theories and practices in subject areas as diverse as history, mathematics, biology, athletics, and the fine and performing arts. (We will have much more to say about this way of thinking about education and the development of students as communal agents in the final chapter of this book.)

The foregoing critical, conceptual, and theoretical considerations, in combination with extant challenges to empirical assumptions linking self-esteem to higher levels of academic attainment and social functioning (e.g., Baumeister et al., 2003), raise serious concerns about the adequacy of elevated self-esteem as a freestanding educational aim or as an educational means for advancing either intellectual or social goals of schooling. However, they do not suggest that the personal development of students is unimportant as an educational goal that might be set alongside more social aims of schooling, such as the promotion of good citizenship, social contribution, and care for others. The sole conclusion that follows from what has been said thus far is that elevated self-esteem is not an educationally valid end in itself. This conclusion may be sufficient reason to move away from classroom activities such as making a "commercial for oneself," in which students are directed to make "advertisements and commercials to sell themselves" (Canfield & Wells, 1994, p. 125) or to participate in "realizing your uniqueness" lessons (McDaniel & Bielen, 1990, p. 156). However, the larger educational questions concerning possible tensions between these emphases and ways of reconciling personal development and the social/institutional goals of schooling are not in any way decided by what has been said to this point. Since it is highly likely that the salience of concerns about elevated self-esteem in contemporary schools is related to such tensions and their resolution, a brief consideration of these complex matters is warranted.

Olson (2003) provides a useful point of departure for a discussion of personal development as possibly incompatible with more long-standing institutional goals of schooling to produce graduates who are able to fit easily into the economic, political, social, and moral life of their communities.

> Although humane feelings and personal morality are important, they are not, in my view, the primary concern of the school; people have a right to think and feel as they like. The goal of the school is much more limited, namely, teaching students how to participate in the bureaucratic institutions of the larger society. Thus, students must be taught how to engage with systematic, disciplined knowledge; to understand how the rule of law imparts both entitlements and responsibilities; and to recognize how the public institutions of the society allow them to pursue and achieve their own personal or local cultural goals. Whether or not they love knowledge and empathize with others is, perhaps, less important than that they know their duty and the rights and privileges that are earned by living up to it. Schools cannot and need not reform human nature. They have a more limited responsibility, namely, teaching the young how to live in a complex society composed of institutions for knowledge, justice, the economy, and the like.... Education teaches one to live with and interact productively with others one may never have met but who share competence with a common set of institutions and a common commitment to explicit norms and standards and the rule of law. (p. 296)

Thus, in Olson's view, it is not the job of schools to teach children to love or esteem themselves and others, to value learning or knowledge, or to develop personally in ways conducive to such caring. Instead, the purpose of schooling is to help children acquire knowledge and the ability to participate in those shared institutional practices within which one identifies as a citizen, professional, friend, colleague, and so forth. Throughout his book, Olson (2003) argues that any educational application of psychological approaches to personal development is doomed to fail unless it recognizes and accepts the institutional nature of schooling. As institutions, schools are responsible to the states that create them. Schools are charged with setting and maintaining standards, procedures, norms, and rules for learning, thinking, and knowing. What contemporary advocates of children's self-esteem seem not to understand, along with their arguably more educationally sophisticated progressive predecessors like Dewey, is that these institutional concerns and practices with respect to learning and knowing cannot be identified with child-centered initiatives that treat learning and development as matters of learners experientially exploring their local world and culture (Olson, 2003, p. 291).

It is obvious that the institutional mandates of schooling cannot be identified with the personal caprice of individual children. Nonetheless, to suggest that thoughtful progressives like Dewey (whom Olson obviously admires) are confused about the social, institutional, and personal developmental goals of education seems unwarranted. In particular, such a critical assessment appears to depend on an overly strong distinction between self and society of the sort that Dewey—together with other early American pragmatists like George Herbert Mead—found untenable.

That schools are institutions with a mandate to prepare individuals for full participation in society is undeniable and certainly is at odds with the elevation of enhanced self-esteem as an educational goal in the absence of a demonstrable causal and rational argumentative association with such mandated ends. However, beginning, at least in part, with the interests and activities of children is not necessarily incompatible with the kind of social/institutional understanding and capability that Olson (2003) champions as the chief aim of schooling. In 1938, Dewey responded to critics of his educational ideas in a way that emphasized his approach to educational development as charting a trajectory from the child's interests and activities to the social/institutional participation of full and active citizenship. Here, as we have previously noted, he stated that his intention in beginning with subject matter found in the current life experience of the learner was in accordance with "the basic principle of using existing experience as the means of carrying learners on to a wider, more refined, and better organized environing world, physical and human, than is found in the experiences from which educative growth sets out" (p. 82).

Dewey's theory of educational development assumed a unique kind of social psychology that he borrowed in large part from George Herbert Mead. Instead of setting social reality against individual psychological development, Mead (1934) understood meaning, mind, and self-consciousness to emerge through participation in routine social actions with others. For Mead, such ongoing interactivity allows developing individuals to take the attitudes and perspectives of particular others and of society in general and apply them to themselves and the physical and social world (Gillespie, 2005; Martin, 2006b). It is precisely because children take and react to perspectives available in interpersonal social activity that they become selves at all. When the constitution of selfhood through social interactivity is fully appreciated, there is no sharp divide between social (including institutional) practices and personal psychological growth and development because the latter is cut from the cloth of the former.

Olson (2003) is correct to suggest that the institutional mandates of schools cannot be identified with the personal experiences of students, but it is only through participation in sociocultural practices (including institutional practices) that learners develop as persons and citizens. Being a particular kind of person is a matter of participating in, observing, and experiencing conventional and institutionalized interactions with others, within which we learn what it is to be decent, honorable, generous, irresponsible, deceitful, and so forth—that is, learning what actions in a wide range of contexts count as one or the other of these characteristic ways of being persons. Our categories of personhood exist in our everyday interactivities within our societies and cultures. When this is clearly understood there is no choice other than to educate experientially, beginning with the child's experiences to date and gradually, as her or his understanding and ability warrant, making available an ever-expanding array of social, disciplinary, and institutional practices and perspectives within which the child can interact with others and, through such interactions, develop increasingly organized, sophisticated, and nuanced understandings of himself or herself and the sociocultural and biophysical world.

Self-development thus occurs together with educational and social development. We are immersed in social and institutional practices from birth, and our participation in them constitutes us as persons—that is, social and moral agents with rights and responsibilities. Valuing and acting honorably, confidently, with pride, and so on are not primarily matters of what is inside us but of what we do in the social world we inhabit with other people. The real tension that Olson (2003) is concerned about is not between the institutional practices of schooling and individual development but between competing sociocultural practices found in contemporary liberal democratic societies. This is a tension between social and psychological practices that privilege individual freedom and development versus those that privilege civic duty and responsibility to others. The problem is that liberal democratic societies embrace both of these sets of practices and their attendant virtues. In critiquing enhanced self-esteem as an educational aim, we are critiquing a set of discernible social practices that currently are highly influential in promoting forms of personal development centered too narrowly on the inner experience of individuals in the absence of appropriately educative concerns for the expansion of such experience through social and intellectual contact with other understandings and perspectives. Instead of encouraging schoolchildren and adolescents to look within to find personal significance, educators and schools should be encouraging students to expand their experience, perspectives, and understanding by looking around and engaging actively with other individuals, objects, and happenings within the sociocultural and biophysical world. If Dewey and Mead were correct, this can be done without sacrificing either personal development or the institutional mandates of school, because educational development of the sort just outlined necessarily includes personal development.

Conclusions

Without evidence that the enhancement of students' self-esteem promotes greater levels of academic achievement or other distinctly educational benefits (cf. Baumeister et al., 2003), there is little empirical support for heightened self-esteem as an educational aim. Moreover, a historical sketch of the emergence of enhanced self-esteem as an educational goal suggests that important distinctions among types of self-esteem—which may be more or less educationally and socially (including morally and politically) productive—have gradually been eroded in more contemporary educational inquiry and practice. Such erosion has resulted, especially in Western nations, in psychoeducational practices and interventions that may be criticized for an overemphasis on psychological individualism—a socioculturally endorsed reification and privileging of the inner psychological lives of individuals. In some instances, it seems as if students are encouraged to pursue their self-interest at the expense of acquiring knowledge and understanding about perspectives and interests different from their own and engagement with these. In consequence, the acquisition and critical consideration of a wide variety of viable and productive perspectives typical of educational development may suffer when enhanced self-esteem is isolated as a major educational aim.

Some (e.g., Olson, 2003) have argued that personal development in general (whether in the specific form of enhanced self-esteem or not) is incompatible with the institutional mandates of schools to prepare students for citizenship and productive participation in the economic, political, legal, and moral structures of society. However, such a position may be predicated on too strong a divide between personal development and education for civic virtue and participation. Early American pragmatists like Dewey (1938) and Mead (1934, 1938) objected to such dualistic formulations. They pointed out that self-development was inextricably bound up with the taking, experiencing, and application of a diversity of perspectives. In this way, they tied self-development directly to the experience of points of view and modes of understanding that went beyond students' current circumstances, knowledge, and self-interest. "[E]xperience does not occur in a vacuum. There are sources outside an individual that give rise to experience. It is constantly fed from these springs" (Dewey, 1938, p. 40). From this point of view, it is not self-esteem per se that is problematic but overly individualistic, narrow, and instrumentally self-interested psychological and sociocultural orientations and practices. When self-esteem is set within such a context, attempts to enhance it might prove to be more dogmatic than educational.

As indicated earlier, we will have much more to say about these matters in our final chapter. However, as a brief foreshadowing of what is to follow, it is important to understand that a recognition of subjectivity (i.e., an explicit awareness and remarking of our first-person experience, concerns, thoughts, emotions, attitudes, strivings, and so forth) does not necessitate or require either a metaphysical individualism which assumes that we exist as psychological individuals before we exist as social beings in communion with others or a sociopolitical individualism which assumes that individual psychological beings are the only things that matter or are genuinely real in societies and cultures. Against these individualisms, it is entirely coherent to argue that individuals come to exist as psychological beings through their embodied participation in the practices of their societies and cultures and that such sociocultural practices (and the traditions, rules, and artifacts embedded within them) have a reality that matters greatly in the constitution of psychological persons (Martin, Sugarman, & Hickinbottom, 2010). However, this being said, it is equally important to emphasize that the tendency of much scientific and professional psychology has been to align with both metaphysical and sociopolitical individualism.

In Chapter 5, which follows, we extend our historical and critical examination of self-esteem and self-concept (which together constitute the expressive self of educational psychology) as psychological concepts and educational goals by focusing specifically on the idea of self-concept and its history as a focus of psychological and educational inquiry and practice. In Chapters 6 and 7, we will turn to the managerial self of educational psychology (see Chapter 3), with a focus on both self-efficacy and self-regulation.

5   Understanding Yourself
ALL ABOUT SELF-CONCEPT

SELF-CONCEPT IS A term used by a wide variety of psychologists to refer generally to one's understanding and evaluation of oneself. It has been linked to and at times identified with related terms such as *self-esteem, self-worth, self-image, self-schemata, self-representation, self-presentation, self-awareness, self-knowledge, self-appraisal, self-perception, self-monitoring,* and *self-efficacy.* However, the most compelling aspect of the large body of research and writing in this area is the promise that it will tell us something worthwhile about ourselves in ways that might be said to constitute and promote our understanding and evaluation of our actions and experiences.

Most of this chapter consists of a brief history and a critical constructive appraisal of selected aspects of self-concept theory and research as these have developed within disciplinary psychology from the late 1800s but especially from the 1950s to the present, with particular emphasis on the past few decades. Of course, as we saw in Chapter 2, conceptions of selfhood have a much longer and more varied history. However, once again, according to many historians and theorists of the self (e.g., Baumeister, 1987; Cushman, 1995; Danziger, 1997a,b; Seigel, 2005; Sorabji, 2006; Taylor, 1989), currently popular conceptions of selfhood and self-concept (which assume an individual's surveillance and understanding of inner mental/cognitive processes, structures, or personality traits) are of surprisingly recent origin. Perhaps not surprisingly, such conceptions of self-concept owe much to popularizations of the theories, research studies, and interventions of scientific and professional psychologists (e.g., Herman, 1995; Pfister & Schnog,

1997). Indeed, it is because disciplinary psychology is so deeply implicated in how we contemporaries understand ourselves that a history, appraisal, and tentative forecast concerning psychological inquiry about self-concept are warranted. Some commentators have gone so far as to suggest that disciplinary psychology itself may be understood as a "technology" or set of discursive, measurement, and intervention practices devoted to the construction and perpetuation of distinctively psychological ways of being a person (e.g., Hacking, 1995; Rose, 1998).

Our overall strategy is to tell the story of the psychology of self-concept through a compilation of the historical analyses and reflections of a number of prominent self-concept researchers (e.g., Harter, 1996; Hattie, 1992, 2003; Keith & Bracken, 1996; Marsh & Hattie, 1996; Pajares & Schunk, 2002, 2005; Roeser, Peck, & Nasir, 2006). Along the way, we will dip into the writings of other historians of psychology so as to raise possible alternative interpretations and conclusions to rival the perhaps more optimistically framed yet nonetheless critical "insider" histories we feature.[1]

Consequently, the brief history of self-concept that we will present deviates somewhat from conventional insider histories. In particular, we will draw attention to a line of psychological inquiry (concerned with motivation, attitudes, and personality) that unfolded during the first half of the twentieth century; it has been mostly overlooked by self-concept historians but we believe it to be highly relevant to a critical historical understanding of self-concept research and theory. We will also include a discussion of recent critical historical work on measures of self-concept (Greer, 2003, 2007) as an example of the kind of detailed theoretical/historical inquiry that we believe can contribute greatly to our understanding of contemporary self-concept research and theory and can help to chart future possibilities for work in this area. Thus, our historical account in this chapter will connect to extant work in the history and theory of psychology in a manner atypical of the progressive yet critical histories written by self-concept researchers themselves.

What we hope to establish by our historical survey is that a number of the persisting difficulties attending self-concept theory and research can be traced to the assumption that the self is a psychological entity within the person rather than simply a person. Even when prominent self-concept researchers have admonished against this tendency to separate selfhood from personhood, the assumption persists in their own work and methods and in the way in which this work is understood within and outside of disciplinary and professional psychology, perhaps especially in applications of self psychology to education. Thus, psychologists and educators talk about self-concepts rather than persons' understanding and evaluation of their own actions and experiences. And when individuals appear to be experiencing difficulties related to their acting and

---

[1] We wish to be clear that we do not regard the eminent psychologists (past and present) to whose ideas and work we refer to be lacking in critical awareness of the strengths and weaknesses of their enterprise. Many trenchant criticisms of self-concept theory, measurement, and research have been made by "insiders" (e.g., Hattie, 2003; Shavelson, Hubner, & Stanton, 1976; Wylie, 1974, 1979).

experiencing, many such difficulties are interpreted as having their genesis in individuals' self-concepts and are explained accordingly. For example, we are frequently quite content to explain Susan's behavioral and experiential difficulties by reference to her self-concept, as in "her self-concept is so low that she cannot learn effectively, and her grades suffer as a consequence." The possibility that the self-concept references the actions, understandings, and experiences of persons is cast aside in favor of understanding the self-concept as an inner source of motivation and psychological resilience or the lack thereof.

In the last part of this chapter, we examine various problems associated with understanding the self as an inner psychological entity. We also recommend and discuss the alternative of construing selves as the understandings and evaluations of persons concerning their own actions and experiences. One particularly interesting difficulty that we address is the possibility that psychological theory and research on self-concept may be contributing to distinctively psychological ways of being persons. These are ways of life that were not available to previous, less psychologically oriented generations. Such psychological perspectives may tend to remove people from their worldly contexts and interactions with others, leading them to orient to their own psychological interiors and needs. What is lost through this interior focus is an active orientation to actions and interactions with others within social and cultural practices. These are practices or ways of interacting that structure things like friendships and family relationships, ways and methods of engaging in particular activities like mathematics or politics, and social life in general. We then conclude by suggesting an alternative framing of persons' understanding and evaluation of their own actions and experiences. The suggested alternative focuses on the holistic interactivity of persons within interpersonal practices. Importantly, these practices provide contextual criteria for framing persons' understanding and evaluation of their actions and experiences—criteria that are not available in isolation from persons' active engagement within their communities and societies.

Because of the close historical relationship between self-esteem and self-concept—an association that we have retained in our conception of the expressive selfhood promoted by educational psychologists (see Chapter 3)—and because we devoted considerable attention to specific educational applications and interventions in the previous chapter on self-esteem, educational theory and practice will feature less prominently in the current chapter. However, several of the examples we use are drawn from educational contexts, and the vast majority of the discussion in this chapter is directly relevant to our central aim of critically exploring relations between psychology and the education of students as psychological selves.

A Short History of the Psychology of Self-Concept

Almost all historical accounts of psychological work related to the self-concept begin with the pioneering work of William James (e.g., Harter, 1996; Pajares & Schunk, 2002,

2005; Roeser, Peck, & Nasir, 2006). James's distinction between the self as knower and agent (the I-self) and the self as known and object (the Me-self) in his famous chapter on self-consciousness (James, 1890, chap. 10) undoubtedly informs much subsequent work on the self-concept (a term that James never used himself). In particular, the general idea that the self is made up of different constituents (e.g., recall from Chapter 2 that James's Me-self contains material, social, and spiritual selves) arranged hierarchically is a basic structural assumption in many contemporary theories of the self-concept, just as James's assumption that the I-self can create and monitor a variety of Me-selves anchors much self-concept methodology and theorizing in psychology. With respect to the general aims of self-concept research, James's framing of self-esteem (a term he did use) has also been extremely influential on subsequent generations of both self-esteem and self-concept researchers. For James, self-esteem is a feeling that "depends entirely on what we back ourselves to be and do" (James, 1890, p. 310), a feeling that depends on the success with which we achieve those things we set out to achieve.[2] Notice that implicit in James's conceptualization and framing of self-esteem is the assumption that self-esteem is as much (or more) a consequence of successful performance as it is a cause of such performance.

Alongside James as the founding father of self psychology, many commentators on the history of self-concept also point to the theoretical legacies of sociopsychological thinkers like Charles Horton Cooley (1902) and George Herbert Mead (1934) (e.g., Harter, 1996; Pajares & Schunk, 2002, 2005) as well as to the influence of ego and identity theorists like Sigmund Freud (1949) and Erik Erikson (1959, 1968) (e.g., Pajares & Schunk, 2002, 2005; Roeser, Peck, & Nasir, 2006) and developmental thinkers like James Mark Baldwin (1897) and Jean Piaget (1965) (e.g., Harter, 1996, 1999). Central to the sociopsychological thought of Cooley and Mead are the roles played by others in the formation of an individual's self-concept. Social interactions with others reveal their reactions to us in ways that we recognize, imagine, and feel (Cooley) or in ways that lead us to react to ourselves as others do (Mead). Thus, our selves and self-concepts have their origins in our social interactions with other persons and society at large.

However, both Cooley and Mead emphasized that we are not passive recipients of others' regard but active agents in our internalization and transformation of others' reactions, attitudes, and perspectives. Mead, in particular, theorized a Me-self that is much more explicitly and thoroughly social than that envisioned by James—a self that is constantly transformed through interactivity and intersubjectivity with others and through the reactivity of the agentic I-self to these encounters. Somewhat uniquely for his time, Mead (1934) also developed the idea of a generalized "other" reflecting the social

---

[2] Hattie (2003) provides an extremely thoughtful and interesting set of observations concerning specific ways in which James's ideas have influenced research and theory on self-concept. Hattie also revisits James's ideas to suggest directions for contemporary self-concept research and theory that he believes might ameliorate some of the difficulties or right some of the imbalances he perceives in this area of psychological inquiry.

processes and conventions of entire communities of others, thus providing a conception of sociocultural influence on our self constructions that goes considerably beyond interpersonal interactivity with particular others (more of this in Chapter 9). Interestingly, both Cooley and Mead tended to think of the self in a holistic way, refusing to draw sharp distinctions between cognitive, affective, and volitional aspects of self-functioning.

Emphasis on the ongoing interaction between social others and one's sense of oneself is also found in the work of the developmental psychologist, James Mark Baldwin (1897). Baldwin maintained that each of us undergoes "constant modification of his sense of himself by suggestions from others," resulting in "changes in the content of one's sense of self" (p. 30) that frequently vary across different relational contexts. Baldwin not only emphasized the importance of sociopsychological processes of imitation in the "other" orientation of young children, whom he regarded as "veritable copying machine[s]," but also recognized the impact of particular social situations in which such sociopsychological processes unfold. "[T]he growing child is able to think of self in varying terms as varying social situations impress themselves upon him" (p. 37)—a point echoed years later by Jean Piaget (1965), who noted young children's tendency to reason and think of themselves from concrete particular to concrete particular.[3]

The influence of the ego and identity psychologies of thinkers like Freud (1960/1923, 1961/1930) and Erikson (1959, 1968) has been remarked recently by Pajares and Schunk (2002, 2005) and Roeser, Peck, and Nasir (2006). The Freudian ego acts as a regulatory center for executive functioning directed at balancing psychological and behavioral tendencies of both conscious and unconscious origin (Freud, 1960/1923). However, Freud's early biological determinism and later pessimism, grounded in the civilized ego's limitations in the face of powerful forces of aggression and destruction (Freud, 1961/1930), placed rather severe restrictions on what the ego could accomplish and highlighted the difficulty of self-understanding. Thus, any equation of genuine self-understanding with sets of consciously available self beliefs was, for Freud, to be resisted.

More directly relevant to contemporary self-concept research and theory, especially its motivational features, is the theory of identity development across the life span developed by Erik Erikson. Roeser and colleagues (2006) have highlighted Erikson's contribution to self theory by citing his conceptualization of the I-self as "an observing center of awareness and of volition" (Erikson, 1968, p. 135), which they (borrowing from contemporary neuroscientific and self-regulatory research) redefine as "a master regulatory mechanism by which attentional, cognitive, and affective resources can be consciously and willfully deployed" (Roeser et al., 2006, p. 399). However, Erikson's primary focus, somewhat reminiscent of that of Cooley and Mead, was on developmental

---

[3] As will become apparent, such highly situational renderings of self-conceptions have recently made a comeback in domain-specific theorizing about the self-concept as well as in the more task-specific idea of self-efficacy.

processes of psychosocial identity development defined within particular social contexts and developmentally sequenced tasks of living. Thus, Erikson's focus, as also noted by Roeser and associates (2006), was "on objective relationships between the person and the environment ... [and] brought needed attention to the cultural and intergenerational nature of psychosocial identity development" (p. 395).

Despite the rich theoretical and conceptual frameworks advanced by James, Cooley, Mead, Baldwin, Freud, Erikson, and others, the behaviorist hegemony within disciplinary psychology in North America, which prevailed during much of the 1930s to the 1960s, dramatically curtailed what came to be regarded (in the absence of programmatic empirical scholarship in the still developing area of self-concept inquiry) as speculative philosophical theorizing incompatible with empirical science. Except for the mention of a few self theorists such as Lewin (1935), Goldstein (1939), Lecky (1945), Bertocci (1945), Murphy (1947), Ramey (1948), and Hilgard (1949), the historical reflections of self-concept researchers (e.g., Harter, 1996; Pajares & Schunk, 2005; Roeser et al., 2006) tend to skip the 1930s and 1940s, moving directly to the humanistically framed self psychologies and empirically focused measurement studies that began to appear and gather intellectual momentum in the 1950s.

In many ways but in one way in particular, this neglect of self-relevant work during the missing years of the 1930s and 1940s deprives the reappearance of self-concept research, following the humanist bridgehead in the 1950s, of an explanatory historical grounding. Fortunately, recent work in the history of psychology by Danziger (1997b), Nicholson (2003), and others has highlighted the relevance to research on self-esteem and self-concept of a great deal of psychological theory and research on motivation, personality, and attitudes from the late 1920s to the 1950s. Although it is not possible to devote much space to this topic, the personality psychology of Gordon Allport provides an excellent example of how ideas and measures related to various psychological traits and constructs, including self-concept, emerged in ways that made possible and legitimated what has come to be regarded as the scientific study of the self within psychology. This was a form of study that effectively moved the self and self-concept from the social relational contexts favored by Cooley, Mead, and Baldwin into a psychological interior to which only individuals themselves had privileged access and on which they could report, especially if assisted by the instruments and measures developed by psychological experts who increasingly claimed the psychological interior as their unique disciplinary turf.

Alongside the behavioral psychologies that captivated American psychology during much of the first half of the twentieth century was a newly forged and less remarked on psychology of attitudes, motivation, and personality. For many prominent psychologists like Allport (1937), the concept of attitude went well beyond a disposition to act. Between the First and Second World Wars, these psychologists began to talk as if attitudes were real entities interior to and possessed by all persons—entities that, by adulthood, became relatively permanent and exerted a causal influence on what persons believed, thought, and did. As previewed in our first chapter, the natural reality of psychologists' conceptions of attitudes was confirmed in the minds of psychologists and others when L. L. Thurstone and Rensis Likert developed various methods of measuring attitudes (Danziger, 1997b).

One such method, which involved asking people to rate the extent to which they agreed or disagreed with a variety of statements concerning whatever it was that was being measured, became especially popular. Although this method was similar to methods then in use for opinion polling, when married to psychological theory to the effect that what was being measured were semipermanent, psychological entities possessed by respondents, it was seen as an important social scientific advance. Disciplinary psychology now had a means of measuring attitudes—and (by extension) motivational and other personality traits and characteristics—that was thought by many to rival sophisticated methods of physical measurement associated with advances in the natural sciences, especially when the responses of large numbers of people were subjected to apparently meticulous quantifications through a variety of psychometric and statistical procedures.

Within the developing tradition of psychological research on attitudes, motivation, and personality, self-concept came to be understood as a causally efficacious property of individuals that was implicated in a wide variety of personal actions and experiences— one that could be measured through individual responses to appropriately constructed psychological measures with requisite psychometric properties. For many, ratings of the extent to which individuals agreed that statements such as "I feel good about myself most of the time" described themselves came to serve as operational indicators of an inner core of self-understanding and experiencing. Moreover, because self-concept could now be measured, it became a tractable focus for the applications of professional psychology in education, psychotherapy, vocational counseling, and industrial/organizational psychology. In all of these areas and more, applied psychologists now could study scientifically how their interventions might positively affect the self-concept and self-esteem of students, clients, job seekers, and employees.

Research on Self-Concept Explodes

By the 1950s, a number of humanistic thinkers in psychology had begun to rebel against the behaviorists' neglect of inner experience and selfhood. Carl Rogers (1957) presented a system of client-centered psychotherapy based on the provision of appropriate conditions for the development of the self and the achievement of self-actualization. Rogers believed that each human being has an inborn tendency to self-growth and actualization and that this must be socially accepted and nurtured. The self theory of Rogers was extremely influential in clinical and educational psychology (e.g., Snygg & Coombs, 1959). It not only connected with the work of Continental phenomenologists and existentialists but also helped to fuel a gradual rebirth of interest in the self among mainstream experimental psychologists. Because of Rogers's emphasis on how individuals view themselves, much of this new mainstream interest focused on the operationalization and measurement of the self-concept, understood as the sum total of individuals' beliefs about themselves or at least those that they could articulate.

By treating the self as self-description, a new generation of self-concept researchers rapidly developed and standardized a variety of paper-and-pencil measures of the self as self-described. For many psychologists, the self was now understood as a set of self-descriptions or, more accurately, as a set of self-ratings on the basis of descriptions supplied by psychological researchers and diagnosticians. Such measures of self-concept simplified the self and made it less abstract and elusive. In effect, where James and earlier psychologists had struggled with difficult ontological questions concerning the self, the self-concept researchers adopted a methodological solution that effectively denied the conflictual, multiple, developmental nature of the self as previously theorized by Freud, James, Mead, and Rogers himself. The self-concept as an empirical psychological self, operationalized in standardized psychological measures, offered a tractable conception of selfhood that seemed to make it readily accessible to psychological experts and their clients.

A voluminous literature reporting the development and administration of measures of self-concept quickly developed, along with a variety of interventions targeted at producing changes in individuals' responses to these measures. By the 1970s, when mainstream psychology's attachment to behaviorist theories and methods had mostly given way to a new wave of cognitive theorizing and intervention, research on self-concept and self-esteem continued unabated, absorbing and reflecting newly developed models of cognitive information processing, schemata, and memory stores.

Although in many ways initiated by humanistic impulses to recognize the uniqueness and emotional experience of individuals, the burgeoning literature on self-concept and self-esteem of the 1960s and 1970s soon reflected the kind of joint commitment to science and humanism exhibited by a previous generation of attitude and personality researchers like Gordon Allport (see also Chapter 4). Self-concept research during this period was a growth industry that merged with and utilized the talents of psychometricians on the one hand (resulting in numerous scales and subscales for the measurement of self-esteem and self-concept—e.g., Piers & Harris, 1964) and the models favored by newly minted cognitive psychologists on the other (resulting in theories of selfhood and self-concept framed in terms of information processes and cognitive operations—e.g., Markus, 1977). Perhaps not surprisingly, with all this activity and the multiplicity of measures and models it spawned, the critical attentions of self-concept researchers turned to questions (framed in both psychometric and cognitive terminology) concerning the dimensional structure and organization of the self-concept—issues that, according to most self-concept researchers who have written about the history of their enterprise, were galvanized by the influential review of self-concept research by Shavelson, Hubner, and Stanton (1976).

The Shavelson, Hubner, and Stanton Review

As Marsh and Hattie (1996) point out, structural models of self-concept have typically been influenced by corresponding models of intelligence, and much debate has attended issues such as the dimensional (unidimensional versus multidimensional), hierarchical, and taxonomic nature of self-concept—debates closely associated with developments in factor analysis, multitrait-multimethod analysis, path analysis, and related statistical procedures. It is generally agreed among contemporary self-concept researchers (e.g., Marsh & Hattie, 1996; Marsh, Craven, & McInerney, 2003, 2005) that research on self-concept prior to 1980 lacked the theoretical and methodological rigor and empirical progress displayed in subsequent research and that an important "lightning rod" for this positive change was the critical yet constructive review of this area of inquiry by Shavelson, Hubner, and Stanton (1976). Shavelson and colleagues drew attention to the general absence of theoretical sophistication in definitions and conceptions of self-concept, the poor quality of measures of self-concept, a general lack of consistent findings, and a variety of methodological shortcomings—all of which they perceived as typifying the state of play in self-concept inquiry at the time of their review.[4]

However, Shavelson and colleagues (1976) also offered suggestions for improving this state of affairs—suggestions that were taken up by a subsequent generation of self-concept researchers in ways that have methodologically transformed psychological inquiry in this area. They provided a working definition of self-concept in terms of a person's self-perceptions formed through experience within the social and natural environment that are potentially useful in explaining and predicting how a person acts. Assuming that a person's self-perceptions were structured or organized, Shavelson and colleagues also postulated a multifaceted hierarchy, with perceptions of personal behavior in specific situations anchoring inferences about the self in broader domains (e.g., physical, social, academic), which in turn supported a general self-concept. Of particular interest, with respect to relationships such as that between self-concept and academic achievement, Shavelson and associates argued (on conceptual, definitional grounds) that academic self-concept would be more highly correlated with academic achievement than social, physical, or general self-concept and that self-concept in a particular subject would correlate more highly with achievement in that subject than with achievement in other subjects.

Shavelson and associates (1976) also noted that if self-concept research were to advance in progressive ways, it would have to do so on theoretical/conceptual, measurement, and empirical grounds simultaneously. To this end, they proposed logical, correlational, and experimental procedures for advancing psychological statistical inquiry concerning self-

---

[4] Interestingly, some 16 years later, Hattie (1992) was to echo these conclusions, extending what he referred to as the "dustbowl empiricism" typical of self-concept research (with a few notable exceptions) considerably beyond the date of the review of Shavelson and associates .

concept. Logical analysis was, among other things, to develop experimentally testable counterhypotheses based on the interpretations of test scores. Correlational analysis (factor analysis, path analysis, multitrait-multimethod analysis) could be used to investigate relations within hypothesized self-concept structures and between self-concept and related constructs. Experimental methods were appropriate for construct validation (testing the validity of interpretations of self-concept responses)—for example, the extent to which interventions theorized to enhance social self-concept actually did so or whether interventions targeted at particular facets of a multidimensional self-concept influenced those facets more than others.

Contemporary Research on Self-Concept

Subsequent work on the framework and proposals offered by Shavelson and colleagues (1976) questioned the assumption that general or global self-concept is more stable than domain- or situation-specific self-concept, with global self-concept displaying considerable variability over time despite the fact that these same measures displayed reasonable internal consistency in any particular administration (e.g., Marsh, 1990; Shavelson & Bolus, 1982). With respect to the much studied and theorized relationship between academic self-concept and achievement, domain-specific academic self-concept was better correlated with achievement than general or global self-concept, and subject-specific self-concept (e.g., mathematics self-concept) correlated even more highly with achievement in specifically related subject areas (e.g., mathematics) (Marsh, 1992; Marsh & Shavelson, 1985; Shavelson & Marsh, 1986).

More generally, research on self-concept during the 1980s and 1990s and into the twenty-first century also began to emphasize developmental features of the acquisition and age-related nature of self-concept, with researchers like Harter (1999) demonstrating that self-concept becomes both more differentiated and more integrated with age (also see Marsh, Craven, & Debus, 1991). Evidence also began to accumulate in support of the idea that ratings of one's self-concept by significant others also tends to correlate more highly with self-ratings on domain-specific than on general measures of self-concept. Complex relationships among self-concept, race, nationality, ethnicity, and gender also became a focus of much recent self-concept research (see Crain, 1996; Marsh, Craven, & McInerney, 2003, 2005), as did research on family self-concept, physical self-concept, social self-concept, and self-concept in multicultural contexts (see relevant chapters in Bracken, 1996 and Marsh, Craven, & McInerney, 2003, 2005). Comprehensive reviews and histories of different measures of self-concept developed during the 1980s and 1990s (e.g., the Offer Self-Image Questionnaire–Revised; the Self-Perception Inventory; the various self-perception profiles for adolescents, children, college students, and learning-disabled students; and the Self-Description Questionnaire II) as well as previously developed measures initially introduced in the 1960s and 1970s (e.g., the Piers-Harris Children's Self-Concept Scale and the Tennessee Self-Concept Scale) have also appeared (e.g., Blascovich & Tomaka, 1991; Keith & Bracken, 1996; Wylie, 1989), as have reviews and histories of self-concept interventions (e.g., Harter, 1999; O'Mara, Marsh, Craven, & Debus, 2006).

Despite being widely viewed as putting self-concept research on a firmer footing and promising course, subsequent research has not supported some aspects of the assumptive framework advanced by Shavelson and colleagues (1976). Perhaps more importantly, despite the laudatory efforts of major self-concept researchers like Herbert Marsh (1990; Marsh & Shavelson, 1985; Marsh, Craven, & McInerney, 2003, 2005) to adhere to the generally sensible framework proposed by Shavelson and associates (1976), critical commentaries by "insiders" like John Hattie (1992, 2003) indicate that some of the difficulties that continue to plague the enterprise of self-concept research in psychology may have deeper roots than can be extracted by the current tradition of theoretically informed measurement construction and construct validation inspired by Shavelson and associates and practiced so diligently and competently by Marsh and others.

A Critical Look at Contemporary Research on Self-Concept

Marsh and Hattie (1996) conclude their chapter on theoretical perspectives on the structure of self-concept with the pleas that "empirical tests, theoretical models and instrument construction should be evaluated simultaneously" and that "appropriate compromise[s] should be supported on the basis of theory, intended purpose, instrument construction, and empirical results" (p. 83). Their overall point is that construct validation of self-concept instruments and measures must be based on explicit theoretical models and pursued within comprehensive programs of research that span theory, analyses of relevant empirical relationships, experiments, and intervention studies (e.g., Marsh & Craven, 2005; Marsh & Köller, 2003).

However, Hattie (2003) has more recently delved historically and critically into a number of basic assumptions concerning research on self-concept that appear to point to deeper difficulties in this area of inquiry. On the surface, Hattie (2003) can be read (and may intend to be read) as advocating a move away from conceptions and inquiries concerning self-concept that derive from the classic model of test theory's dependence on correlation (e.g., high alphas, large factor loadings on a first factor, and notable discriminations among factors) to more contemporary item response models and generalizability theory focused on understanding change and variability across situations. However, much of what he says, including a thought-provoking example of what he refers to as "self-toeness" (see below), points to conceptual and theoretical difficulties concerning the very idea of self-concept that are unlikely to be assuaged adequately by methodological and statistical-theoretical means alone.

Hattie (2003) asks us to imagine a scale for self-toeness that might include items such as "I like my big toe," "I am proud of my toes," " I like to show off my toes to others," " My

toes are important to me," and "I could not bear to part with my toes" (p. 131). He goes
on to say,

> Given that there would be high correlations between such items, it would be easy to
> show via factor analysis and reliability that there is a strong single factor (80% vari-
> ance explained by the first factor, AGFI > .95, alpha < .80, RMSEA < .05, etc.), that
> it is discriminant from other aspects about my self, and that it correlates with other
> related dimensions (e.g., fingerness, eyeballness, and earness). Psychometrically
> wonderful it would seem. (p. 131)

Later, toward the end of his chapter, Hattie (2003) employs a Wittgensteinian
(Wittgenstein, 1953) ploy in asking why we use the concept of self when it is a given.

> A useful question to ask ourselves every time we reach for the "self-concept" lens
> is whether the same or different question would be asked if we left the term "self"
> out of the question. For example, rather than asking [about] the relation between
> self-concept of mathematics and achievement we ask [about] the relation between
> our conceptions of mathematics and achievement. Rather than asking about the
> development of self-concept of physical attributes, we ask about the development
> of conceptions of physical attributes. (p. 141)

Such suggestions are consistent with a more general theme that cuts through many of
Hattie's critical reflections and concerns—that is, that conceptualizing the "self" in
"self-concept" as a kind of interior entity or entities may be counterproductive.

Of course, the nature and ontological status of selfhood have been much discussed in the
philosophy of mind and psychology since Hume (1986/1739) claimed an inability to locate
the self behind his own impressions, sensations, experiences, perceptions, and memories.
More recently, Peter Hacker (2007) has offered a powerful set of arguments for resisting
the idea of the self as an interior entity—arguments that relate directly to Hattie's (2003)
observations. Hacker notes that "A person cannot both *be* and *have* a self ... if the self is
some thing *within* a human being, then he cannot be identical with his self, since the human
being cannot be identical with one of his constituent parts" (p. 261).

> To speak of myself is not to speak of a self that I have, but simply to speak of the
> human being that I am. To say that I was thinking of myself is not to say that I was
> thinking of my *self*, but that I was thinking of me, *this* human being familiar to my
> family and friends. (p. 266)

In Hacker's view, it makes sense to talk about the experiences, understandings, and
beliefs of a person but not as matters that require consultation with an interior entity
called the self or with the perception of such an entity. A person can assess her or his

performance and capability in mathematics, baseball, or ballroom dancing. Nothing sensible is added by requiring that the person observe and report her or his self-concept as a mathematician, baseball player, or dancer. To think otherwise is to reify a psychological interior that is a product of our ways of talking and thinking, not a substantive and determining source of our worldly conduct.

It is precisely such reification, through the application of psychological conceptions and practices of measurement and intervention, to which Hattie (2003) seems to be pointing in his own critical reflections on the state of the art in self-concept research. Consequently, if understood within the context of his concerns with respect to the ubiquitous and in many ways superfluous "self" in self-concept research, Hattie's recommendations for improving statistical-theoretical and methodological aspects of contemporary research on self-concept are unlikely to have much positive impact if the basic idea of the self as an internal entity that individuals can perceive and report upon remains unchanged. The full implications of Hattie's critique cut much deeper than he himself seems prepared to acknowledge.

If there is any question about the continuing commitment of many self-concept researchers to the self as an interior mental entity or entities, the second edition of the *Handbook of Educational Psychology* by Roeser and colleagues (2006) provides sufficient evidence to conclude that strongly mentalistic, representationalist views of self and self-concept remain the norm in this area of psychological inquiry, just as they do in many other areas of contemporary psychology. Thus, Roeser and associates, in describing their "Basic Levels of Self (BLOS) Model," state that

> We describe the intraindividual levels of representation (e.g., temperamental, iconic, symbolic, and phenomenological) that function to motivate (energize) and regulate (direct) learning and achievement behavior in school by reference to the Basic Levels of Self (BLOS) heuristic model. This model assumes the foundational role of temperamental traits, moods, and emotions in shaping "higher order" levels of me-self representation from birth onward. (p. 401)

Roeser and colleagues go on to clarify that their model

> allows for clear explication of several qualitatively different kinds of encoded me-self representations that play critical roles in the diachronic (across time) whole-person processes that are called sense of identity, cognition, emotion, and behavior. The BLOS model also situates the me-self in specific relation to both the I-self and the wider social and physical contexts in which individuals (as I/Me) function as unified wholes. (pp. 401–402)

Thus, although Roeser and associates clearly emphasize the behavioral and psychological activity of whole persons within their biophysical and sociocultural contexts, it is clear that they understand internal representations, processes, and psychological experiences of selfhood as the real driving forces behind the worldly activity of persons. Despite their references to and use of the ideas of James, Dewey, and Erikson, Roeser and coworkers ultimately understand the prime movers of the contextualized activity of persons to be internal self-representations and processes.

An Example

Recent critical historical scholarship by Greer (2003, 2007) examines the historical transformation of the self-concept through the self research and theorizing of psychologists and helps to unpack the enduring appeal of the psychological interior for past and current generations of self-concept researchers. Greer's historical researches lead him to conclude that the transformation of self into self-concept and self-esteem in American personality research has mostly ignored important qualities of selfhood such as agency, intentionality, reflexivity, and moral judgment (all of which have occupied philosophers and scholars from the time of Descartes and Locke).

In particular, Greer (2003) argues that by understanding self-esteem and self-concept as interior personality traits and/or cognitive representations that determine our experience and conduct, self-concept researchers have gotten things backwards. Such confusion is further compounded by measurement procedures and statistical methodologies that yield results interpreted as indicating that personality and/or representational variables such as self-concept and self-esteem account for statistically significant amounts of variance in behavior. Although these difficulties have their source (as indicated above) in the attitude, motivational, and personality psychologies of the 1930s to the 1950s, it was with the advent of cognitive and information processing psychologies from the 1960s onward that the concept of a hierarchical information-processing system began to replace earlier notions of the self as a rational and moral agent.

Although contemporary theories of self-concept and self-esteem bypass well-known philosophical problems of assuming a homuncular self as a knower within, they effectively reduce the moral and rational agency of persons to cognitive psychological processes of schema-driven inferences or comparison-based perceptions about the quality of our actions—"a schematized set of 'self-appraisals'" (Greer, 2003, p. 102). As a more viable alternative, Greer proposes that we move away from ideas of self-concept and self-esteem as interior personality traits and/or cognitive representations and systems and toward understanding self-concept and self-esteem as forms of moral conduct—"recognizing our conduct as a type of social and moral discourse grounded in our responsibility and relationship to each other (e.g., what makes me feel good is inextricably bound to the fact that I exist in this world with 'you')" (2003, p. 104). Instead, however, Greer perceives that "each succeeding generation of self measures presented self-related constructs in an increasingly decontextualized light, with little or no reference to the self" (2007, p. 19), understood as the moral and rational conduct of persons in relation to others and the social world in general.

In his detailed history of the *Piers-Harris Children's Self-Concept Scale*, Greer (2007) extends his critique of self-concept measures and research by noting that the current state of self-concept research is both contradictory and confusing—a state of affairs achieved in large part through linking the idea of a deeply interior self-concept as personality trait and/or cognitive schema to a set of apparently standardized measurement instruments, practices, and statistical analyses (embedded within an "objectified, third-person discourse of prediction and control," p. 20). "The current state of self measures is more a function of the type of research and knowledge-generating practices being employed, and the purposes to which they are geared, than any objective truth about individual psychological reality" (p. 20). In general conclusion, Greer (2007) imagines a critical historical antidote for some of what he perceives to ail self-concept research in psychology: "We must continue to look at these investigative practices, and the products they produce, more in terms of their place in the larger social context, and their historicity, than as the 'best' or most objective way of conducting research" (p. 20)—a view very much in line with our expressed aims in this volume (see Chapter 1).

Self-Concept, Self-Esteem, and Self-Efficacy

As noted in the previous two chapters, researchers of self-concept, self-esteem, and self-efficacy historically have differed with respect to how they define these terms (Byrne, 1996; Greer, 2003; Hattie, 1992; Wylie, 1974, 1979). Some use the terms *self* and *self-concept* interchangeably, while others seem to equate self and self-esteem. Some draw clear distinctions between self-concept (as comprising various kinds of self-understanding) and self-esteem (as comprising various kinds of self-valuation), while others treat both self-understanding and self-valuation as part of self-concept. In the early days of self-efficacy research (Bandura, 1977), most were careful to distinguish clearly between self-concept (and/or self-esteem) and self-efficacy by noting that the latter was an individual's task-specific judgment of confidence in her or his ability to perform particular task-relevant actions (such as approaching feared objects or performing particular physical or intellectual skills) as opposed to beliefs about and/or valuations of oneself more generally. However, as already noted, more recent tendencies to examine more domain-specific—even task-specific—forms of self-concept (and self-esteem) as well as the development of more general measures of self-efficacy (e.g., Scherbaum, Cohen-Charash, & Kern, 2006) have tended to erode much of these earlier distinctions. Consequently, some commentators (e.g., Pajares & Schunk, 2005), although still making distinctions for particular purposes, have begun to refer to both self-concept/self-esteem and self-efficacy as varieties of the more inclusive term *self beliefs*.

Having said this, it also is important to note that there have been recent attempts to differentiate these concepts. For example Woolfolk, Winne, and Perry (2010) acknowledge that

> *self-concept* and *self-esteem are* often used interchangeably, even though they have distinct meanings. Self-concept is a cognitive structure—a belief about who you are. In contrast, self-esteem is an affective reaction—an evaluation of who you are. Sometimes *self-esteem* is considered one aspect of self-concept—the evaluative part. In research, these two concepts are often closely related, some writers use *self-concept* and *self-esteem* interchangeably. However, there is an important conceptual difference. (p. 82)

Whatever distinctions are drawn among terms such as *self-concept, self-esteem*, and *self-efficacy*, it is clear that over time many self-concept researchers have ceased to worry about defining and conceptualizing the self outside of the particular measures, statistical procedures, and cognitivist assumptions they employ, leading historians like Greer (2003, 2007) to comment on the disappearance of the self in contemporary self research. Even researchers like Hattie (1992, 2003), who offer cogent, incisive critiques of conceptual and definitional problems in self-concept research, tend to emphasize and turn (in their own empirical work) to what they regard as improved methods of measurement and statistical analysis as conceptual aids. Yet it should be clear that no amount of empirical research by itself can repair a lack of attention to basic matters of definition and conceptualization. Consequently—in the absence of consensus, clarity, and consistency around key terms and their use—it is not surprising that this area of research continues to display results and interpretations that struggle to achieve coherence.

Perhaps the one exception to the general lack of consistency and coherence in these results and interpretations (as typified by self-concept research of the past and present) is a growing consensus concerning the domain specificity of correlations between self-concept and achievement; that is, the more specific measures of self-concept and achievement are to particular domains of application/activity, the higher the correlations between them tend to be. Extending this conclusion to include efficacy self-beliefs, Pajares and Schunk (2005) comment "when either self-belief is globally assessed, prediction is diminished; when assessments are domain-specific, and especially when they are task-specific, prediction is enhanced" (p. 111). Even more tellingly, Pajares and Schunk continue, "when self-beliefs do not correspond with—that is to say, match—the achievement outcome with which they are compared, their predictive value is reduced or can even be nullified" (p. 111). Nonetheless, Pajares and Schunk conclude that "both self-efficacy and self-concept are powerful motivation constructs that predict academic achievement at varying levels and differing domains" (p. 111). In a manner generally similar to Hattie (2003), Pajares and Schunk, despite noting importantly troubling aspects of contemporary research on self-concept, more or less conclude that progress is being made through a progressive refinement of research measures and procedures that tie self-beliefs more and more specifically to particular domains and tasks.

Replacing Selves With Persons and Self-Concept With Persons' Understanding and Evaluation of Their Own Actions and Experiences

More generally, the critical, theoretical, and historical work of self-concept researchers themselves tends to raise important questions concerning difficulties and challenges in self-concept theory and research but stops well short of the more radically critical challenges articulated by historians of psychology like Danziger (1997a,b), Greer (2003, 2007), and Nicholson (1998, 2003). Nonetheless, the history of this particular area of psychological inquiry is replete with many appropriately informed commentaries (by both insiders and others) questioning the adequacy and even the necessity of conceptions and measures of focal phenomena (i.e., self, self-concept, self-esteem) and the consistency and coherence of research results. Two matters in particular tend to stand out in ways that call for a more critical appraisal that might warrant attention to alternative possibilities for framing (or reframing) psychological inquiry on self-concept and its assumed motivational effects.

The first of these concerns the viability of conceptualizing the self as a psychological structure and/or process interior to persons but nonetheless somehow distinctive from persons themselves. Hattie (2003) recognizes this concern when he asks "whether the same or a different question would be asked if we left the term 'self' out of the question" (p. 141). The second concerns the separation of self-concept and related self-beliefs from individuals' performance on specific tasks and activities. Pajares and Schunk's (2005) recognition of the task-specific nature of high correlations between self-beliefs and specific performances inevitably raises the question of the extent to which self-concept and other self-beliefs are part of particular performances or actions rather than psychological motivators that precede performance and action. Putting these two concerns together, one well might ask whether anything would be lost if self-concept researchers were to talk only about the understanding and performance of persons acting in a variety of different tasks and task domains. Such a radical reframing certainly would do away with many of the conceptual confusions that have been discussed in this brief critical history of self-concept inquiry in psychology, and it would seem to do so without any loss in explanation or understanding of the task-specific nature of findings linking performative competence to particular tasks.

Thus, a more radical reading of the literature in the area of self-concept research in psychology is that such research has attempted to separate the actions and performances of persons from their beliefs about and evaluations of these performances instead of recognizing that individuals' understandings/beliefs and evaluations with respect to their actions are integral parts of the contextualized activity of persons understood as rational and moral agents. If so, it is not surprising that actions and beliefs are highly and consistently correlated only when they share a common task focus, since such a focus is a necessary part of the integrated acting, understanding, and evaluating of persons. One does not go skating without understanding what one is doing and believing that one can do it. If this is so, perhaps the cleaving of the activities of persons into interior psychological aspects and overt performative aspects says as much or more about the assumptions and interests of disciplinary psychology as it does about the worldly comportment of persons. Perhaps it is in the nature of psychology and not in the nature of persons to separate actions from beliefs and to treat parts of persons, rather than entire persons, as agents and explanations. What, if anything, would be lost by replacing selves and self-concepts respectively with persons and the activity of persons (activity which includes their understanding and evaluation of their own actions and experiences)?

In 1739, the Scottish philosopher and historian David Hume concluded, in *A Treatise of Human Nature,* that he could find no substantive self lurking behind his moment-to-moment perceptions. Many subsequent scholars have pointed to the argumentative fallacy (Gregory, 1987) and infinite regress (Ryle, 1949) that seem to follow from the postulation of any sort of interior homuncular entity that perceives and understands. Although no serious contemporary psychologist imagines a little person inside each of us who explains our actions and experiences, talk of cognitive or mental structures and processes, or areas and processes of the brain, making decisions, "feeling down," or perceiving and understanding comes perilously close to classic homunculus difficulties. Such attempts to place the sources and explanations of our actions and experiences in our psychological and/or biological interiors invite reductive accounts that at least parallel such difficulties. With respect to psychological theory and research on the self-concept, if the self is not identified clearly with an individual person but is instead postulated as some kind of cognitive schema, belief system, or other psychological/biological part of a person, a contemporary, arguably more acceptable homunculus is apparent, with all of its attendant difficulties. Thus, to explain the actions and experiences of a person by recourse to his or her self may amount to little more than using what needs to be explained as an explanation (Gregory, 1987) or postponing the required explanation through an apparently infinite series of progressively more miniscule selves/persons within larger selves/persons, metaphorically similar to a set of Russian nesting dolls. As Hacker (2007) argues, the actions and experiences of persons cannot be explained in terms of the actions and experiences of parts of persons because it is entire persons who act and experience, not their parts. And, as has been argued by many contemporary theorists of personhood (e.g., Bickhard, 2008; Martin, Sugarman, & Hickinbottom, 2010), the actions and experiences of persons must be explicated in terms of the worldly interactivity of persons within relevant biophysical, interpersonal, social, and cultural contexts, practices, and processes.

To help to clarify the foregoing line of argument, it is useful to think about how one might explain the actions, motivations, and achievements of baseball players. Clearly, any viable explanation would have to consider the biophysiology and kinesiology of the players; the sociocultural historically evolved rules (e.g., three strikes and you're out, three outs per inning) and strategies (e.g., hit and run, intentional walk, squeeze plays, protecting the plate, hard slides) of the game of baseball; the artifacts (bats, balls, gloves, legal and illegal performance-enhancing substances) and routines/practices (e.g., fielding positions and alignments, pitching rotations, variations in specific rules in different leagues) that have developed around and within the game; as well as the players' preparedness, skill, emotional states, and how effectively they communicate and coordinate. Psychological factors such as a player's confidence and desire, understanding of his personal capabilities and limits, and so forth obviously are part of the requisite explanatory mix. However, is there really anything to be gained by thinking about such psychological matters as "baseball self-concept," "baseball self-esteem," or "baseball self-efficacy," let alone instituting training interventions targeted at such phenomena as if they somehow could be separated from the activity and interactivity (actions, experiences, motivations, and achievements) of baseball players and then treated as important contributing causes to these more holistic, interactive aspects of the performance of baseball players in the game of baseball?

Is it reasonable to believe that such psychological interventions might contribute much above and beyond well-planned practice with teammates within simulated and actual game situations, of relevant skills, strategies, and coordinated game tactics of the game of baseball? Even if one believes that there are important psychological aspects to players' motivation and achievement, might such factors not be better addressed by focusing on the thoughts, feelings, personal relationships, and life circumstances (professional and otherwise) of the persons who are the players?

More generally, what would it mean to take seriously the idea that psychological focus might be shifted without loss and perhaps with more salubrious consequences from self-concept and similar self-beliefs to a focus on persons' understanding and evaluation of their actions and experiences within particular domains of activity/interactivity, from baseball to mathematics? If the self-concept is nothing more than a person's understanding and evaluation of his or her actions and experiences, why not focus psychological inquiry directly on those actions and experiences as understood and evaluated by the individuals and others concerned? Notice that in framing these questions it is assumed that persons are the kinds of things that act and experience and that they are also the kinds of things capable of understanding and evaluating their actions and experiences. Such assumptions are well within commonly accepted definitions of persons as embodied, reasoning, moral agents with awareness and concern about their existence and activity (cf. Hacker, 2007; Harré, 1983; Martin, Sugarman, & Hickinbottom, 2010; Taylor, 1985). Notice also that when the question is put in this way, it is immediately apparent that an investigator needs to know something about the processes of and criteria for understanding and evaluation that persons apply to their own actions and experiences. Moreover, when an interior self is not posited, it is clear that such processes and warrants of understanding and evaluation are capabilities of persons in interaction with the biophysical and sociocultural world. Understanding and evaluating one's actions and experiences require evolutionary and developmental histories of interactivity through which persons emerge (within their worldly exchanges with others and things) with these requisite agentic capabilities.

When such a conceptualization of persons and their rational and moral conduct and capability is transported into sociopsychological sites of particular interest to self-concept researchers, its advantages can be readily appreciated. Let us take the example of classroom learning, with particular focus on academic understanding, evaluation, and achievement. What the psychological investigator now wants to know about are how students understand and experience classroom tasks, activities, and content and how they evaluate their understanding and experience. None of these objects of inquiry requires the positing of an interior self whose attributes and/or beliefs need to be measured as separate from the actions, experiences, understandings, and evaluations of particular persons. It is entirely possible to talk descriptively about the classroom actions, experiences, understandings, and evaluations of students and to interrogate the processes of learning through which different levels and kinds of achievement emerge within the activity and interactivity of the persons involved within classroom tasks and practices, including relevant materials, artifacts, and so forth. All of these are now revealed as the relevant foci and sources for psychological and educational inquiry and knowledge as well as the primary sources of students' understanding and evaluation of their actions and experiences of learning.

Self-concept researchers and historians like Hattie (1992, 2003), Shavelson and colleagues (1976), and Wylie (1974, 1979) all recognize the desirability of doing away with the definitional/conceptual turmoil and confusions (especially as embedded in talk of inner perception/introspection) that have in the past and still continue to beset research on self-concept. Yet the answers they propose are often framed in terms of calls for superior methods of measurement and statistical procedures, as if such increments in technical sophistication could somehow solve the conceptual and ontological problems occasioned by the idea of an interior measureable self equipped with the capability for self-conception and self-evaluation. Even when such authors sensibly warn against the positing of any such a self, in contradistinction to the person whose actions and experiences are of interest, they continue to pursue a research agenda of "patching" rather than reconceptualizing.

Alternative Possibilities

Rather than continuing to attempt to measure an ill-defined self-concept that assumes a dubiously interior metaphysics, we should learn from the past in ways that excise fallacies, confusions, and conceptual/logical difficulties, thus allowing us to work within more clearly conceptualized frameworks that can ensure that our research programs are targeted at what matters and conducted with methods appropriate to those targets. To illustrate this recommendation, consider a possible alternative to self-concept research in the area of social self-concept. In their review of research on social self-concept, Berndt and Burgy (1996) state that "the creation of multidimensional self-concept measures …

has been a mixed blessing [in that] measurement issues have received more attention in recent literature than theoretical issues," (p. 202) definitional issues, and intervention issues. They note that the validity of such measures "should be treated not as an intriguing hypothesis but as a tautology," given that "items on social self-concept scales are often similar or even identical to items on measures of other constructs such as loneliness and social support" and that "little attention has been given ... to the processes by which the realities of people's social lives affect their self-perceptions and self-evaluations" (p. 203). Thus, Berndt and Burgy, like Hattie (2003), worry and suspect that measures of social self-concept may not be necessary to establish that individuals' understandings and evaluations of their social capabilities are rooted in or part of their social interactions and experiences or that changing social interactions and experiences are likely to affect those understandings and evaluations.

At the same time as research on self-concept and social self-concept has focused on multidimensional measures and their validity and relations with other measures, several social developmental psychologists have been undertaking promising research and intervention studies concerning children's and adolescents' social capabilities and their enhancement with little or no attention to social self-concept (or other forms of self-concept) whatsoever.

Educational Examples

For example, Selman (2003) has experimented with raising children's social understanding and ability much more directly by encouraging children to work together within activities chosen both to promote cooperation and engender conflicts that need to be resolved. More specifically, Selman's aim is to "increase children's awareness and understanding of the actions and motivations of others as well as themselves—to be able to take another's perspective and coordinate it with their own, thus linking social thought to social action" (p. 29). As such, Selman's work clearly fits within the social psychological theorizing of George Herbert Mead (1934), who emphasized that persons' understanding and evaluations of their own actions and experiences are forged in the crucible of ongoing coordinated interactivity with others.[5]

What is striking about the work of psychologists like Selman (1980, 2003) is that it manages to approach important questions concerning the self-understanding and evaluation of persons in relation to others without recourse to the construct of self-concept. Consequently, it is instructive to ask what would be added to their theoretical and empirical work on social understanding and ability with the inclusion of measures of social

---

[5] More recently, Gillespie (2005, 2006, 2012) and Martin (2005b, 2006b; Martin, Sokol, & Elfers, 2008) have theorized that the taking and exchanging of social positions and perspectives within routinized, repetitive sequences and practices of coordinated interactivity is a primary source of persons' self understandings and evaluations. We explore such matters more fully in Chapter 9.

self-concept. More pointedly, would the inclusion of a broadly and rather imprecisely defined construct of social self-concept (one that generally claims to probe the internal, subjective sense that individuals have concerning their social standing and competence) be of assistance in helping individuals to develop social understanding and reasonably veridical evaluation of their social capabilities? Or, would such an exercise be functionally superfluous with respect to such an aim?

Another example of how some contemporary researchers have avoided what they regard as unhelpful interior conceptions of selfhood comes from those who have adopted a sociocultural approach to issues of selfhood and identity that treats "identity as a function of our practices, of our lived experiences of participation in specific communities (and therefore our competencies), rather than our beliefs or values" (Hickey & Granade, 2004, p. 233). "Identity in this sense is an experience and a display of competence that requires neither an explicit self-image nor self-identification with an ostensible community" (Wenger, 1998, p. 152). Such an approach is concretized in research by Vadeboncoeur and Portes (2002) and Lave and Wenger (1991) that illustrates how individual and interior conceptions of self-concept can be reconceptualized within sociocultural frameworks. In their analysis of at-risk students, Vadeboncoeur and Portes understand the individual identities of these students as constituted within social and community practices of group membership and intergroup relations. Consequently, students' individual identities are constantly unfolding within an ongoing process of social negotiation in which the individual is an active participant. In short, it is activity with others within school and extracurricular contexts, not interior reflection, that determines how these students understand and evaluate themselves.

Lave and Wenger (1991) provide several examples of the ways in which individuals' performative competences within different communities of practice legitimate different levels of participation (from peripheral to central) in the practices that define such communities. Typically, as individuals enter into new communities of practice (e.g., freshmen starting their first year of high school), they act and are treated as peripheral members of these communities. As they act and react within these environments they learn to coordinate within the web of sociocultural practices, conventions, norms, routines, and niches that, in interaction with their own activities and styles, constitute their identities. Wenger (1998) distinguishes between peripheral and marginal participation-nonparticipation. Being on the periphery is associated with an inbound trajectory of gradually joining into the practices of the community as a full participant. In contrast, being on the margins is associated with an outbound trajectory away from communal participation and acceptance. "Marginal nonparticipation illuminates the complex motivational reality of the disadvantaged students who often get identified as being at risk of school failure," such that "by the time students are labeled 'at risk,' their mutually constituted trajectory may be so misaligned with the knowledge practices of formal schooling that it is impossible to redirect it" (Hickey & Granade, 2004, p. 235).

Both social developmental (e.g., Selman, 2003) and sociocultural (e.g., Hickey & Granade, 2004) approaches to students' competence, motivation, and understanding/

evaluation of their own actions and identities focus on individuals' coordinated interactivity with others within social, communal practices. These approaches and those who adopt them are less concerned with how students think and feel about themselves in reflective isolation than in how they present and conduct themselves in their interactions with others within those practices that define particular areas of human activity, institutional and otherwise. As such, these theoretical frameworks and empirical research programs offer obvious and distinctive alternatives to programs of psychological inquiry anchored in measures of students' self beliefs that are separated from their actual interactive engagement within schools, classrooms, tasks, and projects.

None of what is said here is intended to imply that self-concept researchers are unaware of such alternative possibilities or that they are stubbornly pursuing their own agendas. The historical record of self-concept research, as has been seen, is replete with many critical observations and comments offered by leading self-concept researchers themselves. However, the general fact of their continued pursuit of self-concept measurement and research clearly reflects the individual and collective beliefs of these prominent researchers that many of the difficulties confronting them and their project will be overcome with improved measures and new avenues of inquiry that make more appropriate use of such technological advances. But, as has also been noted, the basic conceptual/definitional and ontological difficulties that beset this field of psychological inquiry appear to run more deeply than such diagnoses and ameliorative strategies assume. For if the only real and clear sense of self-concept can be rendered in terms of individuals' understanding and evaluation of their own actions and experiences in context, it is ultimately unhelpful to invent self entities, structures, and processes that are treated as interior determinants of such actions and experiences. Instead, it seems more sensible to examine systematically and rigorously those actions and experiences as they unfold in real-world situations in the contexts of the lives and circumstances of the persons whose actions and experiences they are.

One important reason for examining the social contexts within which actions and experiences unfold is that appropriate levels and criteria for understanding and evaluation (self or otherwise) are much more likely to be located within our interactivity with others than in our solipsistic individual psychological interiors. An additional benefit of reframing self-concept as part of the worldly acting and experiencing of persons is a potential decrement in what some (e.g., Baumeister, Campbell, Krueger, & Vohs, 2003; Baumeister, Smart, & Boden, 1996; Martin, 2004a, 2007) regard as a tendency of many contemporaries to be excessively self-concerned and self-interested, to the detriment of others and social, communal relations and functioning in general.[6]

---

[6] McLellan (2008), drawing on the critical historical work of Rose (1998) and Hacking (1995, 2006), has suggested that such psychological self-concern has become so pervasive in contemporary education and society that it is now possible to talk sensibly about those who exhibit it as being psychologically constituted individuals who are experientially and strategically focused on their own interests and agendas in ways that go well beyond the more socially sensitive and constrained practices of personhood available to previous generations.

Conclusions

Histories and reviews of research on self-concept conducted by self-concept researchers themselves often have recognized basic definitional and conceptual difficulties that have plagued psychological inquiry in this area. In the face of such concerns, several leading self-concept researchers have advocated more theoretically driven and statistically sophisticated work to create and establish the validity of better measures of general and domain-specific self-concept. Nonetheless, definitional, conceptual concerns continue to attend contemporary self-concept research. A consideration of critical historical work in the area of personality, attitudes, motivation, and self-concept/self-esteem conducted by historians of psychology (e.g., Danziger, 1997a,b; Greer, 2003, 2007; Nicholson, 1998, 2003), other than self-concept researchers themselves, suggests deeper problems concerning the ontological status of the self-concept. In particular, the assumption of an interior homunculus seems to linger in talk and theory that understand the self-concept as a set of cognitive schemata, systems, and subsystems. Such an interior self-conception tends to be associated with a widespread tendency to treat psychological aspects of the actions and experiences of persons as causes of those actions and experiences as opposed to integral parts of the actions and experiences that need to be explained.

The net result of positing various versions of the self-concept as an interior psychological process or structure that determines actions and experiences has been to shift the attention of researchers away from persons' contextualized, situation-constrained understanding and evaluation of their own actions and experiences. Thus, research in areas such as achievement motivation and social development has been unnecessarily deflected from the direct study of patterns of interactivity within which persons and developing persons (students, children) come to comprehend and evaluate their actions and experiences. It is not reflection on our hypothetical interior selves but our coordinated participation in the physical, interpersonal, social, and cultural practices of understanding and evaluation that constitutes our personal understanding and evaluation of our own actions and experiences in various domains of human activity and interactivity, from the building of bridges to the conduct of social negotiations, to the comportment of students in classrooms.

Psychological and educational researchers interested in advancing our understanding of how persons come to effectively understand and evaluate their own actions and experiences in ways that support sustained, motivated performance in schools and other areas of human activity and interactivity, might do two things. One is to reconceptualize and reconfigure the self-concept in terms of persons' understandings and evaluations of their relevant actions and experiences. The other is to avoid attributing primary explanatory and causal force to psychological aspects of actions and experiences and instead to attempt to uncover the sociocultural and biophysical constituents and determinants of our actions and experiences and of our understanding and evaluation of them. Perhaps such a reconfiguration might also have socially salubrious consequences in restraining possibly excessive, dysfunctional levels of self-concern and self-interest.

In the next chapter, we look historically and critically at the idea of self-efficacy, a more recent arrival on the scene of psychological foci in the self-related studies of psychologists and educational psychologists. In some respects, self-efficacy, at least in its original sense of a task-specific judgment of an individual's capability of performing particular actions in particular contexts, moves toward our suggested alternative of focusing more directly on individuals' situational actions and experiences. However, as we shall see in Chapter 6, like self-esteem and self-concept, the notion of self-efficacy still privileges the psychological interior of individuals as an influential causal force that is understood as lying behind rather than being part of the actions and experiences with which it is associated.

6 Being Confident in What You Do
SELF-EFFICACY AND AGENCY

IN CHAPTER 5, we distinguished between self-esteem, self-concept, and self-efficacy while simultaneously noting that psychologists' conceptions and use of these terms frequently overlap. Nonetheless, self-efficacy as initially formulated by Albert Bandura (1977) differs from self-esteem and self-concept in that it consists of an individual's task-specific beliefs in her or his ability to perform particular goal-directed actions. "Perceived self-efficacy refers to beliefs in one's capabilities to organize and execute the courses of action required to produce given attainments" (Bandura, 1997, p. 3). Moreover, self-efficacy is understood as related causally to the ensuing actions or performance with which it is associated. Thus, when athletes believe strongly in their ability to perform at particularly high levels, self-efficacy theory suggests that their performance-related self-efficacy is high and will increase the probability that they will succeed in performing to the level they envision.

According to Bandura, his colleagues, and many other psychologists who work in the area of self-efficacy, there is now an enormous body of evidence across a wide variety of human endeavors in support of the idea that the beliefs individuals hold about their abilities to organize actions and execute particular tasks are related causally to their motivation and performance.

> Efficacy beliefs contribute significantly to level of motivation and performance. They predict not only the behavioral changes accompanying different environmental

influences but also differences in behavior between individuals receiving the same environmental influence, and even variation within the same individual in the tasks performed and those shunned or attempted but failed. (Bandura, 1997, p. 61)

In other words, an individual's self-efficacy is a major determinant of his or her behavior across different situations; those with higher self-efficacy perform better than individuals with lower self-efficacy in the same situations and particular individuals perform better across different tasks and times when their self-efficacy is higher.

Importantly, self-efficacy theorists and researchers understand self-efficacy as the single most important mechanism of human agency. "The power to originate actions for given purposes is the key feature of personal agency," and "Beliefs of personal efficacy constitute the key factor of human agency" (Bandura, 1997, p. 3). It is precisely because of this association with human agency that self-efficacy has become so strongly linked with self-regulation in general and with the managerial self of educational psychology (see Chapter 3). Whereas self-esteem and self-concept are typically joined to a professional psychological rhetoric that emphasizes individual well-being, creativity, and expression (the expressive self of educational psychology—again, see Chapter 3), self-efficacy is related directly to the organization and execution of particular courses of goal-directed action (the managerial self of educational psychology). In Bandura's theory of triadic reciprocal causation, internal and personal psychological factors (cognitive, affective, and biological) interact continuously and bidirectionally with both behavior and environmental events to determine human action and experience. In these ongoing transactions, persons and their agency (most importantly in the form of self-efficacy) are "both producers and products of social systems" (Bandura, 1997, p. 6).

In this chapter, we begin our historical and critical consideration of self-efficacy by tracing its conceptualization through a series of debates between Bandura and a variety of commentators during the 1970s and 1980s. We then move on to a consideration of more recent developments and innovations in self-efficacy theory and research during the last two decades. Many of these elaborations are intended to enhance human agency at both individual and collective levels. To understand the broader context within which self-efficacy theory and research are situated, we examine the sociocultural and historical landscape of America during the 1960s and 1970s and the globalization of many American values and social practices during the last two decades of the twentieth century. In doing so, we give particular attention to attempts by Bandura and other self-efficacy advocates to argue that high levels of individual self-efficacy are essential to the collective communal ability of all human societies and cultures to forge functional adaptations to a host of new challenges facing the world of the future. Such focused attention is warranted given that many recent and current calls for teaching practices and school programs that promote students' self-efficacy are based on such rhetoric.

Debating Self-Efficacy: Bandura and His Critics

Albert Bandura is one of the best-known, most successful psychologists of his generation. Born in 1925 in Mundare, a small village in northern Alberta, Canada, Bandura faced the kinds of educational obstacles often associated with small-town experience, including a limited exposure to instructional resources, teachers, and the world at large. Later in life, Bandura maintained that in such an environment "the students had to take charge of their own education.... Very often we developed a better grasp of the subjects than the overworked teachers" (Stokes, 1986, p. 2, as cited in Zimmerman & Schunk, 2003, p. 432). In consequence, Bandura apparently developed a lifelong belief to the effect that "The content of most textbooks is perishable, but the tools of self-directedness serve one well over time" (Stokes, 1986, p. 2, as cited in Zimmerman & Schunk, 2003, p. 432). And so it would seem they did serve Bandura, who completed his undergraduate studies in psychology at the University of British Columbia and went on to complete his graduate studies at the University of Iowa. During his first (and last) permanent academic position at Stanford, Bandura quickly established himself as an academic star in the discipline of psychology through pioneering work in the area of social learning and modeling, achieving widespread fame for his studies of the observational learning of aggression (the classic Bobo doll studies—e.g., Bandura, Ross, & Ross, 1961). During the 1950s and 1960s, Bandura expanded his program of research on social learning and modeling to include the study of children's cognitive and linguistic development. By the early 1970s, recognition of his work by fellow psychologists resulted in his nomination and election as president of the American Psychological Association, despite a personal history of relative noninvolvement with this primary governing body of American academic and professional psychology. By this time, he had also turned his attention to the study and theory of self-regulatory abilities, especially the study of self-efficacy.

Given that Bandura already commanded considerable attention in both the academy and certain quarters of the larger society, the initial publications of his work on self-efficacy (1977, 1978a,b,c,d, 1979, 1982, 1984) met with a great deal of critical attention from many of the leading psychologists of this period. Although couched in the theoretical and methodological understandings and language of scientific and applied psychology, several major themes emerged in a variety of critical reactions published between 1977 and 1987 that are directly relevant to our central concern in this book with the importation of conceptions of psychological selfhood to educational policy and practice. Four (somewhat overlapping) matters, in particular, deserve our direct attention: (1) whether self-efficacy can be separated from human action as a whole, (2) whether self-efficacy can best be understood as a psychological or cognitive structure within individuals, (3) whether self-efficacy might appropriately be regarded as an internal cause of human action, and (4) whether the self that exercises self-efficacy ought to be identified with the person whose actions are the objects of inquiry. In relation to this last set of issues, we also will consider briefly the adequacy of more recent attempts by Bandura to identify self-efficacy as the primary ingredient of human agency and thus of great importance to our present and future lives as individuals within communities.

Is Self-Efficacy Not Part of Human Action?

In his 1977 article in *Psychological Review*, Bandura distinguishes self-efficacy, understood in this article as "expectations of personal efficacy," from "outcome expectancies," understood as a person's estimate that a given behavior will result in particular outcomes. Thus, expectations of personal efficacy differ from outcome expectations in that the former concern an individual's beliefs in his or her ability to perform a particular behavior while the latter connote an individual's belief that the behavior produced will result in particular consequences. Perhaps not surprisingly, several critics of Bandura's initial conception of self-efficacy objected to this distinction and related distinctions made by Bandura on the grounds that human action does not divide neatly in accordance with such distinctions. In particular, Teasdale (1978) argued that self-efficacy is very difficult to separate from outcome expectations. For example, when individuals are asked to report their self-efficacy with respect to a particular task, such as approaching a feared object or solving a particular problem, the consequences or outcomes of the behaviors of approach or solution are necessarily part of what an individual considers with respect to his or her ability to perform such behaviors. Kazdin (1978) echoed this concern, claiming that it is also impossible to separate self-efficacy from the appraisal of incentives (motivation) and skill (competence), and appraisal of situations and possibilities for acting within them.

Concerns about separating self-efficacy beliefs or judgments from other volitional, cognitive, and performative aspects of human action implicitly point to the difficulty of "atomizing" human action into such components. Although it may be the case that there are many different motor, cognitive, emotional, motivational, and integrative systems involved in human action, it is very doubtful that individuals who engage in actions typically make such distinctions or have any reliable bases or grounds for doing so. Human action as experienced and reported by acting individuals is a more holistic mode of activity. In answering the telephone, running an errand, or looking for something to eat, people typically do not consider whether they are able to do any of these things or whether doing any of them will actually produce the desired consequences; they just do them. In this sense, what Bandura sees as important psychological antecedents for action (i.e., self-efficacy and outcome expectations) are parts of our acting in the world, not psychological antecedents separate from our acting.

Is Self-Efficacy an Internal Cognitive Structure?

Whereas Bandura (1977) initially tended to write mostly about self-efficacy in terms of a person's efficacy expectations, in subsequent publications (e.g., Bandura, 1978a,b, 1979, 1982), he wrote more explicitly about the "self" in self-efficacy. For example, Bandura (1979) stipulates that the self is not a psychic agent that controls action but rather the cognitive structures that provide a mechanism for action. Such a self also serves as the standard by which actions are evaluated and motivated. In different ways, both Rychlak (1979) and Pereboom (1979) objected to such a characterization of selfhood. Rychlak questioned Bandura's dismissal of the self as a psychic agent by drawing attention to thinking as a part of acting, wondering why the thinking self should be divorced from a personal agency or agent that acts in the world and replaced by cognitive structures. Pereboom took a slightly different approach to reach a similar conclusion. Pointing out that thoughts cannot influence the environment unless they issue in actions, Pereboom also questioned Bandura's separation of the self as a cognitive structure from the person as a rational and moral agent with moral responsibility for his or her actions.

In short, it seems difficult to imagine the self understood as a set of cognitive structures and mechanisms experiencing the kind of reasoning and moral considerations typically associated with the actions of persons. As both Rychlak (1979) and Pereboom (1979) argued, such a self seems too removed from the plane of ongoing activity and interactivity within which persons are embedded. Indeed, the postulation of cognitive structures that somehow judge, appraise, motivate, decide, and direct human action raises long-standing questions concerning the nature of the connections between mind, body, and world that enable the connection of thought with effective action. Bandura (1978a) acknowledges that he is committed to an as yet incomplete form of mind-body interactionism, one that he has attempted to develop through his model of triadic reciprocal determinism, in which he (Bandura, 1978d) posits bidirectional causal connections between persons (including, most importantly, their self-efficacy), their behaviors, and the environment. However, even here, it is instructive to note that although cognitive structures of self and self-efficacy are included as parts or attributes of persons, behaviors or actions are treated separately from (even though highly interactive with) both persons and the environment. With such models in place, it is difficult to interpret Bandura as not promoting a highly dualistic conception of cognitive selfhood separated from the activity of persons in the world (more about this below). Consequently, it does not seem unreasonable for some of his critics to draw attention to Bandura's endorsement of a deeply psychological conception of selfhood that treats the self as a set of interior structures that cause human activity.

Is Self-Efficacy an Internal Cause of Action?

However, there are both conceptual and empirical difficulties with understanding self-efficacy as an internal cause of action. Kazdin (1978) was one of the first to raise the concern that self-efficacy, and self-report measures of self-efficacy, could not be separated from the performances or actions with which they are associated. Although Kazdin directed his concern to the fact that judgments of self-efficacy and the performance being judged shared the same task environment, his more general point was that there is a considerable conceptual overlap between self-efficacy and performance or, as stated previously, that self-efficacy is a part of human action, not something separate from it. When seen in this way, what Bandura has done is to take a part of an action (i.e., the sense we have that we can do something, which is often implicitly part of our doing that something), conceptualize this part as an inner cognitive structure, and then attribute causal efficacy to this structure. But is there any reason to do any of this? Or perhaps more helpfully, what is gained and lost in such a conceptual reframing of our well-known everyday ability to act intentionally—a capability that implicitly includes our sense that we can act as we intend with a reasonable degree of predictability?

When viewed in this way, the full force of psychological selfhood is on display in the theory and research on self-efficacy. What Bandura effectively has done is to create an inner psychological cause (i.e., self-efficacy) for our actions by theoretically removing the intentionality and predictability that are part of any action, coining the term *self-efficacy* for what has been removed, and promoting a conception of self-efficacy as an internal psychological cause of the very actions from which it has been separated. However, parts of action, or more precisely parts of what persons do when they act, cannot be causes of that of which they are part. For this to be the case, it would have to be shown that self-efficacy exists independently of the actions with which it is associated. Instead, as Kazdin (1978) has argued (also see Borkovec, 1978; Eastman & Marzillier, 1984), it seems clear that self-efficacy is conceptually linked to action in a part-whole relationship. Self-efficacy is not a cause of my talking or walking; it is a part of my intentional engagement in these activities that has been acquired as my abilities to perform these actions have developed over the course of my life from infancy to adulthood. If we want to look for actual causes of everyday human actions such as walking and talking, we should look to the history of our interactions with others and the world—to those social, cultural, physical, and biological factors that have been implicated in my learning to walk and talk. We should not look for an interior cognitive structure of belief in walking or talking.

In a related vein, several critical commentators (e.g., Kazdin, 1978; Poser, 1978; Biglan, 1987) on Bandura's theory and research in the area of self-efficacy have noted that although Bandura and other self-efficacy theorists and researchers assume that changes in self-efficacy cause changes in behavior, experimental manipulations of self-efficacy always involve manipulations of social and physical aspects of the experimental context or tasks. Such contexts and tasks include information and instructions about self-efficacy and how to respond to instruments measuring self-efficacy, which very likely function as "demand characteristics" (in the form of implicit training and social commitments and incentives to perform and report according to the experimenters' expectations and understandings). Biglan (1987) noted that people tend to behave consistently with both the experimenters' and their own expectations, creating the correspondence that self-efficacy researchers report between efficacy ratings and performance. For example, when individuals respond to a self-efficacy probe and claim that they are confident that they can perform a particular action or accomplish a particular task, they feel an obligation or social responsibility to do so as well as a psychological motivation to "be true to my word." Thus, Biglan suggested that a consideration of social/contextual factors as possible causal determinants of self-efficacy, and the performances to which it is attached, is likely to yield more useful knowledge of our agentic functioning as persons than self-efficacy ratings. Unfortunately, as Jayakar (2009) has noted more recently, the extant empirical literature on self-efficacy does not, for the most part, report the kinds of longitudinal within-person research designs that might establish the exact causes of either self-efficacy beliefs or the behaviors they are purported to enhance.

Another way of approaching the conceptual problems associated with theory and research on self-efficacy has been advanced by Jan Smedslund (1978). Smedslund argued that Bandura's theory of self-efficacy is made up of commonsense ideas that make the theory logically necessary in ways that do not permit possible refutation or require empirical testing. In effect, Bandura's theory of self-efficacy is simply a set of explications of the conceptual network embedded within our ordinary ways of talking. For example, when self-efficacy researchers conclude that individuals with high levels of self-efficacy are more likely to perform well than individuals with lower levels of self-efficacy, such a psychological explication amounts to little more than the commonsense assertion that people who think they can do things are more likely to do them than people who think they can't. Such a "result" is conceptually implicated in a way that conforms to our everyday ways of talking and thinking about our actions. Indeed, it would seem more than passing strange if research on self-efficacy were to discover that this was not the case.

And yet, a recent review of contemporary research on self-efficacy by Jayakar (2009) indicates that although there has been much research on the relation of self-efficacy to performance, contrary to Bandura's repeated claims concerning consistently high correlations between self-efficacy and performance, such correlations are sometimes absent in studies of self-efficacy. In a section entitled "Self-Efficacy Causality" in his 1997 book *Self-Efficacy: The Exercise of Control*, Bandura claims that

> The evidence is relatively consistent in showing that efficacy beliefs contribute significantly to level of motivation and performance. They predict not only the behavioral changes accompanying different environmental influences but also differences in behavior between individuals receiving the same environmental influence, and even variation within the same individual in the tasks performed and those shunned or attempted but failed. (p. 61)

In contrast to this interpretation of relevant research results, Jayakar (2009) concludes that findings concerning self-efficacy and performance have been inconsistent. What is most instructive about Jayakar's conclusion is the reasons that she suggests for these inconsistent findings—namely, that although it seems clear that past performance influences self-efficacy, it may be that self-efficacy does not always influence subsequent performance. The future is, after all, not as easily known as the past, and unanticipated things can and do happen.

However, as Smedslund (1978) reminds us, such "findings" hardly require empirical demonstration. They simply restate conventional wisdom and common sense to the effect that we know what we have done in the past and use such knowledge to act in the present, whereas our ability to predict the future and what we will do in it is imperfect. When self-efficacy is understood as part of our acting in the world (past, present, and future), there is little more to be discovered concerning relations between different aspects of our acting, such as our perceived ability to act and our actions. When such connectedness is missing, it is more likely that some physical impediment (illness), social occurrence (a hike in "green fees"), or other person (the expressed wishes of a spouse) has emerged to make future actions (golfing) less likely, not that one's self-efficacy has changed ("My goodness, after all of these years of golfing, I suddenly don't think I can golf").

Of course what makes self-efficacy apparently plausible as an internal psychological cause is the way in which it is cut off from action and "measured" by psychologists. Just as we discovered in Chapters 4 and 5 with respect to the measurement of self-esteem and self-concept, when psychologists create instruments to measure these "self variables," the very process of responding to these measurement instruments serves to separate that which is purportedly measured from the actions and experiences of which it is otherwise a seamless part. Thus, for example, when self-efficacy researchers ask participants in their research studies to employ the standard methodology of rating their self-efficacy, the idea of self-efficacy becomes reified as an internal psychological structure underlying confidence judgments with respect to particular actions. In this standard methodology, "individuals record the strength of their belief on a 100-point scale, ranging in 10-unit intervals from 0 ("Cannot do"); through intermediate degrees of assurance, 50 ("Moderately certain can do"); to complete assurance, 100 ("Certain can do")" (Bandura, 1997, pp. 43–44). Further separation of judgments of self-efficacy from the actions with which self-efficacy would otherwise seem inseparable is achieved through standard experimental instructions that

establish the appropriate judgmental set. People are asked to judge their operative capabilities as of now, not their potential capabilities or their expected future capabilities. In the case of self-regulatory efficacy, people judge their assurance that they can perform the activity regularly over designated periods of time. For example, recovered alcoholics would judge their perceived ability to refrain from drinking over specified time intervals. A practice item, such as the capability to lift objects of increasing weight, helps to familiarize respondents with the scale gauging strength of efficacy belief and reveals any misunderstanding about how to use it. (Bandura, 1997, p. 44)

Confusing Selves With Persons

Now, in all fairness, in cases such as that of recovering alcoholics, it is entirely conceivable that such individuals might think and worry about their ability to refrain from drinking alcohol over long periods of time. Persons are, after all, sentient beings with self-reflective concern and capability. However, any such thinking and worrying are the actions and experiences of persons. They are not the functional properties of underlying, cognitive and/or self structures residing inside the psychic makeup of people that causally determine what people do. Thinking, experiencing, and acting are predicates that sensibly and logically attach to persons, not to parts of persons, whether conceived as homuncular entities or internal cognitive structures to which persons are somehow thought to give over executive decision making and control of their actions in the world. Such entities and structures are the inventions of psychologists, not characteristics and capabilities of people functioning in their everyday lives.

As argued in the previous chapter, for purposes of education and social life in general, it is simpler, more realistic, and more functional to think about persons thinking and doing things, and the biophysical and sociocultural determinants that enable or inhibit such thinking and doing, rather than about how to manipulate interior selves and/or cognitive structures (as postulated by psychologists) so as to help individuals to learn, develop, and perform. No amount of self-efficacy intervention will help a person to play baseball, do mathematics, or function effectively in social settings if he or she has not acquired the abilities and skills needed to perform effectively in ballparks, schools, or society. To devote valuable time and energy to the cultivation of purported psychological structures like self-efficacy in lieu of the teaching and learning of requisite skills and knowledge is both unnecessary and ill advised.

None of what has been said here should be interpreted to mean that people, including students in schools, do not think about and experience emotional reactions to their actions and experiences. Being reflective, concerned, and goal-oriented with respect to one's life and what one does in life are part of what it means to be a person, understood as a rational and moral agent with first-person perspective, understanding, and experience. Being such a person certainly involves emotional and cognitive judgments of feeling more or less confident in one's ability to do things. However, for the most part, such judgments and feelings are parts of our ongoing stream of activity and interactivity within the biophysical and sociocultural world. Of course we can choose to understand and break up that world in any manner of ways. And psychologists who construct and frame human experience and action in psychological ways are free to do as they please with respect to their own theorizing and research. However, it is extremely important that such disciplinary and professional theorizing and intervention be seen for what they are and what they are not. The conceptions and practices of psychologists are not definitive let alone the best construals of the way the world and the persons in it are. This is an extremely important thing to remember when psychologists encourage the importation of their ideas and practices into important public institutions such as educational systems.

Beyond Self-Efficacy to Human Agency

In more recent years, Bandura (1989, 1995, 1997, 2006) has attempted to expand the scope of his theorizing about self-efficacy in relation to our individual and collective abilities (or agency) to influence our lives and the future of our societies in the face of an increasingly challenging set of social problems, including overpopulation, environmental concerns, poverty, urban decay, and strained international relations. The possibility of using self-efficacy and more collective forms of efficacy to combat such pressing difficulties will be taken up later in this chapter. However, to set the stage for such a discussion, we want to offer a few remarks concerning the idea that self-efficacy is an essential aspect of human agency, understood broadly as the individual and collective ability of persons to act in ways that make a difference in their lives. Of course, in one sense, all of our actions inevitably contribute to our current and future circumstances. However, when philosophers and others refer to the agency of persons, they typically wish to talk about our ability to exercise two-way volitional control (i.e., to act or refrain from acting) according to reason and moral concern.

Human agency is both rational and moral and is a defining characteristic of persons, not a kind of executive ability that issues from some sort of internal psychological structure, such as Bandura (1979) understands the self to be. As mentioned previously, early in the relatively recent history of self-efficacy, Bandura conceptualized the self not as a psychic agent (or, for that matter, an agent of any kind) but as a cognitive structure that provides a reference mechanism for action. As such, the self contains standards by which actions are evaluated and motivated—a kind of neo-Lockean psychological self busily monitoring actions and experiences "behind the scenes," although now conceived as a cognitive structure, not as a homunculus per se. It is also clear that Bandura has continued to consider the self that lies behind self-efficacy beliefs and judgments to be some kind of internal structural entity, given that he (e.g., Bandura, 1997, pp. 42–45), talks explicitly about the dimensional structure of self-efficacy scales that differ in terms of level, generality, strength, precision, and comprehensiveness. Given that such scales purportedly measure efficacy "beliefs about personal abilities to produce specified levels of performance" (Bandura, 1997, p. 45), it must be the case that the beliefs thus measured also have the kind of structure assumed by the scales said to measure them. [We will leave aside for the moment the important matter of whether it is reasonable to use the term *measurement* to describe the attempts of psychologists to gather data that purport to be about internal structures such as self-efficacy by asking people to rate their levels of self-esteem, self-concept, and self-efficacy (see Michell, 1999), but we will return to this point later in this chapter and will take it up in detail in Chapter 8.]

Nonetheless, a reading of Bandura's writings about self-efficacy between 1977 and now reveals a gradual shift in his way of talking about the self and about self-efficacy. Increasingly, he has moved beyond the idea of both as internal cognitive structures (a conception that remains deeply embedded in the measurement of self-efficacy) to discussing self-efficacy as an essential (indeed, *the* essential or core) component of human agency. According to Bandura (2006), "to be an agent is to influence intentionally one's functioning and life circumstances.... People are self-organizing, proactive, self-regulating and self-reflecting.... They are contributors to their life circumstances, not just products of them" (p. 164). So far, so good, in that human agency in these sentences clearly is something that people do. However, immediately following these assertions, Bandura retreats to his more long-standing conceptual practices and begins to elucidate what he understands to be the structure of human agency. Here, he stipulates four components of agency: intentionality, forethought, self-reactiveness, and self-reflectiveness. Not surprisingly, with this move he begins to talk once again, in a neo-Lockean manner, about agents as

> self-examiners of their own functioning. Through functional awareness, they reflect on their personal efficacy, the soundness of their thoughts and actions, and the meaning of their pursuits, and they make corrective adjustments if necessary. The metacognitive capability to reflect upon oneself and the adequacy of one's thoughts and actions is the most distinctly human core property of agency. (p. 165)

The psychological ghost within the machine (surveying, judging, and evaluating its surrounds and its own activity) is back in the executive saddle, with the person carried along in its wake.

Nonetheless, it also is clear that by the dawn of the current century, Bandura is at considerable pains to connect his theorizing about self-efficacy with a broader conception of human agency, one that involves both individual and group or collective efficacy. Indeed, Bandura (2006) now states that "In the exercise of collective agency, [people] pool their knowledge, skills, and resources, and act in concert to shape their futures ... People's conjoint belief in their collective capability to achieve given attainments is a key ingredient of collective efficacy" (p. 165). Thus, just as self-efficacy is the key, essential component of individual human agency, collective efficacy is the core component of collective agency. However, to make sure that the psychological primacy of the individual is maintained even within his more recent conception of collective agency, Bandura immediately adds that "There is no disembodied group mind that believes. Perceived collective efficacy resides in the minds of group members as the belief they have in common regarding their group's capability" (pp. 165–166).

Consequently, collective efficacy is measured by "aggregating members' appraisals of their personal capabilities for the particular functions they perform in the group" or "aggregating members' appraisals of their group's capability as a whole" (Bandura, 1997, p. 478). Thu, collective efficacy is operationally defined as an aggregation of individuals' judgments of their own or the group's capability. So when Bandura (2006) states that "the collective performance of a social system involves interactive, coordinative, and synergistic dynamics that create emergent group-level properties not reducible solely to individual attributes"

(p. 166), he is talking about a kind of social, collective agency that is not captured by his own measurements of collective efficacy. Indeed, it might be argued that his more recent theorizing situates Bandura's approach to human agency within a broader social and political context than typically recognized by many psychologists. However, at least when it comes to his own and the vast majority of extant theory and research methodology in the area of self-efficacy, there can be little doubt that self-efficacy researchers are firmly wedded to a strong form of individualism that effectively reduces social and cultural artifacts, traditions, practices, and institutions to the actions of individuals—actions caused by their personal inner psychological structures and processes, such as self-efficacy.

In the vast majority of the work of Bandura and his colleagues on individual and collective efficacy, social and cultural ingredients of collective efficacy are reduced and restricted to obviously and immediately present interpersonal conditions such as verbal instructions, demographic characteristics of learners, and the presence or absence of specific behavioral stimuli. Bandura (1995, 1997, 2006) obviously intends his work on self and collective efficacy to apply to broader social contexts and circumstances, including family structures, education and school systems, career choice and industrial organization, health and community well-being, multiculturalism, and international relations. Nonetheless, if it is assumed that societies are more than collections of individuals, the empirical and much of the theoretical bases he and others have provided for self-efficacy seem too individualistically, internally, and reductively psychological to warrant such widespread application.

Self-Efficacy, Personal Agency, and Later-Twentieth-Century American Life and Education

Earlier in this chapter, in recounting briefly some basic facts of Bandura's life and career leading to his work on self-efficacy, we implicitly hinted at the possible importance of American social and cultural events during the mid to late 1900s. Indeed, it is highly unlikely that the popularity, both within and beyond disciplinary psychology, of Bandura's conception of self-efficacy can be explained without reference to its cultural background. By the time Bandura published his influential 1977 paper, many in the United States and Canada were still riding the self-actualization wave of the 1960s but beginning to confront some apparently new, challenging, and stark realities of the late 1970s. The so-called "boomer generation" put away its protest placards and carefree lifestyle to embrace the reality that the world was not going to continue to unfold as a gigantic love-in and began to look toward futures of work, family, obligation, consumption, and profit. In making this transition, they required a form of self-belief that went beyond the abstract self-actualization of the sixties toward a more concretely focused self-assertion that seemed to be required both by their advancing years and changes to the American sociocultural landscape. And nowhere was this change of focus and strategy felt more intensely than in California and its many university and college campuses, including Stanford.

As Cushman (1995) put it, by the mid-seventies, many boomers were trading in "the rebellious, unpredictable, colorful, naïve sixties face [for] the increasingly frustrated, angry, bitterly disappointed face of the seventies [in preparation for] the sad, self-involved, acquisitive face of the eighties" (p. 277). Increasingly, self-actualization began to merge with self-promotional strategizing that promised not only a liberating salvation of one's essential self but also the self-managed acquisition of promotions, products, and perks. Consumerism merged with psychological mindedness to yield a sociopsychological world in which belief in one's abilities was essential for success.

In the early 1970s in Stanford's Department of Psychology, two associates of Albert Bandura, Carl Thoresen and Michael Mahoney (who became well-known psychologists themselves), caught the wave of the sea-change in self-understanding perfectly when they published a highly influential article in the *Educational Researcher* entitled "Behavioral Self-Control: Power to the Person." Mahoney and Thoresen (1972) were able not only to articulate a form of self-management attuned to the strategic seventies as much as to the liberating sixties but also to bring together the humanistic and scientific selves of educational psychology (see Chapter 3), capturing both "the empirical rationale and the personal relevance that have traditionally characterized two disparate factions of psychology ... [to] enlarge our understanding of how behavioral principles can be applied to self-control. To this end, self-control researchers might appropriately adopt the slogan 'Power to the Person!'" (p. 7).

Needless to say, the publication of such pieces in leading journals of education did much to prepare the way for the subsequent application of theory and research on self-efficacy to education and schooling. The mature, responsible form of self-expression that self-efficacy instantiated could be linked specifically to particular school tasks and subject matter in ways that promised both scientific rigor and a humanistic concern for the self-development of individual students. When self-efficacy made its debut to the psychological community in 1977, educational institutions had already developed an appetite for the particular combination of self-development it promised. What could be better than belief in oneself, directed to particular school-relevant tasks?

Soon thereafter, research and interventions in schools and other educational settings, aimed at the affirmation and promotion of enhanced self-efficacy as an educational objective, began to flourish. During the first decade of self-efficacy research and intervention in schools, the focus of researchers and psychoeducational personnel was primarily on student achievement, motivation, and study/learning strategies. Enhanced levels of self-efficacy were claimed to be associated with higher levels of academic performance and greater motivation to learn; they were also reciprocally related to good study habits (including perseverance) and effective learning strategies. However, toward the end of the twentieth century, this continuing student focus was supplemented by a number of other educational initiatives. The self-efficacy of teachers, both individually and collectively, was frequently examined and interpreted as an important causal factor in general academic development and overall school success. More recently, Bandura and others have begun to examine the role played by self-efficacy in computer/Internet environments and in the promotion of self-regulated learning more generally (more of this in Chapter 7). Even more recently, large-scale educational efforts through television programming and curriculum design have been initiated in efforts to bring the power of self-efficacy to bear on entire communities of learners and teachers. "Teachers who consider their students' self-efficacy beliefs, goal setting, strategy use, and other forms of self-regulation in their instructional plans not only enhance students' academic knowledge, but they also increase their students' capability for self-directed learning throughout their life span" (Zimmerman & Schunk, 2003, p. 452).

By the end of the twentieth century, self-efficacy, as the core ingredient of human agency, was being trumpeted by Bandura and others as a vital ingredient in the education of students for a better world and in the preparation of teachers to help ensure a flourishing global village capable of confronting its many challenges. Even as concerns were beginning to be voiced about a possible overemphasis on students' self-esteem and self-concept (see Chapters 4 and 5), self-efficacy, because of its tie with self-regulation and self-control as desired attributes of citizens of the twenty-first century, seemed to be gaining in both popularity and prestige.

> Today's world of accelerated social, informational, and technological changes with instant communicative access worldwide provides people with expanded opportunities to bring their influence to bear on events that affect their lives. The exercise of individual and collective agency is contributing increasingly, in virtually every sphere of life, to human development, adaptation, and change. At a broader level, the challenges center on how to enlist these agentic human capabilities in ways that shape a better and sustainable future. (Bandura, 2006, p. 177)

More specifically with respect to education,

> Educational practices should be gauged not only by the skills and knowledge they impart for present use but also by what they do to children's beliefs about their capabilities, which affects how they approach the future. Students who develop a strong sense of self-efficacy are well equipped to educate themselves when they have to rely on their own initiative. (Bandura, 1986, p. 417)

Thus, for Bandura and many other psychologists and educators committed to self-efficacy, the educational cultivation of strong self-efficacy beliefs in students is the most important goal of education. A strong belief in one's ability to learn and adapt to changing circumstances will be the defining feature of those individuals and societies who will survive and flourish in a future that looks increasingly uncertain, unpredictable, and fraught with challenges. On the surface, such sentiments and convictions seem reasonable. After all, who can doubt that the future will be challenging and that individuals capable of adapting to it will flourish (as they have in the past) compared to those incapable of adapting? But what does self-efficacy actually add to our ongoing struggle to make good lives for ourselves, our families, and our communities, let alone good lives for those others who are far removed geographically and ideologically from us?

Although Bandura (1991, 1999, 2004) has written briefly about moral aspects of human action and agency, it must be acknowledged that the vast majority of work in this area of psychological theory and inquiry has been devoted to the mechanics or "nuts and bolts" of self-efficacy—identifying its sources, documenting its effects, and determining how it can be measured and enhanced. Although possibly relevant to our individual and collective ability to confront environmental sustainability, international conflict, and population growth, it seems either highly doubtful or overly simplistic to suggest that enhanced self-efficacy might deal with such challenges in ways that result in collective flourishing. How does self-efficacy help us to decide what actions and projects to pursue in the face of such challenges? Does self-efficacy somehow come prepackaged with requisite levels of understanding, wisdom, and moral concern? Is self-efficacy, despite Bandura's (1995) assurances that it is a universal psychological feature of all humans and their societies, a sufficiently salient and common feature of all the world's sociocultural communities to inspire requisite levels of cross-cultural understanding and commitment? In the face of such obvious concerns, the psychological literature on self-efficacy seems strangely devoid of the moral, political, sociocultural consideration, concern, and wisdom that immediately suggest themselves as necessary aspects of any viable approach to the world's problems.

Before pursuing further the critical question of the adequacy of self-efficacy as a proxy for rational and moral agency, it is instructive to note that several attempts have been made to develop measures of general self-efficacy (e.g., the General Self-Efficacy Scale: GSES—Schwarzer & Jerusalem, 1995) that are not targeted directly at individuals' beliefs that they can perform particular behaviors or tasks. Intermediate-level measures of self-efficacy (in areas such as teacher, health, and social self-efficacy) also avoid task- or behavior-specific efficacy beliefs in favor of more area-general beliefs. For example, items such as "It is difficult for me to make new friends" appear on the Social Self-Efficacy Subscale of the Self-Efficacy Scale of Sherer and colleagues (1982), which consists of several different intermediate-level self-efficacy subscales. Importantly, some recent research (e.g., Fan, Meng, Gao, Lopez, & Liu, 2010; Luszczynska, Gutiérrez-Dona, & Schwarzer, 2005) claims to establish the utility of such general and intermediate measures of self-efficacy in populations other than those of the United States and Western Europe. "Thus, perceived general self-efficacy appears to be a universal construct that yields meaningful relations with other psychological constructs" (Luszczynska et al., 2005, p. 80). And despite identifying "an important component of social self-efficacy that is presumably less relevant in Western societies" (p. 492), Fan and associates (2010) conclude that their efforts to validate a social self-efficacy measure in Chinese populations were generally successful.

However, before concluding that such work does indeed prove the universality of Californian-style self-confidence in the form of self-efficacy, it is useful to consider the comments of Teo and Febbraro (2003) to the effect that

> It is epistemologically premature to suggest that Euro-American conceptualizations of personality ... are universal. These conceptualizations are then sometimes applied to contexts and supposedly support the cross-cultural authority of these conceptualizations. However, they do not prove the cultural validity of the concepts, only their universal administrative applicability.... No studies attempted to explore, for instance, Ghanaian or Chinese personality structure in their own terms rather than through these Western terms. (pp. 683–684)

Indeed, with this in mind, it also is instructive to consider the following remark from Fan and associates (2010): "China's rapid economic development in recent years and the accompanying fundamental societal changes ... all point toward more opportunities for Chinese individuals to express individuality than ever before.... In other words, with modernization, Chinese societies are shifting gradually toward individualism" (p. 476). So perhaps enhanced self-efficacy is not so universal after all, at least in the absence of U.S. global hegemony. Nonetheless, as hinted earlier, there are other reasons to challenge the idea of self-efficacy and the individualism it assumes as adequate bases for moral and rational agency.

In a recent assessment of systems of moral reasoning that have been advanced at different stages in human history, Kwame Appiah (2008) concludes that "through more than two millennia, thinkers have vigorously demonstrated that mere subjective contentment isn't a worthwhile aim" (p. 165). "Because there are so many worthwhile things we could do, because we cannot give every value equal weight, we will have choices to make, in shaping our lives, among values and among paths through the world" (p. 171). "Whether your life is successful ... is not just up to you" (p. 172)—for, "when we see ourselves as socially embedded creatures, whose actions [are] only intelligible in a fretwork of relations with others in our community, we [have] to take seriously those obligations that [arise] from our social roles" (p. 174). Appiah goes on to emphasize that it is "precisely our recognition that each other person is engaged in the ethical project of making a life that reveals to us our obligations to them. If my humanity matters, so does yours; if yours doesn't, neither does mine. We stand or fall together" (p. 203).

We quote rather extensively from Appiah (2008) because we wish to emphasize that his distillation of what he regards as a core ethical feature of our lives has almost nothing to do with our perceived sense of individual and collective self-efficacy. Human agency is simultaneously a rational, practical, and ethical undertaking. When we are acting individually and collectively in attempting to influence the directions of our lives, our judgments of our capabilities to act in particular ways are not what matters most. Instead, it is our ability to recognize each other as persons struggling to live good lives (in the broad sense of doing morally defensible and reasonable things) that matters much more than our subjective psychological sense of our own efficacy. Consequently, when Bandura and other self-efficacy advocates elevate self-efficacy to the apex of human individual and collective agency, they privilege our individual subjective sensibilities over our rational and moral interconnectivities with others. Such a privileging is consistent with the individualism, interiorism, and reductionism of much disciplinary psychology but jarringly inconsistent with the interdependent existence with others that defines our moral commitments and opens to the kind of wisdom that extends ourselves and our understanding through concerned engagement within a multiperspectival social world.

Conclusions: Self-Efficacy and the Education of Human Agency

The increasing popularity of psychological theory, research, and interventions in the area of self-efficacy marked an important turn in psychological self studies toward the end of the twentieth century. The ascendance of self-efficacy signaled a shift away from the more humanistic, Rousseau-inspired self-orientations typical of psychological work in the areas of self-esteem and self-concept toward a more scientific, managerial form of self study and intervention. As the sixties gave way to the seventies and eighties, North Americans and their societies became more strategically instrumental with respect to personal, economic, political, and social life. Life at all of these levels was to be planned, charted, monitored, and evaluated in relation to goals. Increasingly, the apparently self-set goals of many individuals were attuned to the goals of governments, corporations, and their various agencies, especially in the United States and Canada. What was good for the nation and the economy was good for the individual capable of strategic self-governance. Not surprisingly, the promotion of self-managing, entrepreneurial individuals, capable of benefiting themselves in socially approved ways, was taken up by most public institutions in the United States and Canada, including schools (Rose, 1998). Of course, this shift to individual self-management did not mean an end to earlier psychological modes of self-expression. Indeed, in most educational jurisdictions, the new forms of self-efficacy and self-regulation incorporated those aspects of earlier psychological study (in the areas of self-esteem and self-concept) that seemed amenable to such inclusion (see Chapter 3).

In recent years there have been calls to reform educational systems in order to better prepare students as future workers and citizens in the global economy, proposals that assume the personal and social value of students who exude high levels of self-esteem, self-concept, self-efficacy, and self-regulation, usually in combination with a set of skills thought to define agentive engagement and wisdom. For example, according to the *Partnership for 21st Century Skills*, an American organization dedicated to helping students acquire twenty-first-century skills, learning and innovation skills are what separate students who are prepared for increasingly more complex life and work environments in today's world and those who are not. They include: creativity and innovation; critical thinking and problem solving; communication and collaboration. The ability to navigate the complex life and work environments in the globally competitive information age requires students to pay rigorous attention to developing adequate life and career skills such as: flexibility and adaptability; initiative and self-direction; social and cross-cultural skills; productivity and accountability; leadership and responsibility. (2009, p. 2)

Such initiatives appear to emphasize learning that is complex, changing, and contextual. Students are expected to master a number of strategies and attitudes, including balancing short- and longer-term goals, dealing positively with criticism, working effectively with people from a range of backgrounds, and being committed to learning as a lifelong process. Successful students are also those who can apply their skills across content areas, such transferability being regarded as a key competency in a rapidly changing, complex world. When we look at such models of "studenthood" for the twenty-first century, we witness the emergence of the ideal of an efficacious, self-regulated student, psychologically equipped with the confidence, skills, and strategies required to make a difference in the world. Indeed, as we shall see in the next two chapters, the expressive, entrepreneurial individual who combines high levels of both self-esteem and self-regulation has become highly prized in both schools and society at large. In our opinion, psychological theory, research, and intervention concerning self-efficacy have contributed significantly to the vanguard of psychological, educational, and political interest in self-regulation that emerged during the last quarter of the twentieth century, and this contribution continues into the present day.

What should not be overlooked is the powerful association, advanced by Bandura and other self-efficacy promoters, between self-efficacy and human agency in general. By viewing self-efficacy as the essence of human agency, this group of psychologists claimed to hold the key to our individual and collective ability to intervene in the social and physical world in ways that would resolve difficulties and create new opportunities for human betterment. The scientific and professional rhetoric surrounding self-efficacy pointed to a brave new world of self-regulating individuals joining together to make the world a better place for all concerned. No wonder that many schools and educators caught up in this spirit of the times were more than happy to promote and adopt techniques, strategies, and programs targeted at enhancing levels of self-efficacy in their students.

However, as we have seen, self-efficacy, with all of its psychological trappings (even with its links to more general forms of self-regulation and to the kinds of self-directed learning skills thought by many to be the key to enhanced life opportunities in the twenty-first century), is a poor proxy for the kind of human understanding, moral consideration, and wisdom that seem to be required in the face of challenges such as population growth, environmental decay, poverty, and hunger. Believing that we can do things undoubtedly is part of what is required in the face of everyday challenges, both personal and global. But, such beliefs are inextricably part of our acting in the world. They are not interior psychological causes of our actions but aspects of those actions. Methods employed in psychological research and interventions to measure and manipulate such beliefs separate from the actions of which they are part are of questionable value. What is to be gained by beliefs that may not mesh with actions and capabilities, and how might such beliefs be germane to the amelioration of difficulties that confront us individually and collectively?

Even more basically, what would it mean to believe that one is capable of things that one cannot do or never has done? Wisdom, moral consideration, knowledge, and deep understanding are not matters of believing, nor are they reducible to particular sets of skills. They are matters of serious, ongoing, and often painstaking immersion in relevant contexts, practices, activities, and institutions in interaction with others who also are struggling to achieve these essential bases for moral and rational agency. To think otherwise is to fall prey to a kind of psychological and educational "quick fix" that elevates the importance of our psychological lives in separation from our ongoing relations with others, within which we learn and develop whatever forms of genuine expertise and capability we might contribute to our communities and the larger society.

In the next chapter, we examine psychological programs of research and educational application in the more general area of self-regulation, to which self-efficacy contributes but which it by no means exhausts. In doing so, we position both self-efficacy and self-regulation within a longer history of attempts to control and master ourselves through systems of self-governance that aim at individual and collective flourishing.

7 Managing Yourself
SELF-REGULATION AT SCHOOL AND BEYOND

WE NOW COME to the last (in terms of historical chronology) of the major programs of self studies and interventions pursued by educational psychologists—self-regulation or self-regulated learning. Most of us would agree that a primary responsibility of parenthood is to teach children to control their emotions and impulses. But self-control has become much more than the management of emotions and impulses. Whether referred to as self-control, self-discipline, or self-regulation, the management *of* the self *by* the self is considered to be a hallmark of growth and development. By the time children enter school, they are expected to self-regulate basic bodily functions and needs (e.g., hunger). At school, self-regulation broadens to include the regulation of behaviors related to scholastic activities (e.g., the activity of desk work). Teachers and educators are responsible for ensuring that children become independent learners; they rely on the expert knowledge of psychologists to guide them in their attempts to help children become more self-regulated.

In educational psychology, self-regulation is often referred to as self-regulated learning and involves metacognition (thinking about one's thinking), strategic action (planning, monitoring, and evaluating progress against a standard), and motivation (Butler & Winne, 1995; Winne & Perry, 2000). In this context, highly self-regulated learners are cognitively aware of their strengths and weaknesses, possess a toolbox of skills and strategies, and appropriately utilize the "tools" in their toolboxes to tackle academic tasks. For example, when they are reading a passage, highly self-regulated learners will constantly monitor their comprehension and, when they come across a section they do not understand, will apply strategies such as rereading the material, summarizing what it is that they need to understand, or looking up terms to aid understanding. Through all of this, the ultimate purpose of self-regulation is to improve one's individual academic performance—to get better, become more proficient at particular skills and practices, and achieve more of one's educational goals.

Scholarly inquiry concerning self-regulation has both a recent and a long-standing history. Some commentators (e.g., Carver & Scheier, 1998) have located the origins of contemporary research on self-regulation in the cybernetics developed by Wiener (1948) as a science of feedback processes involved in the control or regulation of system functioning and in Miller, Galanter, and Pribram's (1960) test-operate-test-exit (TOTE) model of feedback control. Others (e.g., Weinstein, Husman, & Dierking, 2000) have traced the roots of current conceptualizations of self-regulation to the information processing and cognitive psychologies of the 1970s (e.g., Simon, 1979).

However, various well-developed theses concerning the broad idea of self-regulation as "the many processes by which the human psyche exercises control over its functions, states, and inner processes" (Vohs & Baumeister, 2004, p. 1) have been available since at least the time of John Locke (1632–1704), who is considered by many (e.g., Danziger, 1997b; Seigel, 2005) to have originated modern psychological conceptions of selfhood (see Chapter 2). Indeed, almost all major Enlightenment, Romantic, and twentieth-century philosophers had a good deal to say about matters of self-command, self-discipline, and self-control (cf. Seigel, 2005; Taylor, 1989). Few who have seriously contemplated the nature of human existence have failed to remark on those aspects of life that Adam Smith (1976/1759) referred to as "the great school of self-command" (p. 145). Nonetheless, most psychological and educational research and writing on self-regulation has appeared since the early 1980s—"the vast majority of work in this field has occurred over the past 15 years or so, with self-regulation now the subject of intense professional interest and scrutiny" (Zeidner, Boekaerts, & Pintrich, 2000, p. 749).

With so much past and recent history, it might be assumed that our current inquiries into self-regulation would be marked by increasingly clear and well-developed conceptualizations and methods. Unfortunately, any such assumption fails miserably when set against the extant body of research and writing on self-regulation in psychology in general and in educational psychology in particular. In this chapter, a variety of definitions and conceptions of self-regulation and self-regulated learning in psychology and educational psychology are surveyed and a critical analysis of the conceptual confusion, individualism, psychologism, and omissions that currently beset this area of psychological inquiry in education is undertaken. The aim of the conceptual and critical analysis offered is to reveal assumptions, confusions, and lacunae that limit the possibility of fruitful inquiry into the nature and promotion of self-control in educational and related settings.

Definitions and Conceptions

Two influential handbooks of self-regulation (Boekaerts, Pintrich, & Zeidner, 2000; Baumeister & Vohs, 2004) testify to the diversity of perspectives, conceptions, and definitions of self-regulation in different programs of psychological inquiry:

> At present, there is considerable confusion in the literature with respect to the criterial attributes of self-regulation, its key components, and related constructs from the same semantic domain.... there are almost as many definitions and conceptions of self-regulation as there are lines of research on the topic. (Zeidner, Boekaerts, & Pintrich, 2000, p. 750)

A variety of terms have been used to designate the focal concept of self-regulation, including *self-control, self-management, self-regulated learning, problem solving, behavior management and control, goal-directed behavior, conscious impulse control, mood control, delay of gratification, willpower, agency, metacognitive strategies*, and *executive functioning*. Some researchers draw distinctions between these and other terms while others treat many of them as interchangeable. Some approach the topic from a neo-cybernetic, cognitive science perspective that emphasizes feedback loops, goal states, and error detection (e.g., Carver & Scheier, 1998). Some adopt cognitive neuroscientific frameworks that link executive functioning to neural control processes operating in the prefrontal cortex (e.g., Norman & Shallice, 1986). Still others emphasize processes of self-organization and dynamic systems theory (e.g., Vallacher & Nowak, 1997) or processing and representational dynamics involved in delay of gratification (e.g., Mischel, Shoda, & Rodriguez, 1989). It would take an enormous effort to clarify all of the distinctions that different psychological researchers have drawn explicitly and tacitly between these various terms and frameworks. And yet, it is equally obvious that, in the absence of such an effort, the entire area of self-regulation risks a solipsistic fragmentation in which each researcher or research team works with concepts, frameworks, and methods that defy translation across programs of research that may be united only insofar as they employ some rubric tied loosely to "self-regulation."

Models, conceptions, and definitions of self-regulation in applied areas of psychology, such as educational psychology, have tended toward a mix of cognitive, affective, and behavioral processes, structures, and operations. Many educational psychologists influenced by the social cognitive theorizing of Albert Bandura (1986) consider self-regulation to be a multiphase, cyclical, cognitive-behavioral process involving the self-generation and adaptation of thoughts, emotions, motivation, and actions with respect to personal goals. According to Schunk and Ertmer (2000),

> Self-regulation comprises such processes as setting goals for learning, attending to and concentrating on instruction, using effective strategies to organize, code,

and rehearse information to be remembered, establishing a productive work environment, using resources effectively, monitoring performance, managing time effectively, seeking assistance when needed, holding positive beliefs about one's capabilities, the value of learning, the factors influencing learning, and the anticipated outcomes of actions, and experiencing pride and satisfaction with one's efforts. (p. 631)

The prevalence of such highly inclusive, componential construals of self-regulation in educational psychology is highlighted in Zeidner, Boekaerts, and Pintrich's (2000) conclusion that

> there appears to be consensus...that self-regulation involves cognitive, affective, motivational, and behavioral components that provide the individual with the capacity to adjust his or her actions and goals to achieve desired results in light of changing environmental conditions....Overall, definitions and conceptualizations of self-regulation that appear in...this handbook tend to embody the basic ingredients of goal setting, steering process and strategies, feedback, and self-evaluation. (p. 751)

Despite this very general convergence across conceptions of self-regulation and self-regulated learning, there are many definitional and conceptual matters that are far from settled in this literature. For example, researchers differ considerably with respect to the ontological status of self-regulation and its various components. As we discussed in the previous chapter, some, such as Bandura (1986) and Zimmerman (1989), understand self-regulation as a triadic interaction of personal, behavioral, and environmental processes that emphasizes behavioral skill and self-efficacy (beliefs about one's abilities to engage in particular actions and to perform specific tasks). Although not ignoring the importance of cognitive and metacognitive processes and strategies, such an approach highlights task-specific actions, beliefs, and motives in a way that is tied rather closely to actual performance. On the other hand, researchers such as Weinstein, Husman, and Dierking (2000) and Winne and Hadwin (1998), while not ignoring relevant behavioral skills, tend to emphasize knowledge structures/states, cognitive operations, and metacognitive strategies modeled to a considerable extent on cognitive information processing theories. Here, the defining features of self-regulation seem more a matter of thought and mental life than of action and activity.

Whether self-regulation is more or less in mind or in activity is only one ontological concern. Another is whether self-regulation is best understood as an *aptitude* or as an *event* (Winne & Perry, 2000). Perhaps not surprisingly, theorists and researchers who emphasize metacognitive components of self-regulation tend to regard metacognitive skills, strategies, and dispositions as psychological abilities that develop within individuals over relatively long periods of time and display considerable individual difference.

This is not to say that such scholars are insensitive to what might be regarded as differing metacognitive demands of different tasks and settings. However, such situational factors tend to be understood as constraints on the employment and display of metacognitive abilities or aptitudes possessed by the learner and resident in his or her cognitive life. On the other hand, theorists and researchers who emphasize behavioral skill, motivation, and belief are more likely to treat self-regulation as an occurrence or event that may be contingently related to different situations and patterns of activity. In this case, self-regulation is understood to vary greatly in response to particular educational tasks and contexts and the particular pedagogical supports available.

Still another complex and unresolved conceptual matter that divides researchers of self-regulation concerns the difficult question of distinguishing between the *regulation* of activity and learning in general and the *self-regulation* of such activity and learning. This, in turn, is a matter nested in long-standing debates concerning the compatibility of human agency with biophysical and sociocultural determinism. However, it also relates to how selfhood is understood and to the intended meaning of self-regulation as either regulation that is orchestrated by the self (regulation *by* the self) or regulation that is directed at the self (regulation *of* the self) (Vohs & Baumeister, 2004).

One of the most striking features of the now considerable body of literature in psychology and educational psychology that is concerned with self-regulation is the exceedingly small amount of attention that has been devoted to conceptualizing the self. Although there are various definitions, conceptions, and frameworks of self-regulation, very few definitions, conceptions, and frameworks have been articulated with respect to the "self" in self-regulation. Given this state of affairs, it is perhaps not surprising that so little progress has been made in differentiating self-regulation from the quotidian activity of persons in going about life tasks that require some degree of purposeful planning and execution. After all, aren't most human pursuits replete with many of the characteristics of goal setting, attentional focus, perseverance, strategic action, and evaluation of outcomes that are taken to define self-regulation? In what ways might the activity of persons not be self-regulated? Insofar as all actions are actions of particular persons, what is the point of picking out certain actions as self-regulated, and on what basis might such selection be justified? Similar critical concerns, as we have discovered, are applicable to all four areas of self studies in educational psychology (see Chapters 4, 5, and 6 as well).

In the final chapter of their *Handbook of Self-Regulation*, Zeidner, Boekaerts, and Pintrich (2000), citing a contribution to their volume by Brownlee, Leventhal, and Leventhal (2000), state that

> to distinguish between the two constructs [regulation and self-regulation] we need to know whether the goal originated in the external world or internal world (i.e., the social environment versus the self system), and whether a person sees its

origin as being internal or external. Thus, when a person is setting a goal or defining a relevant procedure, he or she is self-regulating: otherwise his or her behavior is being externally or 'other-regulated.' (p. 752)

A bit later in their text, these same authors, again citing Brownlee and associates (2000), attempt a further distinction when they define regulation of the self as a special case of regulation by the self.

> Self-regulation [i.e., regulation by the self] becomes regulation of the self when the problem-solving process focuses upon the self and leads to its reorganization and redefinition. In the case of regulation of the self, a component of the self is the focus of problem solving (redefinition of old identities, the creation of new ones, the addition or remodeling of existent procedures for managing the self, and illness threats). (p. 752)

Such attempts at distinguishing *regulation* from *self-regulation* and distinguishing and relating *regulation of the self* and *regulation by the self* are standard fare in the self-regulation literature in educational psychology (see Schunk & Zimmerman, 1998; Zimmerman & Schunk, 1989).

But, is it really possible to make such distinctions on the basis of whether or not the goal-setting, strategic acting, monitoring, and evaluation said to attend the worldly activity of human persons is self-generated and self-determined versus occasioned and determined externally by circumstances and others? How do researchers or even actors themselves know when their thoughts, emotions, and motivations are self-determined in ways that go sufficiently beyond the dictates of their bodies, brains, and circumstances? Does such a question even make sense given the integrated nature of human activity in the world? Relatedly, are biophysical/neurological determinants of human activity to be understood as causes "external" to the self (because they are not consciously controlled by the self or "self-system," whatever that might be) or as causes "internal" to the self (because they are inside the person who is acting)? A considerable historical and contemporaneous literature exists that bears directly on such questions as the nature and possible compatibility of human agency (sometimes thought of as "free will") with biophysical and sociocultural determinism, the nature of selfhood, and the extent to which human actions may be said under different circumstances to be consciously engaged. Indeed, such questions and the debates they have spawned occupy much of the scholarly literature in philosophy, anthropology, sociology, and certain subdisciplines of psychology such as evolutionary and theoretical psychology (see Kane, 2002; Martin, Sugarman, & Hickinbottom, 2010; Martin, Sugarman, & Thompson, 2003; Seigel, 2005; Taylor, 1989).

The general failure of educational and other applied psychologists to come to grips with the many thorny definitional and conceptual issues that attend their inquiries into self-regulation (even when these difficulties are recognized) and their apparent failure to engage with the admittedly vast yet highly informative general literature on topics immediately germane to such issues cannot be dismissed as oversights that will be easily remedied. Why this is so will become clear through a critical consideration of many of the confusions, omissions, and problematic assumptions that attend research on self-regulation in educational psychology.

Studies and Measures of Self-Regulation in Schools

Studies on self-control or self-regulation lagged far behind the number of studies on self-esteem and self-concept during the 1960s and 1970s. However, in the 1980s and 1990s, interest in self-regulation increased greatly, with the number of such studies more than doubling during the 1990s (Martin, 2004a). This trend followed the cognitive revolution in psychology that saw psychologists shift their interests and commitments to information-processing views of human functioning. Many research studies examined the self in relation to information processing, problem solving, and general skill acquisition. In this context, psychological research on self-regulation began to flourish, and it is still thriving. The number of investigations of children's academic achievement and self-efficacy (e.g. Schunk, 1981, 1982; Schunk & Hanson, 1985; also see Bandura, 1993) and self-perceptions of ability (e.g., Altermatt, Pomerantz, Ruble, Frey, & Greulich, 2002; Blumenfeld, Pintrich, Meece, & Wessels, 1982; Pintrich & Blumenfeld, 1985) have increased noticeably. Other studies have examined relationships between academic achievement, self-regulation, self-monitoring, and self-instruction (e.g., Arnold & Walker, 2008; Fish & Pervan, 1985; Harris, 1990; Stright & Supplee, 2002).

Self-regulation is now considered to be a powerful predictor of human learning and functioning in almost all areas of life. In education, most of the available studies use a variety of self-regulation measures to focus on the usefulness of self-regulation in promoting students' academic achievement. For example, Albaili (1997) used the Learning and Study Strategies Inventory to examine differences between high-, average-, and low-achieving students and concluded that motivation was the strongest factor in discriminating between these groups. Miller and Byrnes (2001) examined the utility of a self-regulation model of decision making as a predictor of adolescents' academic decision making and concluded that students' decision-making competency and valuing of academic goals were strong indicators of academic achievement.

More generally, psychological research on self-regulation in education has focused on the understanding and promotion of self-regulation in and of itself as a goal of schooling. These studies tend to be intervention-based. For example, as already noted in Chapter 3, Butler (1998) examined the efficacy of an instructional model designed to enhance self-regulation among students with learning disabilities. In another study, Zimmerman (1997) examined the effects of goal-setting and self-monitoring phases of self-regulation on a motor task performed by female students and concluded that shifting from process to outcome goals results in better, more productive forms of self-regulation than focusing on process goals alone.

Whereas measures and research concerned with self-esteem and self-concept focused on self-worth and self-understanding with a general sense of encouraging student self-expression and fulfillment as important abilities and attributes of uniquely worthy human individuals, measures and research in the area of self-regulation have focused primarily on the self's ability to monitor, manage, motivate, strategize, and reinforce itself with respect to the successful completion of specific academic tasks. There have also been explicit suggestions that research in the area of self-regulation can not only benefit learners in classrooms but also have general applicability to lifelong learning and social improvement (more about this in the next section of this chapter). As noted in Chapter 3, the conception of selfhood that underlies the work of educational psychologists in the area of self-regulation is that of the self as strategic manager. Students in classrooms and people in everyday life are pictured as highly rational and deliberate processors of information. The self of the self-regulated learner is constituted of sets of executive skills and strategies attuned instrumentally to the accomplishment of specific academic and life tasks.

The most popular instruments used to measure self-regulation are the Motivated Strategies for Learning Questionnaire (MSLQ) and The Learning and Study Strategies Inventory (LASSI). The MSLQ is a 56-item Likert-style self-report inventory that assesses student motivation, cognitive and metacognitive strategy use, and effort management (Pintrich & DeGroot, 1990). The items on this measure "were adapted from various instruments used to assess student motivation, cognitive strategy use, and metacognition" (Pintrich & DeGroot, 1990, p. 34). The MSLQ was originally designed for college students and has been adapted for use with younger students. Examples of items on the MSLQ are "I expect to do very well in this class" (self-efficacy), "Understanding this subject is important to me" (intrinsic value), "I worry a great deal about tests"(test anxiety), "When I study I put important ideas into my own words" (cognitive strategy use), and "I work hard to get a good grade even when I don't like a class" (self-regulation). These items are almost exclusively focused on students' use of strategies and skills to reach academic goals.

The Learning and Study Strategies Inventory (LASSI) is a 90-item self-report inventory designed to test university students' use of study strategies and methods. The LASSI comprises 10 scales that measure different groups of learning strategies and study attitudes. These scales are anxiety, attitude, concentration, information processing, motivation, scheduling, selecting main ideas, self-testing, study aids, and test strategies (Weinstein, Goetz, & Alexander, 1988). The LASSI is very similar to the MSLQ in its measurement of strategies and skills. Examples of items on the LASSI are "When I begin an examination, I feel pretty confident that I will do well" (anxiety), "Success in school is very important to me" (attitude), "I concentrate fully when studying" (concentration), "When I study, I try to somehow organize the material in my mind" (information processing), "I read the textbooks assigned for my classes" (motivation), "I make good use of daytime study hours between classes" (scheduling), "My underlining is helpful when I review text material" (selecting the main idea), "I go over homework assignments when reviewing class materials" (self-testing), "I make sample charts, diagrams, or tables to summarize material in my courses" (study aids), and "I think through the meaning of test questions before I begin to answer them" (test strategies).

An examination of items on the MSLQ and LASSI reveals a cognitive managerial self made up of component parts and processes. Items on these measures reflect a model of the self-regulated student who has a positive attitude toward studying, utilizes appropriate strategies to perform well, and maintains the motivation to achieve. At the same time, this component self works in relative isolation and is focused on acquiring and improving skills and strategies directed at self-determined goals. According to the conclusions reached in much of the research and reflected in the items on the self-regulation measures, the successful individual is a rational, calculating scientist/practitioner able to scrutinize his or her own practices, consider alternative solutions to a problem, and implement appropriate steps to become and continue to be a successful student. Items such as "I work hard to get a good grade" and "I make sample charts, diagrams, or tables to summarize material in my courses" reflect a self that is an information processor, capable of rational planning, decision making, and execution of skills and strategies to meet rationally and personally determined goals. There is little or no reference to a sociocultural or moral connection to others. Rather, "the central concern is for an individual actor capable of simultaneous action and reflection on this action" (Martin, 2004a, p. 193).

The LASSI has steadily grown in popularity as a tool for measuring students' learning strategies. According to H & H Publishing (2010), over 2,200 high school and postsecondary institutions currently employ the LASSI. It is often used as a diagnostic tool in conjunction with study skills improvement workshops. For example, Texas A&M University (2010) offers the LASSI as a tool for awareness and use of study strategies in conjunction with a variety of workshops aimed at enhancing student academic achievement.

Self-Regulation in and Beyond Educational Settings

How important is self-regulated learning in educational settings? Duckworth, Akerman, MacGregor, Salter, and Vorhaus (2009) conducted an extensive literature review of the impact of self-regulation on learning and achievement. They reported that "self-regulation skills have important benefits for the learning and attainment of children and young people, and…they can be developed and improved with appropriate teaching and support" (p. 1). *The Primary Program: A Framework for Teaching* (British Columbia Ministry of Education, 2010) devotes a section to self-regulated learning emphasizing its importance and impact on student progress and achievement (p. 44). Self-regulated learning was even promoted by President Barack Obama in his 2009 national address to American students to "work hard, set educational goals and take responsibility for their learning" (U.S. Department of Education, 2009a, p. 1). In anticipation of the presidential address, the U.S. Department of Education released a menu of classroom activities for students in pre–K to grade 12. The menu for grades 7 to 12 offers teachers a number of ways to encourage students to take more responsibility for their education. One activity suggests that students discuss questions such as "What ideas do we associate with responsibility, persistence and goals?" (U.S. Department of Education, 2009b, p. 1). Another activity suggests that students create index cards in the form of graphic organizers and post them around the classroom to "create a culture of goal setting, persistence and success" (U.S. Department of Education, 2009b, p. 3).

It is clear that self-regulation is considered a powerful source of student success. Thus, it should come as no surprise that the promotion, practice, and application of self-regulatory skills have broadened beyond their application to academic tasks per se. The Collaborative for Academic, Social, and Emotional Learning (CASEL), an American national organization, is dedicated to establishing social and emotional learning as a fundamental part of education. According to CASEL, "Ours is a social world. The abilities to pay attention, listen accurately, remember what we hear and learn, and engage in thoughtful decision making, are among the most important skills for navigating our world successfully" (Collaborative for Academic, Social, and Emotional Learning, 1998, p. 2). "In a global economy characterized by rapid change, SEL cultivates competencies valued in the workplace, including teamwork, collaboration, problem solving, and perseverance through obstacles" (Collaborative for Academic, Social, and Emotional Learning, 2010, p. 2).

Some education systems already recognize social and emotional skills as core components of learning. For example, the Province of British Columbia Social Responsibility Framework (British Columbia Ministry of Education, 2001) aims to build self-awareness, self-control, awareness of others, empathy, and good relationship skills. The Department for Education, United Kingdom (2010) Social Emotional Aspects of Learning (SEAL) program similarly focuses on the development of self-awareness, managing feelings, motivation, empathy, and social skills to enhance student achievement and well-being. Curricular programs designed to enhance students' self-regulation now range across diverse areas such as leadership development, prevention of mental and physical health problems, and social mediation.

One notable area that emphasizes the development of self-regulatory skills is antibullying education. *Bullying* is loosely defined as involving deliberate physical, verbal, and/or social acts of harm repeated over time that create or reinforce an imbalance of power. Antibullying education programs tend to emphasize a "whole school" approach that involves the entire school community in redirecting negative behaviors into prosocial behaviors in a positive social environment. This approach is seen as proactive rather than punitive and focuses on building self-regulation skills such as self-awareness, self-management, and decision making.

Second Step is a violence prevention program that offers schoolwide and classroom-based plans for enhancing school success and social and emotional development. The program is offered in the form of grade-leveled kits consisting of program guides, DVDs, and lesson plans. The middle-school classroom kit purports to help students make good decisions and learn the necessary skills to stay in school and avoid bullying, substance abuse, and peer pressure. The program promises lessons that take little preparation time and are filled with fun games, activities, and skills practice. It purports to help "students develop the 21st century skills they need to make positive decisions and achieve academic success" (Committee for Children, 2010, p. 1).

We can now see that self-regulated learning provides a framework for linking students' academic achievement with their social and emotional well-being. Indeed, under this "broader" framework of learning (and teaching), self-regulation, self-esteem, self-concept, and self-efficacy come together in the form of skills, strategies, attitudes, and beliefs that conceivably contribute to students' personal, academic, and social growth. The suggestion that self-regulation can be learned by all students is appealing to policy makers, psychologists, educators, and parents alike.

The school as an institution for promoting intellectual and social development is increasingly an institution devoted to personal adjustment and self-fulfillment. As we have shown here, the development of personal skills and abilities is offered to educators and students, often in the form of participation in and completion of programs that consist of apparently "foolproof" steps and procedures that will guarantee students' psychological health. Many of these programs and activities offer a conception of the self as a compilation of personal attributes and skills that can easily be acquired as long as one purchases the right program, activity, or videotape. Whether the broader educational goal is to increase students' intellectual achievement or produce future responsible citizens, often the focus at the school and classroom levels is to help students build their own repertoires of "self" tools (i.e., self-enhancement and self-management skills and strategies) that can be acquired easily and utilized across curricular and extracurricular activities both at school and at home.

In the United States and Canada, the public education of children encourages and celebrates the acquisition of attributes of self-regulation such as independence, autonomy, and self-discipline. An important critical question concerns how well these self-regulated capabilities and attributes serve the interests of communities (the social/institutional mandate of schools) and how well they serve the interests of individual students (the personal development mandate of schools). On the one hand, it would be difficult to imagine responsible citizenship and community involvement in the absence of these individual characteristics. On the other hand, an inwardly focused, detached selfhood that applies such attributes too narrowly, instrumentally, and individualistically can clearly preclude meaningful collaborative participation and engagement in the complex social and political practices of liberal democracies. Although social relations and abilities, such as friendship and empathy, are often mentioned in the educational discourse of self-regulation, an examination of particular curriculum materials reveals that these are often reduced to simplified skill sets that individual students can acquire and apply to enhance their own achievement and social wherewithal mostly for their own ends. In light of this and other concerns noted above, a more critical consideration of self-regulation as practiced in the schools of the United States and Canada is warranted.

Critical Considerations

Conceptual Confusion

As already noted, definitions and conceptions of self-regulation (despite some convergence on components such as goal setting, performance monitoring, and evaluation) vary widely across different programs of inquiry. Moreover, this undesirable state of affairs is compounded by what can only be regarded as misguided attempts to resolve it, either through (1) theoretical integration across incompatible definitional and conceptual differences or (2) conceptually inadequate empirical research. The former strategy risks forcing different conceptions of self-regulation into highly complex models and frameworks of questionable coherence that seem to equate with problem solving, strategic thinking, or cognitive-behavioral functioning in general. The latter strategy confuses conceptual and empirical issues. Both of these confusions are readily illustrated by reference to recent well-intended proposals by Winne and Perry (2000), who offer what otherwise is a highly useful and competently executed summary of measures, methods, and issues in the measurement of self-regulated learning.

As previously mentioned, Winne and Perry (2000) observe that some research-ers of self-regulation in educational contexts treat self-regulation as an aptitude while others treat it as an event. However, rather than contenting themselves with describing this conceptual inconsistency, Winne and Perry propose an integrative model in which self-regulation "has dual qualities as an aptitude and an event.... It is situated within a broad range of environmental plus mental factors, and potentials, and manifests itself in recursively applied forms of metacognitive monitoring and metacognitive control that change information over time as learners engage with a task" (Winne & Perry, 2000, p. 563). They go on to claim that "each of the seven measurement protocols we reviewed—self-report questionnaires, structured interviews, teacher judgments, think aloud mea-sures, error detection tasks, trace methods, and observations of performance—foreground different components of conditions, cognitive operations, standards, and event-related change" (p. 563). The implication is that all of these are components of self-regulation. Such a strategy strives for conceptual integration by means of putting together various measures and their diffuse cognitive and behavioral targets. The claim is then made that the resultant mix is what is meant by self-regulation. Unfortunately, such an approach fails to address the various matters of definitional difference, conceptual differentiation, and clarification raised earlier in this chapter. When Winne and Perry claim that their integrative strategy captures different levels of self-regulation understood as an aptitude and as an event, it is reasonable to ask whether they are talking about different levels of one thing (i.e., self-regulation) or about different things.

Moreover, such a strategy confuses conceptual with empirical matters and misconstrues relations between conceptual and empirical branches of research programs. Winne and Perry (2000), following Cliff (1982) and many other psychometricians and statisticians, believe that empirical "measurement is akin to model building and model testing" (Winne & Perry, 2000, p. 563). This view inclines them toward the conviction that "much basic research remains to develop better models of SRL [self-regulated learning] as guides for developing measures of SRL," a strategy that they understand as "a recursive bootstrapping process" (p. 555). But it is a mistake to think that conceptions of what one is attempting to study can possibly emerge from empirical inquiry alone. In order to study something empirically, one must know what one is attempting to study and what criteria indicate the thing, its presence, and its operations. Without such a conceptual understanding of what is to be investigated, empirical research cannot get off the ground. If the meaning of a particular concept, in this case self-regulation, is not clear, what is needed is not empirical research but a clarification of the concept's rules of correct employment (Hacker, 1986, p. 158). Such clarification requires conceptual investigation into the rules and standards for the correct employment of the concept in question. This kind of conceptual investigation is essential to but separate from empirical identification and study of the focal phenomena.

> The referents of concept " θ" are constituents of reality and, hence, have properties that can, in principle, be discovered through scientific investigation. But these properties have no direct bearing on the rules that fix what concept " θ" does, in fact, denote (if, in fact, it denotes). On the contrary, fact f is a fact about " θ"-things only if it is a fact about constituents of reality denoted by concept " θ," and which constituents of reality are denoted by concept " θ" is given by the rules that fix the correct employments of concept " θ." (Maraun, 2006, p. 284)

If self-regulation is to be a focus of empirical inquiry in psychology and education, what the concept of self-regulation is must be made clear. It is, of course, true that various sciences often study empirical phenomena in advance of such phenomena being fully understood. Frequently, such study is fueled by this very lack of understanding. However, any empirical phenomena studied in this way cannot be understood as relating to any particular concept until the conceptual work that warrants the application of the particular concept to the focal phenomena being examined has been conducted. Again, the conceptual features of a particular concept are logically independent of the empirical features of the phenomena denoted by the concept—in the same way that the grounds for ascribing the concept "widow" to an individual are logically distinct from the properties of widows. To discover, for example, that widows are depressed presupposes the capacity of correctly identifying widows and distinguishing them from those who are not widows. Such identification and differentiation equate to the grounds for ascribing the concept "widow" to individuals.

Empirical investigation will not cure the conceptual ills of psychological research in the area of self-regulation. Indeed, the mistaken belief that it will only adds to the considerable confusion already evident in the scholarly literature on self-regulation and self-regulated learning.

Individualism

Although "some theories of self-regulation…recognize social context as a component of self-directed behavior…the impact of socially mediated factors often assumes a status that is far inferior to individually based components" (Jackson, Mackenzie, & Hobfoll, 2000, p. 275). As the various definitions and examples discussed above would seem to attest, "the interpersonal dimension of self-regulation is still underappreciated" (Vohs & Baumeister, 2004, p. 9). In major handbooks on the subject, such as that edited by Boekaerts, Pintrich and Zeidner (2000), "sociocultural and discursive models are not represented" (p. 756).

This relative neglect of sociocultural historical context in the area of self-regulation is both surprising and problematic. It is surprising given that many past formulations of self-regulation or its equivalent (in the Western history of ideas) have been at pains to avoid overly individualistic construals that would remove self-regulation from our quotidian experiences with other members of our societies. Thus, for example, even Adam Smith, that frequently identified champion of Western capitalism,

> presents the subjectivity that makes the self able to objectify its own existence as intersubjectively formed, developing through the repeated recognition that others are subjects just as are we. Our subjectivity expands through interaction with their ability to judge our actions, and with our awareness of how their viewpoints differ from our own. (Seigel, 2005, pp. 144–145)

In speaking specifically about self-regulation, or what he preferred to call "self-command," Smith maintained that "Our continual observations upon the conduct of others, insensibly lead us to form to ourselves certain general rules concerning what is fit and proper either to be done or to be avoided" (Smith, 1976/1759, p. 159). Like other contributors to the Western history of ideas concerning selfhood (e.g., Locke and Rousseau), Smith recognized clearly that self-awareness, self-development, and self-control not only require but to some extent are constituted within our interactions with others. Consequently, almost all major historical theories of selfhood come replete with social, moral, and political considerations that are glaringly absent in most of the contemporary psychological and educational literature on self-regulation.

That such obvious lacunae in this literature exist is not only surprising but highly problematic, particularly when self-regulation is considered as an educational aim. Educational systems have a social, institutional mandate to prepare students as persons and citizens capable of functional levels of both self-sufficiency and civic participation. An overemphasis on the former does much more than risk endangering the latter. If Smith and other leading thinkers of the past are to be believed (also see contemporary commentators such as Gutmann, 1990, and Schutz, 2000), an overly individualistic emphasis in education also jeopardizes students' self-sufficiency by possibly providing too little in the way of exposure to the interests and perspectives of others with whom a reasonable level of civil coexistence is necessary for both personal and societal flourishing. And yet, on such points as on most matters that touch on our quotidian, political, and moral life with others, the literature on self-regulation in educational psychology is strangely and inappropriately silent.

Educating for life with others must move beyond scripted exercises in psychoeducational materials that emphasize the importance of developing empathic skills, not bullying others, and cooperating in the classroom. Such materials consist of lessons, readings, and activities that attract the interest of individual students in search of skill sets valued by teachers and school administrators. As such, they offer social training for individual students rather than educative experiences of communal engagement and problem solving—experiences within which the perspectives of different students must be considered by all concerned and collaborative strategies determined and implemented. There are, of course, some notable exceptions, but most of these are not derived from the work of educational psychologists in the areas of self-regulation and self-regulated learning but from the efforts of others who work at the intersection of social and developmental theory and educational practice (e.g., Selman, 2003).

Perhaps at least some of the difficulty that contemporary researchers of self-regulation experience in drawing workable distinctions between self-regulation *of* versus *by* the self is that the idea that the self ought to be constrained in the service of communal ends has become unfashionable. In place of this "old-fashioned" idea has arisen a desire to encourage and celebrate individuals' instrumental pursuit of their own strategic goals and interests. This is not to say that contemporary educational psychologists who champion psychoeducational research and interventions in the area of students' self-regulation are actively attempting to foster the development of self-absorbed, self-interested individuals. Nonetheless, the failure to situate self-regulation within its appropriate and necessary sociocultural, historical, interpersonal, and moral context may inadvertently decouple *self-sufficiency* from *civic responsibility* in the minds of otherwise well-intentioned teachers and students. Adequate preparation for the latter necessarily entails an appropriate level of reasoned constraint on the former—a constraint that issues from a recognition of, and concern for the personhood of others.

Psychologism

Psychologism refers to the idea that processes of reasoned choice and intentional action can be explained by underlying mental states or activities. Although not all of the various components contained in componential definitions of self-regulation include or consist of mental states and processes, those emphasizing cognitive and metacognitive strategies and operations most certainly do. As noted earlier, in such models (e.g., Weinstein et al., 2000; Winne & Hadwin, 1998), the defining features of self-regulation are located in thought and mental life as much as or more than in action and activity. In these approaches, it is clear that underlying conceptions of mind, self, and agency are predominately mentalistic. Indeed, the assumption that intentions, beliefs, desires, motives, and reasons are mental entities and processes that guide and otherwise underlie strategic activity in the world is rampant in almost all contemporary models of self-regulation, even those that explicitly highlight the worldly activity of agents.

It is reasonable to assume that the invocation of the term *self* in self-regulatory competencies such as self-monitoring, self-evaluation, self-management, self-reward, and self-motivation references a highly mentalistic conception of selfhood. This is the self that is understood as a kind of agentic neohomunculus (in the guise of cognitive and metacognitive executive structures) operating behind the scenes to determine, monitor, and guide successful performance in learning and other important life tasks. The psychologism evident in contemporary research on self-regulation and self-regulated learning not only reduces much of the strategic activity of human agents to mental states and processes but also locates the origins of strategic activity in these states and processes and places them under subpersonal executive control systems and mechanisms. In effect, psychologism of this kind traps definitions, conceptualizations, and explanations of self-regulation *inside* our bodies and brains. This inward focus shifts the perspective of psychological theorizing and inquiry away from the activity of persons in the biophysical and sociocultural world, a world of materials and practices shared with others, to the interior psychological and neurophysiological processes of individuals.

Unfortunately, "a fully functioning executive/regulatory system could never, by itself, deliver [the] concepts of mental life" (Moses & Carlson, 2004, p. 142) required for inquiry into self-regulation. As so many developmental theorists (e.g., Bickhard, 2004; Chapman, 1991; Duveen, 1997; Gauvain, 2001; Hobson, 2002; Mead, 1934; Tomasello, 1999, 2008; Vygotsky, 1978) have so clearly shown, the sources of consciousness, meaning, mind, and selfhood lie in interactivity with others within historically established sociocultural practices and ways of life. Psychological development would be impossible if we were cut off from the world, as psychologism advocates. If we were to have access to the world only through our mental representations and operations, there would be no way that we might detect errors in such operations and representations. Such an inability would make a mystery of our readily observable ability to achieve progressive refinements in our actions and capabilities. Further, if we understand our minds and selves as inner entities removed from our worldly involvements, the only way of explaining them is to adopt an extreme version of innateness. For if our only contact and commerce with the world is through our mental entities, representations, and operations, all of our primary conceptual structures must then arise by virtue of our biophysical makeup. Innateness of this kind (whether "full-blown" or "seeded") poses many seemingly intractable theoretical difficulties, such as which of our cognitive structures and processes might be derivative from others and how, together with the nature of the structural and functional relations that might pertain among them (cf. Edelman, 1987).

Psychologism of the sort adopted by many researchers of self-regulation in educational contexts deprives us of the raw materials that our mental life, selfhood, and agency require and that their own conceptions of self-regulation demand. It is in our worldly interactivity with others, not in our underlying mental and neural functioning, that the meaning and significance required to fuel our goal-directed functioning might be located. This is not to say that we do not come to represent, strategize, and orchestrate our experiences and actions in thoughtful, reasoned ways that are associated with and even requisite for much of our intentional activity in the world. However, it is to say that such abilities are developmental accomplishments that would be inexplicable without a primary focus on the social character of our existence and interactivity with others. And it is to say further that attempts to teach self-regulation to students and others that ignore the primacy of our situated, interactive life with others (whether in classrooms or elsewhere) ought to be reconsidered (see Chapter 9).

It is also important to emphasize that such reconsideration cannot take the form of only including more and greater attention to social and interpersonal factors in research on self-regulation. Many traditional social psychological approaches leave the psychologized subject essentially intact as an individual entity interacting, at some distance, with external variables and forces. As Jackson, Mackenzie, and Hobfoll (2000) note, even when "some theories of self-regulation, in particular social cognitive models…do recognize social context as a component of self-directed behavior…the impact of socially mediated factors often assumes a status that is far inferior to individually based components" (p. 280). What is required is a more thoroughgoing recognition of the constitution of minds and selves within social interactivity with others. Such alternative models of mind, selfhood, and agency are available within the social-developmental psychologies of those referenced earlier (e.g., Bickhard, 2004; Chapman, 1991; Duveen, 1997; Gauvain, 2001; Hobson, 2002; Mead, 1934; Tomasello, 1999, 2008; Vygotsky, 1978), but they have rarely, at least to date, been drawn upon by researchers interested in self-regulation in educational contexts (again, see Hickey & Granade, 2004; McCaslin, 2004; and Rohrkemper, 1989, for some notable exceptions).

It undoubtedly is the failure of researchers of self-regulation to consider such alternative conceptions that has made it so difficult for them to differentiate between the self-regulation of behavior and behavioral regulation through other means, such as direction by teachers. If psychologism pervades all our thinking about our choices, non-choices, and actions, there is really no viable distinction to be made. If strong forms of psychologism are assumed, all actions are self-determined and self-regulated because the self as an inner executive can always be invoked. Consequently, it becomes both meaningless and redundant to emphasize the self in self-regulation. On the other hand, conceptions of selfhood that recognize its sources in our worldly activity within sociocultural practices are necessarily concerned with the kinds of self–other and self–world differentiations upon which any reasoned conception of selfhood or self-regulation must rest. When selfhood is understood as a socially enabled, developmentally emergent first-person experience and understanding (cf. Martin, 2005a; Martin, Sugarman, & Hickinbottom, 2010; Russell, 1996) that depends on the exercise of both prereflective and reflective forms of personal agency, such differentiations cannot be avoided and must be conceptualized as part of any viable research program. For this reason, it is exceedingly unfortunate that so much research on self-regulation in educational psychology has divorced itself so completely from potentially informative conceptual and empirical research in sociocultural developmental psychology (more will be said about such work in Chapter 9).

What is suggested here should not be interpreted as advocating a strong form of social determinism in which human agency is reduced to social structures and processes. To be viable, educational theory, whether psychological or not, must contain resources capable of supporting human innovation and change at both the collective and individual level. However, the tendency of many educational psychologists, even those who claim adherence to more social, communal forms of selfhood, to elevate individual cognitive activity over interdependency and interactivity seems far too one-sided. Productive participation with others in socially meaningful activities to achieve common goals requires forms of communal agency that go well beyond individual strategizing and problem solving. Once again, given the growing evidence that individuals' development as self-regulating agents is constituted within sociocultural practices of interactivity, this is an extremely important conclusion (Bickhard, 2004; Chapman, 1991; Duveen, 1997; Gauvain, 2001; Hobson, 2002; Martin & Gillespie, 2010; Mead, 1934; Tomasello, 1999, 2008; Vygotsky, 1978).

Summary and Critical Interpretation

Clearly, the various conflations, omissions, and reifications that respectively typify the conceptual confusion, individualism, and psychologism that attend psychological inquiry and intervention in the area of self-regulation can be expected to limit scientific and professional advance. It is not difficult to understand the limitations and difficulties that arise from treating conceptual matters as if they were empirical, selectively ignoring critically important social (including moral and political) dimensions of self-regulation and attributing actions and intentions to mysterious inner entities rather than attending to the worldly activities of agents within their biophysical and sociocultural contexts. The apparent difficulties only multiply in light of the plethora of definitions employed by researchers of self-regulation to specify and characterize their focal phenomenon in ways that resist convergence across major programs of inquiry. Unfortunately, there is also good reason to entertain an additional concern that seems to apply to work on self-regulation and self-regulated learning. This is a concern related to the fostering of student self-surveillance in ways that fit the assumptions and interests of psychoeducators.

How might the widespread use by students and teachers of conceptions and techniques of self-regulation developed by educational psychologists be interpreted? In line with the neo-Foucaultian critical psychology of Rose (1998), introduced in Chapter 1, is it possible that forms of student self-surveillance encouraged by teachers under the guise of promoting student self-regulation might masquerade as student-centered when they clearly serve a narrowed institutional mandate of schooling and the professional interests of psychoeducators? In reading representative selections from the research and intervention literature on self-regulation, one cannot help but be struck by the obvious degree of researcher and/or teacher control exercised over students' *self*-regulation. Even interventions targeted at older adolescents bear the clear imprint of such other-directedness.

> When students are initially learning to self-manage, teachers must provide antecedent strategies that clearly explain outcomes, use examples and non-examples of problem-solving behaviors (i.e., persistence or improvement)…as well as outcome behaviors (i.e., achievement or performance) and self-monitoring accuracy. (Belfiore & Hornyak, 1998, p. 191)

Even when psychological researchers and teachers recognize the degree of external control typically required to stimulate students' self-regulation and attempt to reduce such supports, they most often compensate for any decrements in direct teacher instruction by strengthening self-regulatory structures in the curriculum offered.

> we consider ways that classroom teachers might provide self-regulatory opportunities and requirements for their students through tailored curricular activities….As one example, we describe what we have learned in our collaborative efforts to develop a *curriculum-embedded* approach….This curriculum invited self-regulated learning. It gave students lots of ways to tune in to the various aspects of what it means to self-regulate. (Randi & Corno, 2000, p. 652)

Given such clear evidence of psychologist and teacher determination and control of methods and techniques of self-regulation, it is not unreasonable to raise questions concerning the manner in which student adoption of these methods and techniques might be said to constitute *self*-regulation. Without assuming anything other than appropriate educational and professional intent on the part of teachers and psychologists conducting research on self-regulation and promoting particular methods of student self-regulation in classrooms, it is still possible to reflect critically on the consequences of such inquiry and interventions. A Foucaultian interpretation (Foucault, 1970, 1980) might be that in the absence of any clear and convincing distinction between self-regulation and teacher or psychologist regulation of student conduct and learning, all that has changed is a redirection of responsibility for the maintenance of appropriate levels of student conduct from psychoeducators to students themselves. At best, such redirection may be envisioned as a desirable part of a student's education as a self-governing citizen and responsible person—long-standing and entirely legitimate aims of education that seem little affected by talk of students' self-regulation. At worst, it might be seen as an especially strategic (even manipulative) form of socialization that secures student cooperation on the false grounds that the students mistakenly and uncritically believe themselves to be truly self-directed and determining. In either case, what seems missing is an appropriately open and critical consideration of the dynamic interplay between ourselves and others within those historical and sociocultural ways of life that inevitably and indispensably enable and constrain our personhood. In other words, it is education with respect to the human condition and our modest role as participants within it and possible extenders of it, not techniques of self-regulation, which ought to occupy students in schools.

This chapter completes our historical and critical reviews of major programs of self studies in educational psychology—that is, self-esteem (Chapter 4), self-concept (Chapter 5), self-efficacy (Chapter 6), and self-regulation (Chapter 7). These various programs of theory, research, and psychoeducational intervention all include conceptions of a psychological self as an inner possession of individuals that can be studied scientifically to establish its causal relations to self-worth, self-understanding, self-confidence, and self-management. As discussed in Chapter 2, this is a conception of selfhood as a deeply interior source of our actions and experiences and is a surprisingly recent development in our long history of attempts to understand the nature of our existence and experience in the world. Moreover, as indicated in Chapters 1 and 3, understanding ourselves in these highly psychological ways has a variety of consequences, several of which have attracted the attention of conceptual and critical historians like Kurt Danziger (1997a,b) and Nikolas Rose (1998) and historical ontologists like Ian Hacking (2002). One of the most interesting of these various lines of critical, conceptual, ontological, and historical analyses concerns the ways in which these deeply psychological conceptions of ourselves have functioned to create new forms of self-understanding and personhood. In the next chapter, we examine the ways in which the expressive and managerial conceptions of psychological selfhood, developed and promoted by educational psychologists (see Chapters 3 through 7), have created new ways of being students in the classrooms and schools of the United States and Canada. One particularly powerful example of this is what we will describe as the *expressive, enterprising, and entitled student*. This is a form of personhood that, in some ways, is extremely well suited to life in contemporary liberal democracies with their particular kinds of economic and political structures. However, it is also a way of being that courts various dangers to ourselves and our societies, some of which seem to be increasingly evident.

8 Putting It All Together

THE TRIPLE-E STUDENT (EXPRESSIVE, ENTERPRISING, ENTITLED)

MANY CRITICAL CONCERNS about the self studies of educational psychologists have been raised in the preceding chapters. However, four concerns stand out and tend to encompass most of the others. For easy reference, these concerns can be referred to as *individualism,* psychological interiorism (or *psychologism*), *reductionism* (of both persons and contexts), and *manipulation*. All of these major concerns trade, in one way or another, on the pervasive tendency in educational psychology, especially during the last half of the twentieth century, to conceptualize the self as a psychological entity thought to be resident within individual persons, mostly understood as some kind of cognitive structure, executive mechanism, or existential/experiential core that is not isomorphic with persons but nonetheless somehow serves to govern the actions and experiences of persons. In this chapter, we review these four concerns and demonstrate how they are assumed in, and perpetuate, particular forms of measurement, research, and intervention favored by educational psychologists. These psychological methods and techniques are commonly thought to give scientific status to the pronouncements and claims made by educational psychologists and others with respect to the central importance of selfhood in the education of children, adolescents, and adults, especially in the United States and Canada. However, these measurement, research, and intervention practices are themselves open to well-known but little attended criticisms.

In the latter part of this chapter, we then discuss how the individualism, psychologism, reductionism, and manipulation (flowing from the misleading language and conceptualizations) of educational psychologists and others have created a set of psychoeducational practices in American and Canadian schools that, following Ian Hacking (2002), have promoted the "making up" and flourishing of a particular way of being a student. This new form of studenthood emphasizes the central importance of experiencing and acting in ways that are expressive of a uniquely interior self. These are ways that are strategically instrumental with respect to the attainment of personal goals and demand both expression and enterprise as entitlements that accrue to students as basic rights—rights students can expect and request in their interactions with peers, teachers, and school administrators.

When we describe and discuss this way of being a student, we do not claim that such a form of student selfhood is achieved in all or even most cases. Rather, we intend to be read as claiming that the ideal of the expressive, enterprising, entitled student has become a way of being a student that now exerts a significant influence on the thinking and practices of contemporary teachers, parents, school administrators, educational policy makers, the public at large, and, of course, students themselves. Moreover, we claim that this new ideal owes a great deal to the conceptions, research, and intervention practices of educational psychologists. However, having said this, we also recognize, following Nikolas Rose (1998), that psychological forms of selfhood are especially well suited to the governance strategies employed in contemporary liberal democracies as joined to economies of commodification and consumption. We conclude this chapter with a brief consideration of what we regard as some significant educational and social disadvantages, even dangers, of such an ideal. We also recognize that, despite a recent backlash (to be discussed in the next and final chapter), the "triple E" (expressive, enterprising, and entitled) student ideal is not entirely without possibly redeeming educational and social value if it can be reconceptualized in ways that transform it from an individual to a social virtue (a project forming the main aim of Chapter 9).

Individualism, Psychologism, Reductionism, and Manipulation

Individualism

The individualism evident in programs of psychological research concerned with self-esteem, self-concept, self-efficacy, and self-regulation is "self-evident" in the very terms that describe these popular areas of psychological and educational inquiry. As discussed in Chapter 4, many psychologists, educators, and policy makers who promote the educational enhancement of the self-concerned beliefs, understandings, attitudes, behaviors, assessments, and judgments that make up students' self-esteem and self-concept (as well as their self-efficacy and self-regulation) are quick to suggest that respect for others, cooperation, and general social concern and responsibility somehow automatically attend the elevation of self-esteem and self-concept. However, there is no convincing evidence that such correlative social enhancements are necessarily forthcoming (e.g., Baumeister et al., 2003) when students' and others' self-esteem and self-concept are elevated. Moreover, given the narrowly self-focused content and strategies of many programs aimed at such elevation (e.g., Canfield & Wells, 1994; also see Stout, 2000, for additional examples), it is difficult to imagine how enhancements to individuals' self-esteem might benefit anyone or anything other than individual students themselves. After all, imagining all of the ways in which you are uniquely special or thinking about all of the things you want to achieve doesn't necessarily seem connected to concerns for social justice or community development. Of course, it is entirely possible that a particular student's life goals might involve these and other more social, communal ends. However, if this is the case, the content of such aims very likely issues from aspects of this person's life experience other than the self-esteem programming in which she or he has participated in school.

But as we have seen, after the 1960s, belief in high levels of self-concept and self-esteem as necessary foundations for almost any undertaking in Western life achieved an almost taken-for-granted status. In psychotherapy, social work, community development, and education, considerable energy and resources were targeted at ensuring that such presumed foundations were in place. A positive self-regard was considered to be almost synonymous with any kind of competence that might possibly be seen to benefit anyone. Unfortunately, as the twentieth century wound down and the twenty-first century began, the excesses of narcissistic attachments to oneself and one's interests and projects—without explicit regard for more communal undertakings and goals—were increasingly noted (e.g., Lasch, 1978; Twenge, 2006; Twenge & Campbell, 2009). Moreover, as historically inclined scholars (e.g., Guignon, 2004; Taylor, 1989) have pointed out, prior to the 1960s, relatively scant attention was paid to matters such as self-esteem, with little obvious detrimental impact on everyday social life compared to the deteriorations in common civility and respect for others widely noted in more recent decades (e.g., Stout, 2000).

Clearly, individualism for its own sake does not necessarily relate and certainly does not automatically translate into social commitment and engagement. In fairness, many advocates of self-esteem, self-concept, self-efficacy, and self-regulation did not necessarily assume such an automatic yield. Instead, they understood an enhancement to an individual's self-esteem as somehow to be laying the psychological groundwork for a healthy recognition and regard for the self-esteem needs and personhood of others (e.g., Maslow, 1954; Rogers, 1957). However, even in expressing such altruistic processes and ideals, the basic orientation to human life and affairs that permeated most broadly humanistic perspectives in disciplinary and professional psychology was undeniably individualistic. In particular, psychology as a science and a professional practice takes individual experience and action as its subject matter and not only understands individuals as the basic units of social communal life but also appeals to causal resources and sources within individuals as the driving forces behind any form of psychological or social development.

Psychologism (Interiorism)

Consequently, in the theories, research, and interventions of psychologists working in education and elsewhere, individualism has most often been accompanied by what we have previously (see Chapter 7) called interiorism or psychologism. The core feature of psychologism is the attribution of the primary causes of the perceptions, experiences, knowledge, and actions of individuals to structures, processes, and/or operations internal to their mental lives. In recent years, the neural activity and patterns studied by cognitive neuroscientists provide good examples of such attribution, whereas in previous decades (dating from the 1950s through to the 1990s), information processing and computational processes and structures were asserted by cognitive psychologists as primary causes of human experience and action. Even when sociocultural influences on individuals' psychological development and learning were acknowledged, any such "external" causes tended to be understood as secondary to the real or ultimate inner causes resident in the mind and brain, providing at best a facilitative grooming of internal dispositions bequeathed through our bio- and neurophysiology.[1] Consequently, as was seen in Chapters 6 and 7, self-efficacy and other self-regulatory phenomena were treated as internal structures or schemata, computation-like information processes, or executive functions built into our cognitive structures and/or cortex, even while the vast majority of research data and intervention practices in education and other areas of human functioning were drawn from the overt actions and verbal reports of individual students and others.

One especially salient consequence of psychologism is an unfortunate tautology or vicious circularity in the kinds of explanation favored by cognitive psychologists and applied cognitive psychologists. Chapters 3 through 7 are liberally sprinkled with examples in which self-esteem, self-concept, self-efficacy, and self-regulation are inferred from the behaviors and interactions of children and adolescents in classrooms and schools, and then used as explanations for these same and similar actions. Thus, for example, educational psychologists and those influenced by them often speak about a wide range of apparently problematic behaviors (including behaving shyly, aggressively, selfishly, intolerantly, arrogantly, and fearfully) as caused by overly low or high levels of self-esteem, a poverty or overabundance of self-regulation, and so forth. However, in everyday educational contexts there is little evidence to sustain such explanations other than the behavioral displays of students that serve as evidence of both difficulties and the purported causes of these difficulties. As we shall see later in this chapter, much of the research conducted by educational and other psychologists fails to supply sources or criteria of evaluation and assessment of psychological phenomena such as self-esteem and self-regulation that do not tap the same data or sources of expert judgment as employed by the researchers themselves.

---

[1] Evidence for the secondary status accorded to sociocultural phenomena in psychological inquiry into development and learning includes the frequency with which such phenomena are treated as "mediator or moderator variables" in this large body of research.

An even more radical critique of psychologism calls into question the very existence of psychological phenomena like self-concept and self-efficacy, at least as internal entities that are anything more than inner aspects of our experience and actions in the world. Thus, in Chapter 5, we questioned what was to be gained by attributing individuals' understanding and evaluation of their experiences and actions to their self-concepts as opposed to observing, reporting, and drawing inferences from their actions and the ways in which they describe their experiences. Just as Hattie (2003) joked about explaining our assessment of the state and condition of our toes by attributing such an evaluation to our "self-toeness" structure, we might well wonder about explaining our assessment of the state and condition of students' classroom conduct in terms of their academic self-concept, especially if this is understood to implicate or point to some ill-defined inner structural entity resident in our psychological (mind) and biological (brain and body) interiors.

Reductionism (of Persons and Contexts)

Rather than understanding our learning, development, knowledge, experience, actions, and interactions as the activities and accomplishments of the kinds of embodied, enculturated persons that we are, much psychology seems anxious to reduce the holistic complexity of our lives to subpersonal aspects of ourselves that somehow can be understood outside of the sociocultural contexts in which our actions and experiences occur. In much psychological research and practice, the activity and interactivity of persons is reduced to aspects of our individual interiors that apparently can be probed through questionnaires, scales, and checklists completed at a temporal and spatial distance from our active immersion and participation in the activities and interactions that encapsulate and define our actions and experiences. For example, in commonly employed psychological measures of self-regulation, students are asked to rate the extent to which they believe their usual classroom experiences and/or actions are captured in sentences such as "When I study, I try to organize the material in my mind," and "My underlining is helpful when I review text material" (see Chapter 7). It is difficult to understand what is to be gained from the use of such instruments compared to the direct observation of students' studying. Indeed, as an apparently objective, scientific source of relevant data, direct observation by appropriately trained expert observers should have much to recommend it against the out-of-context attempts of even well-intentioned student informants to report accurately about what they do when they study. Without direct access to either the actual activity of students or the usual contexts in which such activity occurs, data such as these seem to reflect the inquiry practices and convenience of psychologists more than they do the activities of students as they go about their daily participation in important educational practices such as studying. Indeed, it is difficult to understand how the reduction of the learning activity of students in classrooms and other relevant life contexts to ratings on psychologists' measures of self-regulation does not run strong risks of distorting the reality of what psychologists claim to be studying and/or ameliorating.

Reducing the contextualized activity and experiences of persons to what is measured by psychological instruments such as those frequently employed in the self studies of educational psychologists in the manner just discussed seems highly problematic. However, it becomes even more problematic when the activity and experiences of persons active in the world are explained by recourse to mechanisms such as self-efficacy, self-concept, or self-esteem beliefs. As argued previously (see Chapters 4, 5, 6, and above), such beliefs are not separate from the actions from which we infer self-efficacy, self-concept, or self-esteem. We do not tend to attempt things that we do not think we can do. We do not, at least typically, claim to be what we are not. And even if we do at times over- or underestimate our self-worth when set against our demonstrated competence, the contexts in which such erroneous estimates take place typically tell us a great deal about what is going on when these estimates are invoked as part of our ongoing action and experience.

When we fail to think critically about psychological measures and interventions that reduce and decontextualize our actions and experiences, our attention is drawn away from the sociocultural contexts and interactions within which our actions and experiences are acquired and within which we achieve our collective and individual ways of being the kinds of persons that we are. In education, surely the way to understand students' actions and experiences as learners is to examine educational materials, curricular content, teaching strategies, teacher–student interactions, participation in classroom discussions and projects, and so forth. Why do we (as individuals and as a society) want to rely instead on the reductive, decontextualized measurement and research practices of psychologists who claim to be able to measure things like self-esteem and self-regulation using paper-and-pencil questionnaires that students complete when not involved in classroom lessons, studying, or other educationally relevant tasks?

Manipulation (Misleading Conceptions and Language)

We believe that an important partial answer to questions such as this can be found in the way in which the conceptions and language employed by psychologists, in this case by educational psychologists, serve to focus our attention on purportedly interior psychological mechanisms and structures said to constitute our true core selves. When we become convinced that such selves exist and motivate our everyday actions and experiences, it seems reasonable, even essential, to turn inward to understand why we act and feel the way we do. When this tendency of "looking inward" is firmly in place, whenever we encounter difficulties in our attempts to understand our functioning and experiencing, we are more than ready, even anxious, to accept various forms of psychological expertise to help us feel better about our lives, our inner lives in particular, and to manage our lives in general. In so doing we open ourselves to the theories and ministrations of psychologists by framing our difficulties in ways amenable to their ideas and practices. In effect, we become convinced that we need to understand and govern ourselves in psychological ways. And with such conviction, we readily and uncritically accept that treating and managing ourselves as inward-looking psychological beings is in our own best interests.

At the end of the previous chapter, in discussing the ways in which teachers and psychologists have attempted to help students in classrooms to self-regulate their learning, we offered a tentative neo-Foucaultian analysis of such attempts to promote student self-regulation. By pointing out that in many such programs the range and kinds of goals and strategies of self-regulation were actually determined and monitored by the psychoeducators who create and run them, we asked what exactly in these programs constitutes student self-regulation. If the answer to such questions is nothing more than students ensuring that they act in accordance with the goals and mandates of psychoeducators, what we are left with is a kind of self-governance or self-policing of the sort that Michel Foucault (1977) famously illuminated by referring to Jeremy Bentham's eighteenth-century plan for a Panopticon—a type of prison in which an authority is able to observe prisoners without their knowing whether or not they were being watched. In consequence, the prisoners follow the rules and policies of the authority even in the absence of the authority.

Foucault (1977) used the Panopticon as a metaphor for the ways in which self-governance in liberal democracies is promoted as a means of helping citizens to achieve personal autonomy and freedom in ways consistent with the wishes of governmental authorities. Foucault suggested that contemporary psychological methods of self-regulation are especially well suited for the management of people in contemporary democracies. Others, like Pfister and Schnog (1997) and Rose (1998), have suggested that many of the theories and practices of scientific and professional psychology, especially those related to self-esteem and self-regulation, are now used routinely by governments and corporations to encourage citizens to pursue instrumentally individualistic goals of material acquisition and consumption as a means of keeping them politically docile:

> What the liberal corporate order had accomplished was a way of ruling, not so much by dictatorial oppression or by using brute force to get Americans to go to work, but by creating "psychological" and "individual" significance and by allowing "freedom" to be popularized and enacted as the challenging of taboos (rather than the challenging of the liberal corporate order). (Pfister, 1997, p. 200)

The taboos that Pfister has in mind are various preoccupations with narcissistic self-satisfaction. Obviously, psychological practices and techniques of self-regulation and self-esteem in school classrooms are not used to encourage the challenging of social taboos. However, in general outline, it seems plausible to consider the employment of such practices as means of helping students to act in accordance with classroom and school policies and goals by insisting that such compliance is really a highly desirable form of self-governance.

Obviously there is much more to student life in contemporary classrooms than what is suggested by the foregoing Foucaultian analysis. However, the general implication is that the expressive, enterprising student (prized in psychoeducational programs aimed at elevating students' self-esteem, self-concept, self-efficacy, and self-regulation) is also a student who is extremely well adapted to the complex, contemporary array of educational goals that encompass the development of students as both productive members of liberal democratic societies and as individuals who must find personal fulfillment in their lives. What better way to bring such overarching goals together than by promoting the development of students as expressive and enterprising individuals who fit easily and well within societies with political and economic structures that require precisely these kinds of individuals?

> The purpose of the British Columbia school system is to enable learners to develop their individual potential and to acquire the knowledge, skills, and attitudes needed to contribute to a healthy society and a prosperous and sustainable economy. Schools in the province assist in the development of citizens who are thoughtful, able to learn and to think critically, and who can communicate information from a broad knowledge base; creative, flexible, self-motivated and who have a positive self image; capable of making independent decisions; skilled and who can contribute to society generally, including the world of work; productive, who gain satisfaction through achievement and who strive for physical well being; cooperative, principled and respectful of others regardless of differences; aware of the rights and prepared to exercise the responsibilities of an individual within the family, the community, Canada, and the world. (British Columbia Ministry of Education, 1989, p. D-94)

The relatively seamless manner in which personal and sociopolitical goals are combined in the education of the self-governing student has a powerfully beguiling effect on our acceptance of psychological ways of being students and ultimately citizens—ways that help us to understand and govern ourselves as we fall in line with existing educational, corporate, and governmental agendas, all for our own good, which also is the good of our society and nation. Of course, exactly how all of this is possible or even coherent is seldom is articulated.

The Role of Psychological Measurement, Research, and Intervention

A closer critical examination of the measurement, research, and intervention practices of educational psychologists will help to elaborate the various concerns summarized thus far in this chapter. In this section, we will explain how deeply implicated psychological methods of measurement, research, and intervention are in the forms of individualism, psychologism, reductionism, and manipulation we have described. In so doing, we will also raise a number of troubling questions concerning the appropriateness of these methods and their claims to provide forms of applied psychological knowledge of use to educators and others.

Measurement

A good place to start a critical consideration of psychological measurement is to remind ourselves of what *measurement* means. When scientists measure the size, speeds, and distances of and between objects, they rely on exacting specifications of metrics or standard units of measurement. In our everyday lives, when we measure floor areas for the installation of carpets or amounts of ingredients called for in various recipes used to prepare foods, we too rely on standard units of distance, volume, and so forth. In fact, most dictionary definitions of *measure* are stated in terms such as dimensions or quantities ascertained by comparison with a standard unit or measuring device. Importantly, measuring is distinct from counting. We can *count* the number of words in this sentence, but we do not *measure* the number of words in this sentence. We have no recourse to standard units or metrics with which to measure words in the way that we might measure the physical dimensions of the page upon which those words appear. The same applies to our thoughts, ideas, attitudes, opinions, emotions, and experiences. Assuming that we have a sufficiently clear definition of a particular idea, we might be able to count the number of times that this idea occurs to us over a period of a week or a month, but we certainly are not able to measure ideas in terms of standard units of length, volume, electrical current, or thermal conductivity. In fact, the vast majority of psychological phenomena having to do with experience, intentional action, mind, and selfhood do not lend themselves to being measured in anything like the conventional meanings of *measuring* or *measurement* (see Michell, 1999, for a full discussion of these matters).

When Gordon Allport and other early personality psychologists (see Chapter 5) adapted items and formats previously used to survey public opinions and attitudes to the "measurement" of personality traits such as self-concept, they did not develop scientific measures in the sense of creating standard units that might be applied to ascertain the physical dimensions of individuals' self understandings, let alone of the self-concept of a person understood as an internal psychological entity of some kind—not at all. What they and subsequent generations of personality psychologists prototypically did was to count the number of times that a particular individual rated particular statements prepared by personality psychologists (including themselves) as more or less applicable (typically on a five-point scale ranging from a start point such as "1—not at all" to an end point such as "5—always") to his or her life experience as he or she generally understood it. Then, by grouping together different items or statements that the personality psychologists thought to be related in some way (e.g., which they thought all related to a particular facet of an individual's self-understanding such as self-confidence or social self-concept) and counting and tallying individuals' ratings on this group of items, they claimed to have achieved a quantitative measure of a particular aspect of an individual's self-concept.[2] At a higher level of aggregation, by counting and tallying individuals' total ratings on several groups of such items, they then arrived at overall and average self-concept scores for a group of individuals. However, as already argued, there is a most important sense in which none of these basic steps in the creation and use of a personality scale or instrument to measure the self-concept (and other self-related phenomena such as self-esteem, self-efficacy, and self-regulation) has anything to do with actual measurement in the sense of the application of an objectively defined, standard metric. Instead, what is happening here is the creation of a system of rating, counting, and tallying that relies entirely on the subjective impressions of individuals who complete the "measures" or instruments created and administered by psychologists.[3]

Given that self researchers in educational psychology rely almost exclusively on psychological "measures" of self-esteem, self-concept, self-efficacy, and self-regulation, it is extremely misleading to describe their basic data (i.e., the individual and collective ratings and scores that they employ in their research and which are derived from their paper-and-pencil instruments, such as the Piers-Harris Self-Concept Scale or the Coopersmith Self-Esteem Inventory) as objective data points derived from actual measurements. In fact, quite the opposite is actually the case—that is, the basic data employed by self researchers in education consist mostly of the subjective ratings of children, adolescents, and adults of how they and others see and understand them. No one, including research psychologists, has any idea of the extent to which different individuals respond to the same items on these psychological questionnaires ("measures") in comparable ways. For example, I might interpret rating descriptions like "most of the time," "strongly agree," or "always" with respect to statements such as "I feel good about myself" to mean that I feel good about myself 100 percent of the time; whereas you might interpret these same rating descriptions to indicate that the state of well-being described in such statements need apply to only 70 percent of your total life experience. Moreover, whereas I might make my rating based on the last several weeks of my life, you might make your rating based on what you estimate to be your average experience over the past several years. We might also differ to a great extent in our respective abilities to observe and report accurately on our experiences, on the contexts we assume in making our responses, and in any of a large variety of other ways that are likely to influence the ratings we make. And, of course, others who complete ratings on the same psychological instruments or

---

[2] Typically, psychologists who do this kind of work make this claim because they believe that the rating scale is isomorphic with an underlying dimension of interest; they interpret the rating as an indicator of a position on that dimension and therefore not "merely" a count of a given behavior or thought.

[3] Also, note that in the case of any such psychological measurement, both the existence of what is measured and its magnitude must be inferred. In the case of commonplace physical measurement, most often neither of these inferences is necessary—the existence of the thing measured is obvious and a determination of magnitude requires only a comparison based on the application of a standard metric.

questionnaires might differ in their manner of responding from you and me and each other in these and other ways, which remain entirely unknown to psychological researchers and to those who read their research reports and attempt to base their educational and other practices on the results reported. When understood in this way, such data are not all that different from the declarations that you, I, and our friends might, and frequently do, make about ourselves and each other when we gather around the kitchen table, in the local pub, or at a community event. Although psychologists might want to think of themselves as physical scientists of the self and mind, their typical measurement practices aren't even close to those of their more scientific brethren.[4]

But what about the counterclaim made repeatedly by different generations of "measurement" psychologists when they assert that their personality "measures" achieve an acceptable degree of objectivity (that is, independent verification based on nonsubjective standards) through their painstaking procedures of test validation—procedures they employ to establish the reliability and validity of the results yielded by such "measures"? After all, is it not worth noting the high correlations psychologists are typically able to demonstrate among the different instruments they use to elicit/count/tally the self-ratings of subjects in their studies? Surely such convergences must count for something.

It is certainly true that test validation is taken very seriously by research and applied psychologists in education and elsewhere. Indeed, an enormous number of articles, manuals, texts, and guidelines have been prepared by psychologists in an attempt to gather evidence in support of the consistency (reliability), accuracy (validity), and objectivity of their various instruments. Unfortunately the truth about the vast majority of this work is that it trades on (even conflates) two rather different kinds of objectivity.

Most contemporary scientific forms of objectivity assume an independent criterion to which results might be compared. This is clearly the case when a common metric is used in the physical sciences. Such a metric and procedures for its application can be utilized and results checked across many different laboratories and scientific bodies independently of the scientists engaged directly in the relevant measurements. However, for psychological measures such as those we are discussing here, objectivity is not assessed by criteria independent of the enterprise of psychological testing and test validation. Instead, a different notion of objectivity is in play, one saturated by the very procedures and practices used in psychological testing and test validation. A primary source of subjectivity in

---

[4] But, some readers might ask, what of the physical pictures and measures of brain activity from functional magnetic resonance imaging and electroencephalographic recordings employed by contemporary cognitive neuroscientists? Although such data have seldom been used by educational psychologists, it is possible that their use might increase in the future. If so, however, neuroscientists who record particular patterns of neuronal firing, excitation, and inhibition cannot be said to be measuring self-esteem, self-concept, and the like. They are collecting images of biochemical/electrical activity in brains. Even if such images prove to be consistently correlated with particular actions and experiences thought to be indicative of high levels of self-esteem, it would be incoherent to consider them to be instances of self-esteem per se. Self-esteem refers to a person's self-assessment, not to particular patterns of neuronal activity in the brain.

psychological inquiry utilizing personality measures (such as measures of self-esteem) has already been broached—that is, the fact that the very conditions under which such measures are taken are not known, since they depend on the interpretations, moods, assumptions, and circumstances of individuals making the ratings, which are then counted and tallied to create individual scores and scores for groups of individuals. Such subjectivities cannot be corrected by psychologists because their exact nature is unknown to those who administer measures of self-esteem (and so forth) and perhaps to the respondents themselves. For it is surely the case that few if any of us are aware, on a moment-by-moment basis, of the various social and psychological factors that might be influencing our subjective judgments and responses. No amount of test validation can change this basic state of affairs.

What typically happens in the test validation practices endorsed and employed by psychologists is that results from the application of one measure of self-esteem (or whatever is the focal psychological construct of interest) is compared with results yielded by other measures of self-esteem completed by the same individuals or individuals sampled from the same kind of group or a larger group (population) of individuals. Using statistical methods that correlate the test scores of different groups of individuals who are expected to have similar and dissimilar scores on a variety of measures thought to tap the same psychological construct—and dissimilar scores on a variety of measures thought to tap different psychological constructs—psychologists attempt to provide evidence of acceptable or unacceptable levels of convergent and divergent validity. In other words, they attempt to show by such correlative practices that the instrument or test they have developed or decided to use provides information that more or less agrees with other tests or instruments they regard as having good psychometric properties. That is, they are considered to have these properties in the sense that they appear to measure what they are intended to measure and not other things and that they measure what they measure with acceptable degrees of consistency and accuracy.

However, such attempts at test validation (and many others like them) not only fail to remove the basic subjectivity in psychologists' data (which is attributable to the subjective nature of individual responses to such tests) but the psychometric data yielded by the various approaches to test validation also fail to meet usual criteria assumed to constitute scientific objectivity. This is so because the vast majority of tests with which a particular psychological test is compared (in the sense of comparing convergences and divergences in the results or data they yield) are constructed with similar sets of assumptions, theoretical frameworks, and methods to those employed in the construction of the particular psychological test of interest. In other words, all the data used to provide indications of objectivity of particular psychological measures are produced by essentially the same community of research psychologists utilizing the same methods of test construction and the same statistics to count, group, tally, and yield various aggregate and relational scores and statistics. And none of these is based on actual processes of measurement that can be connected to common metrics relating to a real world independent of the world of measurement devices and practices constructed by psychologists for their own interests and purposes. Unlike the world of rocks, plants, and animals, the world of psychological measures is one that is mostly created by psychologists who share the practices and assumptions required to construct psychological tests and measures as well as the procedures claimed to validate them and their use.

Research and Intervention

As if the foregoing measurement issues were not enough to open the self research projects of psychologists to critical consideration, there also exists great confusion among psychologists about what their research does and does not allow them to conclude. In particular, most psychologists appear to assume that evidence of individual differences that they produce through their research endeavors (conveniently ignoring the spate of measurement concerns just discussed) provides empirical support for them to claim expertise with respect to understanding and predicting the actions and experiences of particular individuals. These claims even reach the point where many applied psychologists (as we have seen in the previous chapters) are fully prepared to intervene in the psychological lives of individuals (in classrooms and elsewhere) with respect to matters such as self-efficacy, self-esteem, self-concept, and self-regulation. But does psychological research that reports differences between individuals with high versus low levels of self-esteem, self-concept, self-efficacy, or self-regulation really allow psychologists to apply the results of such research to psychoeducational interventions in the lives of individual students?

James Lamiell (1987, 2003, 2010) has studied such matters over a period of 30 years and has concluded that attempts of this sort are based on a fundamental error in logic. "The ontological reality that twenty-first-century personality psychologists must finally come to terms with is that the between-person differences that have so preoccupied them for about a century *simply do not exist at the level of the individual*" (Lamiell, 2010, p. 17, italics in the original). To say, for example, that among students high in self-esteem the probability of their doing well on a final examination is .60 is simply to say that given 100 individuals high in self-esteem, 60 may be expected to do well on the examination. This is an empirically testable proposition. It is, however, one that is entirely silent on whether or not any particular student in any group of 100 students will do well on the final examination. Any claim to know or be able to predict how a particular student will achieve based on knowledge of what is the case for groups of individuals is simply nonsensical (i.e., it makes no sense).

Knowledge of group differences in academic achievement between individuals with high versus low levels of self-esteem (or self-concept, self-efficacy, or self-regulation) is different from knowledge of how self-esteem and academic achievement might relate for any particular individual. In fact, in many studies that inquire into such matters and report differences in academic achievement that may be attributable statistically to differences in levels of psychological constructs such as self-esteem, it is typically the case that many individuals with high levels of self-esteem perform poorly on the relevant achievement measures and that many individuals with low levels of self-esteem perform well. There is simply no way of knowing how particular individuals will perform based on knowledge of how groups perform. Again, knowledge of aggregated individual differences between groups of students with high versus low self-esteem carries no implications whatsoever for predicting or intervening at the level of individual students.

> To repeat for clarity and emphasis: the knowledge generated through the study of *individual differences variables* [such as self-esteem] does *not* entitle claims to knowledge about what has transpired with *any one* of the individuals the differences between whom have been made into the object of investigation. The aggregate statistical knowledge yielded by such studies is in fact, and quite literally, knowledge of *no one*. (Lamiell, 2010, p. 7, italics in the original)

The group-based research of educational psychologists is entirely irrelevant to knowledge about the educational progress of individual students and intervention with respect to their learning. This is an unassailable point of logic based on the nature of the research methods, designs, and statistical procedures employed in much mainstream research in educational psychology. When one adds into the critical points raised in previous chapters (and summarized earlier in the current chapter) concerning problems of individualism, psychologism, and reductionism in psychological research in education, it is not unreasonable to question the entire psychoeducational enterprise of "educating selves" as it unfolded during the latter half of the twentieth century, especially in the United States and Canada.

The relative ease with which psychologists' "measures" of self-esteem, self-concept, self-efficacy, and self-regulation can be administered to groups of students and scores on such measures associated statistically with indicators of academic achievement and student satisfaction understandably makes such work attractive to many psychologists, whose careers and reputations have come to rest on precisely this kind of investigation. However, educators and the public should know much more about the nature of such inquiry and what can reasonably be expected from it before concluding that it forms an adequate basis for the forging of educational policy and classroom practice. As we have attempted to demonstrate here, there is no scientifically compelling reason for accepting many of the educational pronouncements of educational psychologists at face value.

The Ideal of the "Triple-E" (Expressive, Enterprising, and Entitled) Student

Consequently, many of the measurement, research, and intervention practices of educational psychologists can and should be considered critically with respect to their relevance, appropriateness, and utility for the education of students. However, in thinking critically about psychologists' typical practices in these areas, it is equally important not to neglect the larger picture concerning the overall impact of such initiatives on students themselves. At the end of Chapter 2, we introduced the work of philosopher and historian of psychology Ian Hacking, especially his ideas concerning what he has termed *historical ontology* and the ways in which psychological theories and practices of research and intervention can be implicated in changing the ways in which we understand ourselves and act as particular kinds of person. In this section of Chapter 8, we argue that the various theoretical positions and programs of inquiry and intervention we have examined in Chapters 3 to 7 have been influential in changing the ways in which pupils in schools understand themselves and act as students. Our central claim is that psychological ideas and practices adopted by many teachers, school administrators, parents, and others have created a new way of being a student; we refer to this as the "triple E" (expressive, enterprising, and entitled) student ideal. In making this claim, we want to be clear that we do not intend to say that all students educated in American and Canadian schools during the latter part of the twentieth century were students of this kind. Rather, it is our contention that this particularly psychological way of being a student began to function as a kind of regulative ideal for student self-understanding and conduct.

Psychologist and educational theorist David Olson (2003; Olson & Bruner, 1996) describes three popular historical approaches to teaching and learning, each of which assumes a particular kind of student. The approach with the longest history is one in which learners observe others who are able to do things and thus gradually come to participate in the conduct of the tasks they observe older, more capable others perform. This is mostly a kind of informal, everyday set of transactions in which children are guided and helped to act in ways that approximate and gradually approach the skilled performances of adults in a wide range of activities essential for the well-being of family and community groups. As they observe and participate in increasingly competent ways in these activities, children make the transition from observer to doer, from learner to competent performer. In such teaching and learning, the idea of "studenthood" that dominates is that of an attentive helper and imitator who, through processes of observing and assisting more competent performers, is gradually initiated into the social and cultural practices of the community. In this model of teaching and learning, learners are not so much actual students who attend to the lessons of their teachers but apprentices who learn by seeing the ways in which things are accomplished and then playing out and practicing the routines and enactments they have observed around them. In human societies, it is through experiencing and acting within the ongoing practices of a community, sometimes under supervision and at other times on their own initiative, that children and adolescents mature into full-fledged contributors to their societies. In this way of learning, learners are observers, participants, and actors who gradually come to understand what others are doing without much in the way of formal instruction.

A second long-standing form of teaching and learning that has joined and often surpassed "learning by doing" is found in numerous versions of didactic teaching, in which pupils are presented with facts, rules, principles, and methods to be absorbed, regurgitated, recalled, and applied. In this approach, students are regarded as empty vessels to be filled with knowledge, while knowledge itself is understood as a commodity that can be organized and transmitted in ways that students will absorb, remember, and use when it is appropriate for them to do so. This is a model of education as formal enculturation whereby sociocultural knowledge and methods are transferred to the minds of students through the intermediary of the expert understanding and pedagogical practices of teachers. Such knowledge is typically represented in a cultural "canon" consisting of standard works that it is the teacher's responsibility to transmit and the student's responsibility to assimilate. The task of the teacher is to decide how to break this knowledge into teachable chunks. In sixteenth-century Italy, all subjects were divided into bits of knowledge that were drilled through repetition into the minds of students, who then were expected to assemble them into wholes, building up understanding just as a mason might construct an edifice by laying one slab atop another (Grendler, 1989). The pupil assumed in such pedagogy was a blank slate or empty vessel but one somehow capable of retaining the knowledge that was inscribed upon or poured into it.

There is little room in such an approach for thinking of students as uniquely individual learners. Instead, in this view, being a student is mostly a matter of decoding, storing, and reproducing that which was taught. Where pedagogical adjustments might have to be made, teachers typically proceed on a basis of comparing and classifying students into groups of more or less capable learners and altering what is expected of individual students based on their ability classifications. The good pupil is by definition the student able to reproduce what has been received through instruction. In more recent enactments of this pedagogical approach, reconstruction has sometimes been set alongside or in place of reproduction. However, the essential conception and function of the student as knowledge recipient remains unaltered. Neither view of the student—defined either as someone who must learn by observing and doing or one who is understood as a receptacle for knowledge—leaves much room for considering students as individual learners who might differ one from the other.

This very cursory overview of historically previous ways of being students perhaps allows a greater appreciation of the extent to which psychological methods of education that emphasized the expressive and managerial selves of students (see Chapter 3) have helped to transform the very idea of studenthood. By the end of the nineteenth century, when disciplinary psychology had begun to flourish, traditional transmission models of education were increasingly in receipt of harsh criticism. As recounted in the previous chapters, early educational psychologists like John Dewey urged greater concern for students as individuals and decried what they referred to as "factory" and "banking" approaches to education, which treated all students as if they were exactly the same in background and ability and insisted on the same outcomes in terms of knowledge retention and reproduction. As psychological influences in education became more pronounced throughout the first half of the twentieth century, teachers were encouraged to be more concerned with how individual children thought, how they came to think about what they did, and how they might be helped to think in more personally creative and socially productive ways (see Olson, 2003).

Children were now to be understood as uniquely individual learners who could be expected to develop and represent ideas in highly idiosyncratic ways depending on their personal experiences and beliefs. Increasingly, children and adolescents were treated, for educational purposes and purposes of individual development, as if they were in possession of their own unique perspectives, which they must be taught to recognize, value, express, and adjust on the basis of their own and others' evaluations. In this third, more psychologically informed approach to teaching and learning, teaching is transformed from transmission to invitation and facilitation. It is now the teacher's job to capture the attention and interest of the student in ways that invite the student as a valued, individual psychological being to create his or her own understandings in relation to learning content and activities and to facilitate the expression and discussion of his or her theories of whatever is under study. It is within such transformations of the activities of teaching and learning that, during the second half of the twentieth century, the self research and theories of educational psychologists gained prominence and influence.

It is in this context that new, highly interiorized, individualized, and contextually reduced forms of psychological studenthood began to emerge. Consistent with our analysis of the social and educational landscape of mid-century America and Canada during the 1900s (see Chapter 3), we believe that these new psychologically inspired ways of being students are well captured in the adjectives, *expressive, enterprising*, and *entitled*. As bearers of idiosyncratic inner selves that are understood as primary sources of learning and creativity, students must be helped to get in touch with their true selves and to learn to elicit and express their intuitive insights and understandings. To do so, they must gain confidence in their feelings and intuitions (their inner senses) as reliable guides and creative sources for what is true and valuable in their experiences in the world. The attainment of such confidence and comfort with their inner experiences comes only with relatively unconditional acceptance of themselves as reflected in high levels of self-conception and self-esteem. And it is these positive understandings and valuations of their inner selves that allow students to express and direct themselves in their classroom activities.

In addition to self-expression, the psychoeducational model of teaching and learning also emphasizes the importance of strategic action in pursuit of methods of inquiry, understanding, and accomplishment consistent with students' expressed interests and goals. Consequently, high levels of self-efficacy and self-regulation are also required for students to keep their focus on their self-determined learning targets, understood as natural consequences of their self-expression. Thus, students must be helped to become both self-expressive and self-managing (or enterprising) in deciding and organizing their learning in ways that are consistent with their inner wishes and desires. The cornerstone of effective learning is the belief that students must be in charge of their own learning. Jones, Valdez, Nowakowski, and Rasmussen (1995), quoting Covey (1989), describe characteristics of students who are responsible for their own learning: "It means more than merely taking initiative. It means that as human beings, we are responsible for our own lives. Our behavior is a function of our decisions, not our conditions. We have the initiative and the responsibility to make things happen" (p. 71).

Consider President Obama's national educational address (Obama, 2009) to American students:

> I want to start with the responsibility you have to yourself. Every single one of you has something that you're good at. Every single one of you has something to offer. And you have a responsibility to yourself to discover what that is. That's the opportunity an education can provide. Now, I know it's not always easy to do well in school. I know a lot of you have challenges in your lives right now that can make it hard to focus on your schoolwork. Maybe you live in a neighborhood where you don't feel safe, or have friends who are pressuring you to do things you know aren't right. But at the end of the day, the circumstances of your life—what you look like, where you come from, how much money you have, what you've got going on at home—none of that is an excuse for neglecting your homework or having a bad attitude in school. That's no excuse for talking back to your teacher, or cutting class, or dropping out of school. There is no excuse for not trying. Where you are right now doesn't have to determine where you'll end up. No one's written your destiny for you, because here in America, you write your own destiny. You make your own future. (p. 1)

The expressive, enterprising student at the end of the twentieth century was not understood to equate with the student as depicted in the prototypically 1960s' sense of engaging in radically free self-expression. The enterprising student certainly is an expressive student, but one who also is self-disciplined and self-directed to make decisions and solve problems on his or her own, without being told what to do. However, being told how to do things is a different matter. Thus, teachers (see Chapter 7) actively encourage expressive and enterprising students with strategies designed to help them set attainable goals, process and use information effectively, and act with self-assurance and self-confidence. In short, while teachers may be reluctant to indicate directly what students should be interested in, there is no shortage of classroom time devoted to helping them become focused on their own thinking, learning, and decision-making processes; supplying them with strategic tools for goal setting, progress monitoring, and evaluation; and encouraging them to engage in troubleshooting and problem solving. The key to teaching expressive, enterprising students is to give them all of the general psychological tools they need to accomplish whatever it is that they might want to accomplish. Consequently, the expressive, enterprising student is a model of self-sufficiency operating within existing community and social conventions even as her or his strategic efforts often aim at *extending and altering such norms and accepted practices.*

Enterprise Education and Twenty-First-Century Skills: A Canadian Example

The concepts of "enterprise," "enterprising individual," and "entrepreneur" are traditionally understood in relation to business and economics. Yet in recent years, the "enterprise" framework has spread beyond these areas to all spheres of life. According to the Organization for Economic Co-operation and Development (1988):

> An enterprising individual has a positive, flexible, and adaptable disposition towards change, seeing it as normal rather than a problem. To see change in this way an enterprising individual has a security borne of self-confidence, and is at ease when dealing with insecurity, risk, difficulty, and the unknown. An enterprising individual has the capacity to initiate creative ideas, develop them, either individually or in collaboration with others, and see them through. An enterprising individual is able, even anxious, to take responsibility and is an effective communicator, negotiator, influencer, planner, and organizer. An enterprising individual is active, confident and purposeful, not passive, uncertain, and dependent. (as cited in Center for Educational Research and Innovation, 1988, p. 33)

Enterprise education is intimately tied to twenty-first century learning initiatives that claim to "be a dramatic departure from the factory model education of the past" (Partnership for 21st Century Skills, 2009, p. 1). Under this new model, curricula are connected to students' interests, experiences, and life in the real world. Learners are unique individuals and are active, responsible participants in their learning. Teachers create classroom cultures of inquiry, serve as collaborative facilitators, and focus on what students "can do." Whether this new kind of self is referred to as an enterprising student or a twenty-first-century learner, the core components are identical: critical thinking and problem solving, creativity and innovation, adaptability, lifelong learning, teamwork and collaboration, initiative, self-direction, an entrepreneurial spirit, communications skills, literacy, and use of technology (Partnership for 21st Century Skills, 2009).

Some American and Canadian school systems have already incorporated this model of learning into their policies and practices. "Enterprise Education" is commonly presented as a course of organized sets of activities within a subject curriculum that can be incorporated into other subject areas. According to Enterprise Education for high school students in the Government of Newfoundland and Labrador Department of Education curriculum:

> In a complex society faced with rapid change, individuals need generic skills to thrive and succeed. This course focuses on transferable skills, such as reasoning, communication, problem solving, opportunity identification and evaluation, innovation, creativity and technological literacy. These skills are critical to enable students to succeed in a dynamic society, where they have to adapt to new situations and challenges at many levels. (Government of Newfoundland and Labrador Department of Education, 2010a, p. 5)

Enterprise Education can be taught as early as kindergarten. According to New-foundland's Department of Education, "the emphasis of Enterprise Education at the elementary level is on refining personal development skills and enterprise management skills" (Government of Newfoundland and Labrador Department of Education, 2010b, p. 48). Students practice enterprise skills in a variety of individual and collaborative learning contexts. "Some activities focus on developing a positive self-image. Others are problem solving, which require students to be enterprising and self-sufficient" (Government of Newfoundland and Labrador Department of Education, 2010c, p. 1). For example, an activity entitled "My Many Talents" engages students in grades 3 and 4 in identifying activities (related to their body parts, such as brain, ears, hands) that they can do well in class. They write their responses on cards and then have small-group discussions. Enterprise skills that students practice during this activity are risk taking, team building, confidence, and review and reflection (Government of Newfoundland and Labrador Department of Education, 2010c).

This example of students working together depicts a coming together of enterprising individuals. At the classroom level, teachers are expected to play a prominent role in developing students' skills and attitudes as enterprising individuals. For example, teachers may use their expertise to guide students in their practice of educational activities in order to enhance enterprise skills. Teachers are often encouraged to match students within group projects so that individual students can shine by practicing those skills that they are good at. In this way, students "sell" themselves to one another ("Suzy is good at writing", and "I'm a good listener"). But such forms of cooperation may not be particularly concerned with the common good of groups of learners. For the most part, they are targeted at achieving goals set in terms of the learning and development of individual students. When all is said and done, they target the production of enterprising individuals, not cooperative groups.

With the help of experts (e.g., psychologists, therapists, educators), enterprising individuals are free to choose a life of personal responsibility and to create lifestyles that promote self-fulfillment. Thus, to make an enterprise of oneself is to maximize one's own assets, develop a future for oneself, and shape oneself in order to become what one wishes to be. Under this view, enterprising individuals are the new workers who strive to align their work life with their personal life—people whose work provides them with satisfaction and a means for becoming even better enterprisers. That is, enterprising individuals choose work that allows them to display, practice, and hone their unique skills (e.g., organizing, goal setting, creative thinking). In this way, work merges with lifestyle and becomes personally meaningful. The enterprising individual sees lifelong learning as fundamental in order to remain competitive in an ever-changing world. A successful enterpriser is, in psychological terms, self-motivated, self-regulated, and self-adapting.

When the third element of entitlement is added to this new way of being a student, it is as if the educational system in the later-twentieth century has moved into the twenty-first century in a way that is directly targeted at producing students who will fit in easily, function smoothly, and be welcomed in many private, corporate, and public governmental roles within a modern, corporate-friendly liberal democracy. Such entitlement issues from the clear emphasis discernible in many educational writings and policies in the latter part of the twentieth century to the effect that student expression and self-direction are not only appropriate educational goals but also both rights and responsibilities of individual students. The self as an expressive enterprise requires that students have both the responsibility and the right to make projects of themselves and their goals. Freedom to pursue personal development and self-determined goals is increasingly understood as a right that students can demand of their educational and social systems and as a responsibility that they have to themselves. The responsibilities and rights of students to shape their own lives is confirmed in education policies, such as the British Columbia education mandate (British Columbia Ministry of Education, 1989), which defines the duties, rights, and responsibilities of students as "the opportunity to avail themselves of a quality education consistent with their abilities, the opportunity to share in the shaping of their educational programs, and the opportunity to determine their career and occupational goals" (p. D-95).

In similar fashion, the *Alberta Steering Committee Report* (Alberta Education, 2010) on the "Vision for the Educated Student" declares that in order for children to reach their full potential, they "must be the center of *all* decisions related to learning and the overall education system. Children and youth of all ages should be supported as individuals—emotionally, intellectually, physically, socially and spiritually" (p. 6).

That such entitlement can have deleterious consequences is by now well documented. Commentators like Stout (2000) and Twenge and Campbell (2009) offer detailed accounts of the numerous ways in which entitlement of this sort might and often does unfold into invidious, narcissistic excess marked by the erosion of cooperation and basic civility. In education, such excess commonly takes the form of students challenging the legitimate exercise of teacher authority, issuing unreasonable demands for special treatment, and finding it almost impossible to accept let alone benefit from well-intentioned but critical feedback. At the community and social levels, many commentators report experiencing not only declines in general civility and respect for others but seeming escalation in disruptions and difficulties occasioned by individuals acting aggressively in pursuit of their own self-interest without concern for the common good.

Nonetheless, it should also be clear that such undesirable, even dire consequences are not necessarily and always associated with individual or group expressivity and enterprise. Although the expressive, enterprising person may act in ways that are clearly antisocial, the logic of a self attuned to its inner experience and strategizing is more amoral than immoral. Furthermore, as a number of historians of psychology have pointed out, when such ways of being persons are harnessed to cooperative causes, such as the American civil rights and feminist movements (see, for example, Herman, 1995), skills and the abilities of expressive interactivity, planning, and strategic enactment have proven invaluable in achieving major social gains in the status of minorities. As we shall argue in the next chapter, there is considerable potential for collective good resident in certain attributes of the "triple E" self, but for such potential to be unleashed, these abilities must be disentangled from the psychological individualism, interiorism, and reductionism within which they are currently entwined. Moreover, the mostly unintentional forms of manipulation that pervade many educational strategies and efforts to develop students as persons committed to both their self-development and the common good must be replaced or made transparent to all concerned. In particular, it must be recognized that, as William Damon (1995) put it, it is not possible to pursue any kind of self-development or self-esteem worthy of the name "in isolation from one's relations to others, because it does not exist apart from those relations" (p. 80). Therefore, the approach we will take emphasizes the necessarily communal constitution of selfhood/personhood and reconstructs the idea of human agency (understood as the ability to act intentionally and purposefully to achieve particular ends) in more communal, less individualistic ways.

9 There Is Another Way

EDUCATING COMMUNAL AGENTS

IN THIS FINAL chapter, we take up the challenge articulated at the end of the last chapter with respect to proposing a conception of students that moves away from the "triple-E" ideal of twentieth-century educational psychology and toward the alternative ideal of students as communal agents. Our conception of communal agency is grounded in an alternative form of social and psychological theorizing that has its roots in the historically and culturally informed social and developmental theorizing of the American pragmatist George Herbert Mead. Of critical importance to any viable conception of communal agency is an understanding of the ways in which psychological aspects of personhood can emerge only within historically established cultural traditions and social practices. It is our interactivity with others within such traditions and practices that enables and constrains our experiences and actions as psychological beings. Rather than seeing us as psychological beings first who are then being socialized to conform with societal conventions and rules, Mead (1932, 1934, 1938) emphasizes the primacy of interactions and coordinations within cultural traditions or ways of living that encompass a vast array of social practices, routines, conventions, and regulations.

What we believe mainstream educational psychology got fundamentally wrong was to conceptualize our selves (our psychological being) as isolated from and prior to our coordinated sociality within communities of others. When this error is corrected, it is clear that our selfhood and agency (now understood as important sociopsychological aspects of our personhood) are evolutionary and developmental accomplishments that have emerged over the course of our history as a species and develop as we mature over our individual lives. We are first social and then psychological, and our psychological personhood arises only within our coordinated interactivity with others.

An important advantage to such an understanding of personhood as historically, culturally, and socially constituted (i.e., made up through our interactivities with others across time and contexts) is that it does not deny that we come to experience ourselves and to function as psychological beings. Consequently, it is possible to retain much of value that inheres in a more social interpretation of the influential work of educational psychologists. For example, it is not necessary to deny the existence, even the importance, of our psychological selfhood and agency so long as these are not understood as interior, entirely individual entities to which our personhood can be reduced. By retaining the actuality of our psychological experience as socially interactive individuals who develop first-person perspectives and understandings of the world, others, and our selves, the conception of communal agency we endorse continues to speak to many of the legitimate concerns, interests, and rights of students as individuals but without the problems of individualism, psychologism (interiorism), reductionism, and manipulation summarized in the previous chapter. By emphasizing the necessarily historical, cultural, and social embeddedness of our psychological lives, our approach to communal agency replaces self-absorption and self-interest with personal and social goals and ideals that include the social virtue of collective flourishing as a primary life goal.

Our plan for this chapter is to begin with a very brief account of the widespread backlash to the education of selves that began toward the end of the twentieth century and has continued since then. In doing so, we will mention the dissatisfaction with the individualism and decontextualized nature of most psychological conceptions of selfhood and agency as expressed by a few educational psychologists critical of their own field. However, we do this in full recognition of the fact that the work of most educational psychologists in areas such as self-esteem, self-concept, self-efficacy, and self-regulated learning continues to celebrate mostly individual ends and continues to exert a powerfully pervasive influence on contemporary education and student life. In large part, such persistence is a consequence of a failure to recognize how deeply ideals of autonomous, independent, interior, and natural selfhood are embedded within our twenty-first-century worldview. At the same time that many of us bemoan the seemingly narcissistic selfishness and indulgence that surrounds us, we demand our rights, recognitions, and entitlements as sovereign individuals. In our opinion, a conception of communal agency that is thoroughly embedded within the necessity of our social relations with others as sources of our agentic capabilities and recognizes it fully can help to resolve unnecessarily strong oppositions between our individual and collective interests and commitments. If we can educate so as to help and encourage students to understand themselves as tied to their communities and others in ways that are indispensible to both their own development and that of their communities, we will have come a long way toward the goal of a sustainable future for our societies and our children.

After considering various alternative conceptualizations of more communal forms of agency, we adopt and describe a form of communal agency that derives from the theoretical social psychology of George Herbert Mead (1932, 1934, 1938). We then go on to detail educational implications, orientations, and practices associated with Mead's perspective and our interpretation, elaboration, and extension of it. Finally, we revisit our critical history of educational psychology with respect to the education of selves as unfolded in the preceding chapters, reminding readers of the purposes, themes, and methods we have employed in this book and inviting their continued participation in discussions concerning aims and methods of education with respect to student development and social progress. In particular, we invite further consideration and discussion of the role of disciplinary, scientific, and professional psychology in our schools.

The Backlash

As noted toward the end of the previous chapter, the end of the twentieth century witnessed growing concerns about the social consequences of our culture of self-esteem and self-interest, with particular concern directed at the educational systems and schools of the United States and Canada. Fueled by the writings of Stout (2000), Twenge (2006; Twenge & Campbell, 2009), and others, many educators and members of the public worried that an overly strong emphasis on student self-esteem was inflating grades, negatively affecting student conduct, and contributing to school failure. To many, it seemed as if narcissism was on the rise in our schools, and its consequences were being felt in all corners of modern life, including degradations in civic, vocational, political, and economic life that seemed attributable to self-interest running amuck. Unnecessary material consumption, celebrity mania, and environmental decay were all linked to the unfettering of self-esteem and self-absorption. A review in the *New York Times* following the publication of Twenge and Campbell's 2009 volume summarized such concerns.

> The evidence Twenge and Campbell have compiled is compelling and appalling.... [They] marshal statistics, polls, charts, studies and anecdotes to assemble a complete picture of the epidemic's current state of contagion, brought on by the Internet, reality television, a booming economy, easy credit and other developments over the past decade. The authors dismantle the prevailing myths that have made us inclined to tolerate and even encourage narcissism: that it's a function of high self-esteem, that it's a function of low self-esteem, that a little narcissism is healthy, that narcissists are in fact superior, and that you have to love yourself to be able to love someone else. (Brubach, 2009)

Other reviews, like one in *Booklist* (Bush, 2009), were even more damning, referring to the self focus in education and society in general as a "scourge that has affected us all, witness Wall Street greed and the mortgage crisis with its overblown sense of materialism

and entitlement.... The nation needs to recognize the epidemic and its negative consequences, and take corrective action (p. 6)."

Interestingly, very few public commentators pointed to what we regard as the important role played by psychological tests, research, and interventions in the elevation of
self-esteem, self-concept, self-efficacy, and self-regulation as laudable educational and
social goals in and of themselves. Given this general gap in the public web of blame, it is
especially important to note, as we did in Chapter 3 and will elaborate here, the concerns
of a few prominent educational psychologists about these same matters. During the final
two decades of the twentieth century, several educational psychologists began to express
dissatisfaction with what they had begun to regard as overly individualistic, decontextualized, and instrumental conceptions of selfhood that had become enshrined in programmatic research in areas such as self-concept, self-esteem, self-efficacy, and self-regulation.
As Salomon (1995, p. 106) put it, "Our main...focus needs to change from the study of
isolated and decontextualized individuals, processes, states of mind, or interventions to
their study within wider psychological, disciplinary, social, and cultural contexts." To this
end, some educational psychologists have employed the ideas of scholars like Vygotsky
(John-Steiner & Mahn, 1996; Tappan, 1998) and Dewey (Bredo, 1994; Prawat, 1995) to
advance conceptions of selfhood and self-understanding that are more socially and dia-
logically constructed through interaction with others, both within and outside of classrooms. Others have distributed and situated psychological processes within and across
classroom interactions, materials, and media (e.g., Brown, Collins, & Duguid, 1989). Still
others have developed conceptions of collective agency that understand the constructive
powers of classroom and other groups as more than the sum of the individual psyches
included within them (e.g., Martin, 2006a).

There also are encouraging signs in some of the literature in educational psychology
(that which has emerged during the first decade of the twenty-first century) that less
individualistic and mentalistic conceptions of selfhood and agency are being endorsed
and pursued by a still small but obviously growing number of educational psychologists
working in areas such as learning, development, and motivation. For example, Walker,
Pressick-Kilborn, Sainsbury, & MacCallum (2010) now actively advocate a more sociocultural, communal approach to motivational research, in areas like the regulation of learning, that focuses on the co-construction of classroom practices conducive to cooperative
interactivity and the achievement of both individual and group goals. (See also recent
works by Arnold & Walker, 2008, Hidi & Renninger, 2006, and McCaslin, 2009.)

Theorizing a More Communal Agent

Common to many of these attempts to reconstitute the work of educational psychologists in a more sociocultural direction is the idea of a communal agent, a socially formed
yet self-interpreting and self-regulating partial author of his or her own choices and
actions. Alternative conceptions of the self as historically and socioculturally situated are

currently available from a variety of contemporary sociocultural theories. These include but are not limited to Vygotskian (Cole, 1996; Wertsch, 1998) and hermeneutic (Martin, Sugarman, & Thompson, 2003; Richardson, Fowers, & Guignon, 1999) conceptions of selfhood that tie the self to collective life with others. Such sociocultural and historical conceptions of the self place it in a very different light from that reflected in the mainstream research of psychologists as considered in the previous chapters. In such alternative formulations, the individualistic, autonomous, instrumental self is eschewed in favor of a socioculturally situated and constituted self, meaningfully connected to its community yet capable of modestly contributing to transformations in sociocultural practices and traditions and the creation of alternative possibilities for living with others.

A reconsideration of persons as historically and socioculturally situated yet capable of new possibilities eases the tensions between the autonomous, self-governing individual and the socially dependent, committed citizen. For example, Fairfield (2000) presents a hermeneutic-pragmatic philosophy that defends liberalism but eschews the classic liberal view of the self as ontologically prior to the culture and social life in which it exists. Amy Gutmann (1990) compares the implications of elevating individual freedom over civic virtue (liberalism) versus civic virtue over individual freedom (communitarianism) in the education of children. She contends that democratic education prepares citizens to contribute as equals to mindfully reproduce (not replicate) their society and examines the ways in which democratic education maintains a creative and productive tension between civic virtue and individual freedom. For Gutmann (1990), democratic education and educational practices require the interpretation and application of standards of nonrepression (repression is defined as the restriction of rational inquiry) and nondiscrimination (discrimination is defined as the exclusion of children from educational goods for reasons not related to legitimate social purposes of such goods). On this view, individual rights are dependent on their ends (with respect to the flourishing of communities of equal and engaged persons) and do not trump that of which they are in aid.

Martin and Sugarman (1999) posit a self that is a kind of understanding constituted by biological, historical, and sociocultural forces but underdetermined by those forces. On their view, we are born with biological capabilities and a limited prereflective agency from which psychological development proceeds. In the general manner envisioned by Vygotsky (1978, 1986), conversations, interactions, and other sociocultural practices and relations are appropriated, internalized, and transformed into psychological tools for thinking and understanding. Thus, individuals learn to talk and relate to themselves in the same manner that others talk and relate to them. Immersion and participation in sociocultural conventions and practices constrain the ways in which persons can talk and relate to one another. These constraints are linguistic, epistemic, moral, and ethical. At the same time, these practices allow for the development of a reflexive awareness of oneself as both subject and object in ways that enable individuals' self-generated interpretations to contribute to their subsequent thoughts and actions.

The various symbolic and relational tools that individuals accumulate through their appropriation of sociocultural practices and conventions enable and constrain the personal theories individuals construct and hold about their experiences, themselves, and others....In developing our theories about ourselves, we identify with certain socially supported conceptions of personhood, and are drawn to act in some ways more so than others....Thus, socially countenanced theories of what it is to be a person act to constrain the shape our personal interpretations, values, and beliefs can take....Nonetheless, the substantive content and constellation of interpretations, values, and beliefs held by an individual, form something with a unique construction. Because of this underdetermination of personal theories by their sociocultural origins, there is a great deal of latitude in the way each individual uses a theory of self, or ideal of personhood, to reference a unique experiential history and reflect on past, present, and future intentions, expectations, and actions. (Martin & Sugarman, 1999, p. 22)

On this view, persons are embedded within their social surroundings. Decisions, actions, and thoughts are directed not merely toward instrumental gratification of individual needs and desires but rather are meaningfully related to particular others, families, communities, and society at large. "It would be dysfunctional for an individual to develop beliefs about things like truth, beauty, honesty, responsibility, and rights, that bore no resemblance to extant forms and practices for such social, cultural, and moral phenomena in his/her society" (Martin & Sugarman, 1999, p. 116). Our self-understanding is socioculturally generated, yet capable of a socially constrained agency conducive to a kind of personhood capable of fostering joint commitments to common, not just individual, goals and goods.

Disciplinary psychology, through its discourse and practices, has become infused in the contemporary lives of Western individuals in search of their selves. Today, changes to psychological discourses and practices can be expected to stimulate changes in our broader conceptions of ourselves as persons and citizens. But this does not need to be an undesirable state of affairs. The current state that leans toward self-esteem, personal growth, and personal happiness as isolated forms of self-improvement can also form the basis of community and collective action (Herman, 1995). Rose (1998) encourages us to imagine an ethics that is collective and does not look to celebrate or govern the self. Although our liberal ideals celebrate an individualistic, autonomous self, they can also celebrate dependency, mutuality, collective action, and commitment to others, and it is important that psychology and education have something to say about the latter as well as the former.

Consequently, it is understandable that some hermeneutically oriented psychologists (e.g., Fowers, 2005) have found inspiration in the ancient works of Aristotle, especially in his virtue ethics as set forth in *The Nicomachean Ethics* (Aristotle, 1962) and in his *Politics* (Aristotle, 1996). Aristotle warned against an excessive concern with individual goods and self-interest—"it is not good that each one of the citizens should consider himself to be his own: all should believe themselves to belong to the city—for each one is part of the city" (1996, 1337a, pp. 27–29). Aristotle recognized that the systems and ideals of democracy, justice, and law that are necessary to ensure individual rights and freedoms are shared goods. Individual rights and freedom are not available in the individual but in publicly endorsed practices and sociopolitical structures. These act as necessary frameworks that are constantly realized and refined through communal action. Such shared goods and activities supersede individual goals because they serve to constitute and support individual rights and freedoms. The best form of life is one in which these constitutive shared goods are richly interwoven in sociopolitical life and in an education that aims to produce citizens capable of participating within, contributing to, and constantly transforming for the better such communal goods and collective means of achieving or striving toward them.

That some educational psychologists have turned to the social cognitive theorizing of past thinkers like Lev Vygotsky and John Dewey in their search for ideas concerning the education of communal agents steeped in but not fettered by communal goods is entirely understandable. In different ways, these influential scholars have emphasized the dynamic interplay between psychological individuals and their social contexts as the basis for personal and educational development and learning. Nonetheless, none of these individuals has focused as directly and consistently on communal agency as did George Herbert Mead, a close colleague of Dewey's at the University of Chicago, whose theories of social and educational development have been relatively neglected by psychologists in general and by educational psychologists in particular.

Mead's (1932, 1934, 1938) approach to communal agency is unique in that it is situated within a much more precisely elaborated social psychology than can be found in Dewey's work. Moreover, this is a social psychology in which a co-constructive, reciprocal interrelation between selves and their societies opens to a democratic pluralism unavailable to Vygotsky's cultural historical theorizing. Finally, as we will document, Mead's perspectivism affords a heretofore little explored set of possibilities for integrative theorizing across personal, interpersonal, social, and cultural levels of human experience.

In recent years, Mead's ideas concerning the development of agency and selfhood within sociality have begun to command renewed interest in social and developmental psychology (e.g., Gillespie, 2005; Hobson, 2002; Martin, Sokol, & Elfers, 2008). One potentially valuable line of reinterpretation and reconsideration concerns an attempt to understand Mead's writings on the sociopsychological and educational development of selfhood and agency in terms of the philosophy of perspectival realism that he developed in the last 10 years of his life—a framing and interpretation of his work that has not previously received a great deal of attention in the social sciences, even in sociology, where Mead's status as a symbolic interactionist has been well established through the efforts of Blumer (1969) and others.

A Neo-Meadian Alternative

The Perspectival Realism of George Herbert Mead Related to Education

In an address to the Educational Section of the American Association for the Advancement of Science in 1909, Mead proclaimed that education could not be studied successfully

> by a scientific psychology unless that psychology is social—[that is] unless it recognizes that the processes of acquiring knowledge, of giving attention, of evaluating…must be studied in their relation to selves in a social consciousness. The child does not become social by learning, he must be social to learn. (Mead, 1964, p. 122)

He also said that "It is impossible to fully interpret or control the process of instruction without recognizing the child as a self, and viewing his conscious processes from the point of view of their relation to his consciousness to his self, among other selves" (Mead, 1964, pp. 116–117).

Mead regarded education as a process that began with students' own perspectives as lodged in their life experiences. "To find out whether the idea is an appropriate one for education, you must find out whether it is a part of the child's own world. Therefore we must know the child's world" (Mead, 1910/11, p. 187). For Mead, the terms *self* and *the child's own world* do not connote psychological entities internal to individuals but refer to understandings of and action orientations to the child and the context of his or her life that derive from the child's interactions with others. Through formal education, students' experiences, perspectives, and understandings are supplemented, coordinated, and expanded through the taking up of other perspectives made available within problem-solving activities with others. The primary task of the teacher is continuously to confront children with problems and problem-solving situations that are intelligible and approachable from within their existing perspectives and experience but in which children's social problem-solving activity results in their occupation and coordination of a broader range of social and disciplinary perspectives. In this way, over time, students' perspectives ideally are expanded and organized so as to approximate something of the society's and culture's historically established knowledge and understanding of whatever topics and courses of study are pursued.

Mead believed that the best method with which to approach problems of any kind was a general method of developing, testing, refining, and combining functionally efficacious perspectives through social interactions. He understood this as a method that adhered broadly both to the scientific method and to the practices of a democratic society. Consequently, the teacher should not only select appropriate problems for learners of different levels of social, emotional, and intellectual development but also help students to attend to, consider, experiment with, and coordinate the variety of perspectives that are stimulated by these problems and problem-solving activities.

The foregoing thumbnail sketch of Mead's general educational theory has been articulated using language and ideas taken from the philosophy of perspectival realism that Mead developed in the last decade of his life. During this period of time, Mead began to use the phrase, "being in the perspective of the other" interchangeably with "taking the role or attitude of the other." For Mead, perspectives are to be understood as holistic (perceptual, conceptual, emotional, esthetic, and physical) orientations to situations with a view to acting within them. Perspectives arise through human activity in the biophysical and sociocultural world. "The perspective is the world in its relationship to the individual and the individual in his relationship to the world" (Mead, 1938, p. 115). In effect, human reality is a perspectival reality. It is made up of the sum total of perspectives that have arisen within the historical, worldly activity of members of the human species.

It is important to emphasize that for Mead, perspectives may be assessed in terms of their functional utility in rendering situations intelligible and problems manageable. In other words, perspectives vary in their usefulness for particular purposes. When, through ongoing human activity in the world, certain perspectives (action orientations) emerge that prove to be especially effective in confronting and ameliorating commonly experienced difficulties and achieving frequently pursued aims, they may be "objectified" into conventionalized sociocultural practices. Because such practices both enable and constrain the actions of individuals and collectives, they and the perspectives they maintain may be considered real and influential. Such practices typically become part of sociocultural traditions that are transmitted from one generation to the next. As such, they become constitutive of the kinds of persons we are and the kinds of societies we are immersed in. From a phylogenetic point of view, such cultural practices and traditions are interactive with our biophysically evolved bodies and brains in complex ways that make us hybrids of our culture and our biology. From an ontogenetic point of view, it is our interaction with others (initially caregivers, and later peers, teachers, and others) within these practices and traditions that allows us to develop as self-conscious persons and agents. Perspectives that have withstood tests of time and function thus make up much of our sociocultural world. Moreover, our activity within this world may be described in terms of our participation within the complex matrix of first-person (self), second-person (others), and third-person (sociocultural) perspectives in which we constantly are caught up as we interact with others within the practices and institutional arrangements of the broader society and historically established culture.

Since the human world is a social world, most perspectives are located and develop within our interpersonal interactions with others, nested within broader sociocultural practices. However, once perspectives have been experienced within particular sequences of interactivity, they need not remain fixed to a particular situation. When recalled in other times and settings, specific perspectives may be used imaginatively, merged with currently experienced perspectives, and employed as a basis for increasingly complex, differentiated, and abstracted forms of thought and action. Nonetheless, all perspectives have their origins in our social interactivity with others. They arise and are maintained within social, collective acts involving two or more individuals, and they focus on social, collective objects (including persons, events, and ideas, as well as physical things) whose meanings are shared by the participating individuals. Such social objects are what they are because they are embedded within the matrix of social acts that makes up the life of a society. For Mead, communication and meaning require the conventional, shared use of significant symbols (i.e., language) that require the taking of perspectives.

Significant symbols require more than the sharing of singular perspectives as manifest in the evocation of the same reaction (meaning) in different individuals. As Gillespie (2005) has argued, language as a collection of significant symbols functions because it rests on simultaneously experienced dual perspectives. "It is through the ability to be the other [be in the perspective of the other] at the same time that he is himself [in his own perspective] that the symbol becomes significant" (Mead, 1964, p. 244). Consequently, when it is interpreted within Mead's later perspectival realism, the vital importance of the significant symbol is that its use positions an individual simultaneously within two or more perspectives. Indeed it is this ability to occupy multiple perspectives that is basic to Mead's social, developmental, and educational thought as it concerns the ontogenetic emergence and education of selves as communal agents.

The Development of Agency Within Sociality

Mead's theory of self-development and agency is unequivocally developmental. During ontogenesis, self-consciousness and reflective forms of agency emerge from the inter-activity of infants and young children within conventional social practices and acts in which they occupy, exchange, and eventually come to differentiate and coordinate different positions and perspectives. "The self is something which has a development; it is not there, at birth, but arises in the process of social experience and activity, that is, develops in the given individual as a result of his relations to that process as a whole and to other individuals within that process" (Mead, 1934, p. 135). Of critical importance to selfhood and agentic self-determination is the reflexivity of the self. It is this self-reflexivity that distinguishes adult human contextual activity from more basic forms of environmental sensitivity and reactivity exhibited by other animals and human infants. For Mead, self-reflexivity only can arise through interacting with others within ongoing social processes and practices. Prereflective consciousness relates to a world that is there, but *reflective consciousness* or *reflexivity* refers to the world as it is experienced by a self that is capable of being both a subject and an object to itself.[1] Self-reflexivity is perspectival.

---

[1] A prereflective infant or young child is conscious of activities and experiences, but does not think about them outside of the immediate contexts in which they occur. An older, reflective (or reflexive) child, adolescent, or adult is able to think about activities and experiences removed from immediate contexts. Self-reflection or self-reflexivity refers to thinking about oneself (i.e., the person that one is) in ways that are abstracted from particular situations. Obviously the developmental shift from prereflection to reflection is gradual, with considerable overlap, and is never complete. Even when reflection and self-reflection are attained, one continues to operate in both nonreflective and reflective ways. None of us can be reflective or self-reflective about all aspects of our lives.

According to Mead, it arises through a process of taking the attitudes or perspectives of others toward oneself. During ontogenesis, the human infant becomes "an object to himself by taking the attitudes of other individuals toward himself within an organized setting of social relationships" (Mead, 1934, p. 255).

For Mead, two important, closely related processes of perspective taking are indispensable to the developmental emergence of selfhood, self-understanding, and agency. One of these is the simultaneous occupation of one's own and another's perspective. The other concerns reacting to the multiple perspectives that one is in. Early in human development, perspective taking is exceedingly rudimentary and occurs in the form of performing particular functions within conventional sequences of action. For example, a young infant, initially with the help of a caregiver, may repetitively push a ball toward the caregiver, who returns it to the child. Through repetition of such routine sequences of interactivity, infants gradually comprehend and anticipate the meanings of the various constitutive social gestures and differentiate the others and objects involved.

Gillespie (2005) elaborates the close relationship between social activity and perspective taking in Mead's thought.

> A social act refers to a social interaction that has become an institution, with established positions (i.e., buyer/seller, teacher/student, parent/child, boss/subordinate) that are stable over time. The introduction of both time and social structure is a breakthrough. Although the perspectives of self and other within any ongoing social act are necessarily divergent, if one takes into account time and a stable social structure, then it is possible that at some previous point in time, the positions of self and other were reversed. Given this, each participant in a social act may, by virtue of previous responses while in the position of the other, already possess the attitude of the other.... It is because self and other are often in the same situations, or social positions and acting toward the same objects, that the child comes to acquire the same attitudes that others have. (pp. 27–28)

As the social interactions of the developing child widen, the child gradually takes on the perspectives of others that have been encountered within the social practices extant in the communities within which she or he exists and participates, eventually taking the perspectives of what Mead calls generalized others (i.e., those standard orientations to situations that are endorsed by most members of a community and enshrined in social rules and regulations). In other words, through interactions with others within routine sequences of conventionalized interactivity, the child is able, actually and/or imaginatively, to occupy an increasingly diverse array of perspectives that have been experienced directly and vicariously. Moreover, as hinted earlier, with the acquisition of language as a system of significant symbols capable of coordinating the perspectives of language users, opportunities for the communication and simultaneous engagement of multiple perspectives grow by leaps and bounds. For example, as Gillespie (2006) points out, in many contemporary cultures, there is a clear longitudinal developmental sequence that connects the game of hide-and-seek to obvious precursors such as "peek-a-boo," and successors, such as treasure hunts and more abstracted narratives that revolve around hiding/ seeking and escaping/chasing (e.g., as evident in many cinematic and real-life dramas). At more advanced levels, actual position exchange and occupation give way to vicariously engaged processes of narrative and personal imagination that serve to elaborate and coordinate the various perspectives involved. Opportunities for increasingly sophisticated forms of perspective taking abound across developmental trajectories that typify a wide variety of human interactivity, yielding opportunities for the development of sophisticated and nuanced forms of self-understanding and self-reflexivity.

Simultaneous occupation of two or more perspectives (as enabled by actual position exchange, recollection, and imagination) allows the child to become both subject and object in her or his experience. What this means is that children are able self-consciously to take first-person (personal, experiential) perspectives on those second-person perspectives (of particular others with whom one has interacted) and third-person perspectives (of the broader society) that they have experienced socially and have applied to themselves in a way that constitutes their self-understanding. Mead's self thus has two distinctive aspects: (1) a "Me" that is constituted by the perspectives of others based on past experience, and (2) an "I" that reacts to the "Me" and the immediately present context. It is the reactivity of the "I" to the "Me" that constitutes the particular form of self-reflexivity that for Mead constitutes human agency.

The distinction between the "I" and the "Me" combines both temporal and social features of self-development and agentic capability. The "Me" is an objective self that contains perspectives and possibilities for social interaction that have been extracted from a past history of social interactivity. The "I" is the self as subject that reacts to the "Me" in the immediate moment of experience. In doing so, the "I" reconstructs the "Me" of the next moment to which the "I" of the next moment will react. Thus, for Mead, "the immediate moment of action brings together a concern of the present with both recollections of relevant past activity and anticipations of a future in which the concern or problem to which the action of the present is directed is resolved or somehow made manageable" (Martin, 2006b, p. 71). Median selves emerge through processes of perspective occupation, exchange, simultaneity, and coordination that create an ongoing, dynamic interplay between objective "Me's" and subjective "I's" within constantly unfolding social contexts.

Unlike many contemporary cognitive developmental accounts of perspective taking, Mead does not give perspective taking a mentalistic interpretation. For Mead, perspectives are relational, not mental entities. One is in and part of perspectives by virtue of one's interactivity with others within historically established sociocultural practices and traditions. The agency exercised by a self-conscious person is a reaction of a self-interpreting being to those perspectives she encounters through her immersion in such practices and traditions. "In short, agency is a reaction to the situation in which one finds one's self, and that situation always is a social situation. For Mead, both selfhood and agency arise developmentally through perspective taking (positional exchange, simultaneity, and coordination) within social acts" (Martin, 2006b, p. 72).

To explain the novelty and creativity he associated with agency without in any way denying its social origins, Mead (1932) emphasizes the emergent uniqueness occasioned by interactions among various spatial temporal perspectives. In the immediate present, the agent brings together the perspectives of a reconstructed past, based on the recollection of relevant past experiences, with the perspective of an anticipated future that is based not only on such recollection but also on a consideration of action possibilities afforded within the immediate present. The agent's simultaneous occupation of, and reaction to, these different spatiotemporal perspectives is a source of creative activity that goes beyond the past, and opens to an imagined unfolding future. In such moments, the agent's actions are simultaneously conditioned and free, depending on the particular spatial temporal perspective adopted. By holding and reacting to these different spatiotemporal perspectives simultaneously, the agent is both determined and determining.

When set within debates among and concerning various contemporary poststructural, critical, and postmodern discussions of agency, Mead's approach may be understood to offer an account of agency that is remarkably free of assumptions concerning preexisting, essential entities and foundational certainties. In what Butler (1997) refers to as a postliberatory era, Mead's theory of agency recognizes the sociorelational constitution of agentic selves while resisting the conclusion that all such theorizing is unavoidably linked to maintaining existing practices of domination and marginalization. This is not to say that Mead's approach is neutral and does not carry the stamp of his time and interests. Rather, it is to claim that the perspectivism that Mead embraces provides a uniquely open template for a pluralistic approach to persons, circumstances, and ideologies. That such an approach was used by Mead (1934) himself to support a liberal democratic worldview that celebrates tolerance of and engagement across differences is undeniable. Nonetheless, in principle, Mead's social developmental theory of agency offers a thoroughgoing social ontology of selfhood and reactive, creative agency subject to pragmatic fashioning within a wide variety of social, economic, moral, and political ways of life. Mead's self is a communal agent by virtue of its social constitution, multiple perspectivity, reactivity, and creativity. The educational implications that flow from such a strongly relational, socially constituted, and continually emergent conception of perspectival selfhood and agency are both theoretically informative and practically suggestive.

The Education of Communal Agents

In recent years, some educational psychologists have drawn on the works of Vygotsky, Dewey, and others in an effort to develop conceptions of selfhood that might promote the personal development of students without sacrificing their sociocultural development as productive and engaged members of their societies and communities. As mentioned at the outset of this chapter, the general attempt in such initiatives has been to balance or even to replace conceptions of selves and agents as isolated, decontextualized individuals pursuing self-serving instrumental ends with conceptions of selves and agents as sociocultually embedded, active, and committed. Nonetheless, to date the kinds of communal selves and agents proposed in the recent writings of educational psychologists stop well short of the more thoroughly collective conceptions of agency and selfhood found in some branches of contemporary educational philosophy, sociology, and policy studies (see Schutz, 2000). To recognize this state of affairs is not to advocate strong forms of social determinism that would reduce human agency to social structures and processes. As mentioned previously, any viable psychological approach to education must support human change and innovation at both collective and individual levels.

It is within this context of striving to balance agency with effective communal inter-activity with others, and to direct it toward this end, that Mead's perspectival theorizing concerning selves and agents has been sketched. A perspectival reading of Mead's theory of the sociopsychological development of agentic selfhood is replete with implications for the education of communal agents. Mead's conception of agency unfolds and is conditioned within sociality yet is not fully determined by social processes and structures. Mead's reflexive self emerges through interactivity with others within historically established social and cultural practices. However, its reactivity to the socially situated and acquired perspectives that constitute it at any given moment enables an irreducible self-determination capable of going beyond those perspectives.

Particular educational significance attaches to the idea that the agentic potential of the Meadian self is enhanced through participation within an increasingly complex and coordinated matrix of cultural, social, and psychological perspectives (see Martin & Gillespie, 2010). This being so, the task of education with respect to the promotion of communal agents may be understood as the purposeful cultivation and coordination of cultural, societal, interpersonal, and personal perspectives within educational settings that realistically represent actual contexts of communal problem solving, deliberation, and engagement. Indeed, for Mead it is the provision of such ongoing, graduated educational experiences that is required to prepare students for their roles as democratic citizens and responsible persons. This is an educational sequence, as it was for Dewey (see Chapter 4), that begins with the students' immediate situations and perspectives and moves gradually and progressively to enlarge and place them within the broader social context of human sociocultural perspectives, understandings, and accomplishments.

To fully appreciate the kind of educational development envisioned by Mead, it is helpful to consider briefly the dynamic relationship he believed to hold between fully functioning members of a society and the society itself. As has been seen, at the heart of Mead's social psychology is activity with others in a biophysical and sociocultural world. We come to understand ourselves and others by taking perspectives that are embedded in the world in ways that go well beyond individual subjective views and judgments. It is through acting with others that such perspectives come to constitute us as understanding and agentic selves. The development of selves and societies is possible only through the ongoing dynamic exchange and emergence of perspectives at social, interpersonal, and personal levels of reality. There is no personal development outside of social development, and the development of a society always coincides with the self-development of its members. Perspectives and their exchange do not come about by abstract imaginings of others' experiences, minds, or worlds that result from adopting particular sorts of introspective or empathic strategies, nor do we come biologically pre-equipped with selves inclined to such strategic imaginings. Rather, it is primarily through our worldly activity with others that we come to know ourselves, others, and our world at all. We are caught up in action before we come to understand and reflect. Recognition of this basic fact of human existence has significant moral, political, and pedagogical implications.

For Mead, the moral worth of a society can be judged in terms of the degree to which members and institutions in the society are able to adopt multiple perspectives. This, in turn, may be determined by the extent to which they are able to engage in problem solving and perspective taking in ways that are communicatively open and reflect a genuine concern for the well-being of others. The highest level of political organization is reached when the suffering of others ceases to be regarded as an object for love or help but as the occasion for achieving a political remedy for that suffering. To Mead (1915), this is the heart of democracy. A democratic society fosters the social conditions that enable the greatest possible degrees of participation and expression by all members of the society. None of this assumes a social harmony of interests but instead insists on the importance of democratic-experimental methods of collective problem solving supported by communicative capabilities that permit the free and open exchange of perspectives. There is no guarantee of progress beyond the achievement and maintenance of this highly valued engagement and exchange with others.

So what, then, is the role of education with respect to the development of effective, responsible communal agents capable of entering into significant and necessary public debate with others? This question might best be approached through a consideration of three pillars of Mead's educational philosophy and psychology: (1) the social nature of education, (2) the educational situation as related to the student's experience and development, and (3) the teacher as mediator between the student's developmental process and the broader social process.

The Social Nature of Education

Not surprisingly, given Mead's social ontology of selfhood and agency as sketched above, he understands education as vital to the development of individuals within the social process of the society and community. Although the social development of agentic selfhood already has been initiated within the conventional interactions, play, and games of childhood, it is education that is charged with enabling individual students to assume the perspectives of the broader society. By gradually expanding the child's participation in increasingly wider, more encompassing, coordinated, and integrated systems of perspectives, education makes possible forms of selfhood and self-understanding that are embedded within the sociocultural history and current practices, knowledge, and values of the immediate community, the nation, and humanity writ large. It is through education that self-development reaches its most elaborated and full expression. And, because all self-development, according to Mead, carries agentic potential in the form of the reactivity of the self[2] to those perspectives within its orbit, it is through education that persons are able to achieve forms of thought and action capable of transforming the sociocultural practices and perspectives of the larger human community.

In his course at the University of Chicago entitled The Philosophy of Education, Mead articulated "a psychological statement of the act" (Mead, 1910/11, p. 81). In doing so, he lays out a description of the stages through which human thought and action develop within the biophysical and sociocultural environment together with methods that humans have developed to promote conscious intelligence in others. This statement encompasses historical attempts to integrate and promote the development of individuals within their societies. It stands as "an historical account of the methods and materials man has employed to educate, to teach people to think, know, explain, and deal effectively with the objects of their environments" (Renger, 1992, p. 148).

In brief, Mead believed that human cultural history is best understood as the implementation of progressively more sophisticated practices, materials, methods, and institutions for attempting to ensure effective interactions with an ever-changing world. To this end, each sociocultural and scientific advance has been accompanied by related attempts to integrate individual members of society, especially younger members, into the successive patterns and perspectives of analytic, reflective, and critical thought required for effective participation in their changing worldly contexts. "As different explanations of the world arose, different methods of instruction [education] had to be developed and the form in which the objects of man's environment were presented to individual members of society had to change accordingly" (Renger, 1992, p. 149).

Thus, for Mead, historically established cultural and social practices are replete with perspectives that human beings employ to orient themselves to the situations in which they find themselves, with a view to acting effectively within those contexts. And it is the task of education to help individual members of societies to develop forms of agentic selfhood that take up and embody those perspectives that have proven most effective in dealing with the biophysical and sociocultural world. However, education conceived in this way not only enables individuals to function effectively with others within the world but also, in a graduated manner that culminates in more advanced levels of educational accomplishment, provides them with opportunities and means for reacting to extant perspectives with a view to transforming them in ways that are potentially beneficial to their societies. Thus, the communal activities of educated persons contribute to the

---

[2] It is important to remember that Mead uses the term *self* not as a mentalistic entity but to refer to the self-understanding, experience, and action tendencies of a person.

sociocultural, scientific, and esthetic development of societies themselves. In this way, education is a sociocultural process, attached to a set of institutional arrangements and practices, which is charged with the personal development of students as well as their participation in the ongoing development and transformation of their societies and communities. There is no inconsistency or choice between goals of education focused on either personal or societal development. For Mead, both are part of the educational act as embedded within those historical social processes through which societies have emerged and continue to transform themselves. Moreover, it is through the activities of communal agents—who act within and through those perspectival practices and structures that constitute both communities and selves—that such transformation is possible.

Education in Relation to Students' Experience and Development

By the time children enter school they typically have sufficient facility with language that they are able to communicate with each other in ways that help them to coordinate their actions and perspectives to achieve some degree of rudimentary cooperation in problem-solving situations. Enhanced facility with language, achieved through greater educational experience, affords increasingly sophisticated and precise forms of interpersonal coordination and intrapersonal reflection. These, in turn, enable forms of perspective taking that may be more and more abstracted from the immediate concrete experiences of learners. Mead understood reflective thought to arise from attempted resolutions of conflicts among different perspectives with respect to particular situations and problems. Accordingly, Mead's primary educational method consisted of presenting sequences of problems that encouraged students to discuss, apply, and evaluate alternative perspectives to resolve them. To Mead, such careful consideration and testing of a range of perspectival orientations, embedded within problem spaces that were meaningful and interesting to learners, paralleled the general form of the scientific method that he so valued.

For educational purposes, the most productive problem situations are those that are social, grounded in students' life experiences, and congruous with students' levels of social, emotional, and intellectual development. Reflective thought arises out of interactivity with others within conventionalized sequences of social action and develops through the consideration and coordination of alternative perspectives in situations where problems are encountered that disrupt conventions and existing perspectives. Such problems must occur within the life experience of learners so that they are both interesting and meaningful. However, to have educational value, the problems selected and presented must somehow relate the spontaneous activities and perspectives of the learners to those broader sociocultural perspectives associated with appropriate forms and levels of disciplinary and general knowledge relevant to the problem situations employed. Like Dewey, Mead understood education as a process of growth from the child's immediate experience outward to commonly accepted yet always changing perspectives endorsed by communities in general and within specialized areas of human accomplishment such as mathematics, history, and so forth. As students' social, emotional, and intellectual functioning develops, they may be presented with increasingly challenging problems that encourage further development and organization of their perspectives. Over time and at higher levels of education these may begin increasingly to approximate more closely those perspectives associated with expert practice in relevant areas of human accomplishment.

The Teacher as Mediator Between Student Development and Social Process

> Back of all instruction lies the relation of the child to the teacher and about it lie the relations of the child to the other children in the schoolroom and on the playground.... To use Professor Dewey's phrase, instruction should be an interchange of experience in which the child brings his experience to be interpreted by the experience of the parent or teacher. This recognizes that education is interchange of ideas, is conversation—belongs to a universe of discourse. (Mead, 1964, pp. 117–119)

Mead made these statements, together with those cited earlier in this essay, in his address to the Education Section of the American Association for the Advancement of Science in 1909. In that same address he goes on to assert that it is the teacher's job to make "the subject-matter of...instruction the material of personal intercourse between pupils and instructors, and between the children themselves" (p. 119). In particular, through teacher–student and student–student conversations embedded in appropriate problem-solving situations, teachers immerse students in the larger meanings and perspectives of society as a whole—intellectual, social, and moral. No less than intellectual growth, "values and moral standards which guide an individual's conduct must be discovered in the process of living through the 'intelligent' resolution of problematic moral situations" (Renger, 1992, p. 155).

However, once again, Mead is clear that individual development and social/moral development are not exclusive but fully integrated aspects of communal life with others. He therefore advises that exactly the same approach to education that imports a sense of community practices and perspectives will also encourage individuality within those communal orientations. By selecting and arranging social problem-solving contexts that are appropriately educational (i.e., appropriately matched to both students' experience and levels of development and to relevant perspectives of the broader society), the teacher creates opportunities for students to explore alternative perspectives and to react to them in ways that afford much scope for creative and innovative thought and action. The teacher's own contributions to the instructional conversations that occur within these problem contexts can do much to ensure that an appropriate balance is maintained between the exploration of the perspectives of different students and those available in materials and resources that the teacher has selected to mediate between students' perspectives and those housed within relevant disciplinary practices. A modification of an example taken from Davydov (1990) shows how such teacher mediation may help students to position their own views within a history of past and contemporary perspectives extant within areas of activity directly relevant to the problem at hand.

Imagine a group of middle school students given the problem of explaining why any line drawn from the midpoint of any circle to anywhere on the circumference of that circle must be exactly the same length as any other line drawn from the midpoint of the same circle to any other point on the circumference of the same circle. After considerable discussion of students' ideas and consideration of their possible strengths and weaknesses, the teacher tells them a little about the mathematician and philosopher Spinoza and his perspective on circles as figures "described by the rotation of a line with one end free [moving] and the other end fixed" (Davydov, 1990, p. 251). She then places a number of pairs of compasses on a table in the classroom that is also equipped with paper, pencils, and other supplies.

This simple example provides a useful illustration of the pedagogical approach that issues from the reinterpretation, integration, and extension attempted here of Mead's considerable but scattered writings on education. Of critical importance for current purposes is the way in which Mead's thought concerning the social/communal origins and agentic nature of selfhood leads to a particular understanding of educational aims and processes. This is an understanding of education as conversationally abetted problem-solving activity in which the experientially acquired perspectives of a group of learners and the disciplinary perspectives of the broader society are mediated through teacher-selected materials and interventions. It is this pedagogical mediation of perspectives that stimulates students' agentic activity within sequences of teacher-arranged problems. Understood in this way, pedagogy is a social situation and interaction marked by a matrix of coordinated perspectives that links the personal experience of the child to the accomplishments and limits of the larger society and culture.

Some Strengths of a Meadian Approach to the Education of Communal Agents

The social, cultural, experiential, and mediational aspects of Mead's approach to education as interpreted here, through the lenses of his later perspectival realism, obviously share much with accounts of education that have been drawn from the works of John Dewey and Lev Vygotsky. However, unlike the ideas of these others, Mead's thought contains a clear theory of the sociopsychological development of agentic selfhood. This is a self-as-agent that is constituted within and continues to operate through communal interactivity yet which, because of its self-reactivity, always carries the possibility of going beyond conventional social practice and understanding. This is an agency that is at once determined and determining. Moreover, as has been illustrated here, Mead's account of human agency is one that may be linked closely to both educational theory and practice.

Mead thus provides an account of communal agency that is more thoroughly social, more holistic, and more fully theorized than anything available in the work of the other theorists mentioned here (as important and relevant for education as their work has been and continues to be). At the very least, Mead's account is one that should be considered by those educational psychologists who are anxious to remedy what they regard as that discipline's "isolated and decontextualized" approach to the education of persons as communal agents (e.g., Salomon, 1995, p. 106).

The potential of Mead's ideas to transform the conceptions of selfhood extant in much theoretical and empirical literature in educational psychology may be illustrated briefly by considering programs of research on students' self-esteem and self-concept on the one hand and students' self-regulation and self-efficacy on the other. Whatever advances may be linked to research on self-concept and self-esteem, it is clear that much of this work does indeed risk elevating students' self-concern over both concern for and cooperative interaction with others. As mentioned previously, classroom activities that have been directly linked to a concern for students' self-esteem include such obviously self-centered activities as making "advertisements and commercials to sell themselves" (Canfield & Wells, 1994, p. 125) and participating in "realizing your uniqueness" lessons (McDaniel & Bielen, 1990, p. 156). What a Meadian approach makes clear is that self-esteem and self-concept are not educational ends in isolation from engagement with the perspectives of others, societies, and the organized knowledge and methods of different disciplines and domains of knowledge and inquiry. It is only through such engagement that self-development can be meaningfully integrated and constantly coordinated with a communal agency that potentially benefits society and its members.

With respect to another major program of self studies in educational psychology concerned with enhancing students' self-regulation of their own learning, Mead's approach can help to ensure that students' self-regulation is grounded powerfully in disciplinary traditions of knowing without sacrificing agency and innovation. Such an approach helps resolve a key tension in the extant literature on self-regulation concerning how to assist students to acquire by themselves appropriate standards against which to assess their learning progress. In general, by highlighting both interactions with others and with disciplinary materials and resources, Mead's approach contextualizes the agentic person within human communities present and past. In so doing, it helps students to position themselves and their current activities within that complex of historically established sociocultural perspectives that so far has been achieved and to comprehend, adhere to, and potentially (at higher levels of education) critique and reformulate criteria and standards implicit and explicit within those perspectives and associated practices.

One of several promising lines of research suggested by Mead's perspectival approach to communal selfhood and agency as developed here would be to examine shifts in students' perspectival orientations to and actions within problem situations that are representative of the kinds of challenges faced and overcome by more mature learners and advanced practitioners in particular domains. For example, at what ages and under what instructional conditions might students of history begin to consider alternative interpretations of historical facts and to seek additional information to assist them in resolving apparent discrepancies and differences? It is relatively easy to imagine such work contributing to our understanding of the two primary educational trajectories: (1) from immediate to more remote experience and (2) from first- and second-person perspectives of self and immediate others to broader third-person disciplinary and sociocultural perspectives as highlighted in Mead's educational theory.

Mead's conception of the communal agent as a developmental product of the graduated immersion of human biological individuals into the practices and perspectives of their societies and cultures leads to a unique view of education. This is an understanding of education as the promotion of personal growth in a way that is grounded in the immediate experiences and perspectives of learners but which gradually helps learners increasingly to go beyond their own experiences and perspectives. The means of educational advancement are teacher orchestrated, intensively engaged interactions with others and materials/resources from which students can acquire much broader and more organized perspectives on themselves, others, and the world. The words of Philippe Meirieu (2005) are once again relevant—"*À l'école, on apprend à passer progressivement de son point de vue et de ses intérêts personnels à la recherche du bien commun* (p. 72)." ["At school one learns to move progressively from his own point of view and personal interests to search for the common good."] Helping children to take and evaluate different perspectives in cooperation with others within problem situations was, for Mead, the major means of education, one that helped students to develop as both persons and citizens by realizing and extending their agentic personhood and communal agency.

At higher levels of educational development, Mead envisioned a constantly evolving and expanding perspectival repertoire as the mark of an educated person who was truly cosmopolitan and open to the tensions, pluralities, and contested character of human interaction across ways of living that both unite and divide us. Mead's perspectival theorizing offers a powerful model of the ways in which personal and interpersonal experiences and orientations are nested and emergent within, yet reciprocally interactive with, social and cultural levels of human acting and knowing. Mead's unique contribution was to theorize agency within sociality in a nonreductive manner that does not diminish the power of either collective or individual contribution to the human mosaic. As interpreted herein, Mead's educational theory promotes the development of such a communal agency as the primary aim of education.

> To be a person is always ... to be craving an image of what it is to be human.... Our very nature is to be embedded in a project of self-confirmation that is inseparable from a project of supporting and being supported by the development of others whose identities cannot be separated from our own. (Russon, 2003, p. 144)

Educational Psychology and the Education of Persons

More than 100 years have passed since Mead's address to the Education Section of the American Association for the Advancement of Science in Boston in December 1909. Consequently, it may seem odd to some readers that we have chosen to reinterpret Mead's views on selfhood, community, and education as a means of presenting an alternative framing of these subjects and their interrelationships more than 100 years later. Surely there must be more recent educational proposals that could be used to combat the late-twentieth century and continuing current predominance of students' self interests over their social interests and development, an imbalance which we have argued is at least in part the result of the impact of psychological theory, research, and interventions on educational thinking and practice. Perhaps unfortunately, our choice of alternative educational philosophies and approaches that might serve to demonstrate the difference between the education of self-centered and self-interested students and the education of communally oriented students boiled down to a choice of Mead over theorists like Dewey and Vygotsky, most of whom lived and labored in, or much closer to, Mead's time than our own. To us, this state of affairs is further testimony to the extent to which, over the course of the last century, disciplinary psychology has pursued a social science of the individual, with increasingly little regard for understanding necessary constitutive relations between individuals and their societies, relations within which both individuals and societies continuously develop.

As a possible antidote for the individualism, psychological internalism, and reductionist decontextualizing we have examined in the theories, research, and intervention practices of mainstream psychology, Mead's approach to the education of communal agents helps to demonstrate the considerable distance that must now be traversed if psychology is to become a more helpful partner to education, at least with respect to promoting common rather than solely individual goods. In our opinion, there currently is considerable evidence that many psychologists are making transitions to more integrative, coordinated perspectives concerning the interplay between the personal and social development of children and adolescents during the school years. We have been especially heartened in this regard by current trends not only in social, cultural approaches to psychology (see Kirschner & Martin, 2010 for a collection of relevant examples) but also by theories of social interactivity and coordination in developmental social psychology (e.g., Carpendale & Lewis, 2006) as well as in educational psychology (e.g., Packer & Goicoechea, 2000).

Toward the end of Chapter 1, we said that we would

argue that the self-conceptions adopted and promoted by psychologists during the latter half of the twentieth century may be described as broadly scientific and/or humanistic, but that in either case the underlying idea was and remains that of a detached, masterful self that is focused on its own interior experience and its instrumental expression.

We went on to say that in consequence, such "psychological conceptions of selfhood tend to be highly self-serving and focused away from our morally saturated concerns and practices as citizens engaged with others, some of whom might be quite different from ourselves." In the immediately preceding chapter, we discussed the emergence of a new student ideal based on psychological conceptions, theories, and research and intervention practices in schools—that of the expressive, enterprising, and entitled student, inwardly self-focused and outwardly strategically self-interested. Between Chapters 1 and 8, we presented a combination of historical and theoretical discussion of various "self-related" areas of psychologists' research programs in education (self-esteem in Chapter 4, self-concept in Chapter 5, self-efficacy in Chapter 6, self-regulation in Chapter 7) and also relevant historical (Chapters 2 through 7) and twentieth-century sociocultural contexts (Chapters 3 and 6 in particular) as well as the measurement, inquiry, and intervention practices (Chapter 8) of psychologists, all of which have enabled what we have described as the psychologizing of studenthood in the latter part of the twentieth century.

We realize that psychology itself is a set of ideas, strategies, and practices that has emerged and continues to unfold within our broader sociocultural traditions and ways of living. So it would certainly be both misleading and unfair to say that psychology is alone in promoting the self-related understandings and practices we have held up to critical consideration. However, it would be equally inappropriate to neglect the special role that psychology has created and come to occupy as a major (especially in many Western societies like the United States and Canada) repository of accepted expertise and wisdom with respect to individual experience and action, a socially sanctioned expertise that extends well into our everyday consciousness concerning how best to live our lives. Consequently, we think it both reasonable and appropriate to hold psychology and its practitioners to a high standard with respect to bearing considerable responsibility for the ways in which contemporary persons, in and outside of schools, understand and conduct themselves.

However, our primary hope is that in discussing the topic of the probable impact of psychology on the educational experiences and development of students in schools, we will have succeeded in engaging readers in a critical consideration of how disciplinary psychology functions in contemporary liberal democratic societies. Although our topic has been the educational development of students, we would be most gratified if others were to direct their attention to relationships between scientific and professional psychology in this and other areas of our lives. In this critical and constructive spirit, we conclude with a quotation in which Eugene Stelzig comments on the understanding of self-understanding held by the early Romantic writer and polymath Johann Wolfgang von Goethe (1749–1832):

> For Goethe, the goal of self-understanding is not to be pursued or achieved through the passive and protracted introspection of a self withdrawn from its world, which he dismissed as sterile self-absorption, but by exploring the dynamic and dialectical relationship between self and world. His most paradigmatic statement on this issue

comes in a late essay (1823): "I here confess that the great and significant demand, know thyself, has always appeared questionable to me as a ruse of secretly allied priests who wish to confuse humans with unattainable demand and to misdirect us from an active involvement with the outer world to a false inner contemplation. Humans know themselves only insofar as they know their world, of which they only become aware in themselves and of themselves in it." The "world" includes the natural cosmos, which he studied in his scientific investigations...but the "world" includes as well the sphere of human culture....(Stelzig, 2000, p. 128)

References

Adelman, C. (2000). Over two years, what did Froebel say to Pestalozzi? *History of Education*, *29*, 103–114.

Albaili, M. A. (1997). Differences among low-, average-, and high-achieving college students on learning and study strategies. *Educational Psychology*, *17*, 171–177.

Alberta Education (2010). *Transforming Education in Alberta: Inspiring Education Steering Committee Report*. Retrieved August 15, 2010, from http://www.inspiringeducation.alberta.ca/Home/tabid/37/Default.aspx

Allport, G. W. (1937). *Personality: A psychological interpretation*. New York: Holt.

Altermatt, E. R., Pomerantz, E. M., Ruble, D. N., Frey, K. S., & Greulich, F. K. (2002). Predicting changes in children's self-perceptions of academic competence: A naturalistic examination of evaluative discourse among classmates. *Developmental Psychology*, *38*, 903–917.

American Psychological Association (2008). *About APA*. Retrieved July 10, 2008, from http://www.apa.org/about

Ames, C., & Felkner, D. W. (1979). Effects of self-concept on children's causal attributions and self-reinforcement. *Journal of Educational Psychology*, *71*(5), 613–619.

Anderman, L. H., & Anderman, E. M. (Eds.). (2000). Special issue: The role of social context in educational psychology: Substantive and methodological issues. *Educational Psychologist*, *35*, 67–141.

Appiah (2008). *Experiments in Ethics*. Cambridge, MA: Harvard University Press.

Aristotle. (1962). *Nichomachean ethics* (M. Ostwald, Trans.). Indianapolis, IN: Bobbs-Merrill. (Original probably published c. 350 BCE.)

Aristotle. (1996). *The politics and the constitution of Athens* (S. Everson, Trans.). Cambridge, UK: Cambridge University Press. (Original probably published c. 335–322 BCE.)

Arnold, L. S., & Walker, R. A. (2008). Co-constructing classroom environments that improve academic outcomes. In P. Towndrow, C. Koh, & T. H. Soon (Eds.), *Motivation and practice for the classroom* (pp. 165–184). Amsterdam: Sense Publishers.

Ash, M. (2005). The uses and usefulness of psychology. *Annals of the American Academy of Political and Social Science, 600,* 99–114.

Baldwin, J. M. (1897). *Social and ethical interpretations in mental development: A study in social psychology.* New York: Macmillan.

Bandura, A. (1977). Self-efficacy: Toward a unifying theory of behavioral change. *Psychological Review, 84,* 191–215.

Bandura, A. (1978a). Reflections on self-efficacy. *Advances in Behaviour Research and Therapy, 1,* 237–269.

Bandura, A. (1978b). Self-efficacy: Toward a unifying theory of behavioral change. *Advances in Behaviour Research and Therapy, 1,* 139–161.

Bandura, A. (1978c). On distinguishing between logical and empirical verification: A comment on Smedslund. *Scandinavian Journal of Psychology, 19,* 97–99.

Bandura, A. (1978d). The self system in reciprocal determinism. *American Psychologist, 33,* 344–358.

Bandura, A. (1979). Self-referent mechanisms in social learning theory. *American Psychologist, 34,* 439–441.

Bandura, A. (1982). Self-efficacy mechanism in human agency. *American Psychologist, 37,* 122–147.

Bandura, A. (1984). Recycling misconceptions of perceived self-efficacy. *Cognitive Therapy and Research, 8,* 231–255.

Bandura, A. (1986). *Social foundations of thought and action: A social cognitive theory.* Englewood Cliffs, NJ: Prentice Hall.

Bandura, A. (1989). Human agency in social cognitive theory. *American Psychologist, 44,* 1175–1184.

Bandura, A. (1991). Social cognitive theory of moral thought and action. In W. M. Kurtines & J. L. Gewirtz (Eds.), *Handbook of moral behavior and development* (Vol 1, pp. 45–103). Hillsdale, NJ: Lawrence Erlbaum.

Bandura, A. (1993). Perceived self-efficacy in cognitive development and functioning, *Educational Psychologist, 28,* 117–148.

Bandura, A. (Ed.). (1995). *Self-efficacy in changing societies.* New York: Cambridge University Press.

Bandura, A. (1997). *Self-efficacy: The exercise of control.* New York: Freeman.

Bandura, A. (1999). Moral disengagement in the perpetration of inhumanities. *Personality and Social Psychology Review, 3,* 193–209.

Bandura, A. (2004). Selective exercise of moral agency. In T. A. Thorkildsen & H. J. Walberg (Eds.), *Nurturing morality* (pp. 37–57). Boston: Kluwer Academic.

Bandura, A. (2006). Toward a psychology of human agency. *Perspectives on Psychological Science, 1,* 164–180.

Bandura, A., Ross, D., & Ross, S. A. (1961). Transmission of aggression through imitation of aggressive models. *Journal of Abnormal and Social Psychology, 63,* 575–582.

Barrett, P. (2001). *Friends for life kit.* Bowen Hills: QLD: Australian Academic Press. Retrieved July 10, 2008, from http://www.friendsinfo.net/ca.htm

Battle, J. (1976). Test-retest reliability of the Canadian Self-Esteem Inventory for Children. *Psychological Reports, 38*(3), 1343–1345.

Baumeister, R. F. (1986). *Identity: Cultural change and the struggle for self*. New York: Oxford University Press.

Baumeister, R. F. (1987). How the self became a problem: A psychological review of historical research. *Journal of Personality and Social Psychology, 52*, 163–174.

Baumeister, R. F., Campbell, J. D., Krueger, J. I., & Vohs, K. D. (2003). Does high self-esteem cause better performance, interpersonal success, happiness, or healthier lifestyles? *Psychological Science in the Public Interest, 4*, 1–44.

Baumeister, R. F., Smart, L., & Boden, J. M. (1996). Relation of threatened egotism to violence and aggression: The dark side of high self-esteem. *Psychological Review, 103*, 5–33.

Baumeister, R. F., & Vohs, K. D. (Eds.). (2004). *Handbook of self-regulation: Research, theory, and applications*. New York: Guilford.

Belfiore, P. J., & Hornyak, R. S. (1998). Operant theory and application to self-monitoring in adolescents. In D. H. Schunk & B. J. Zimmerman (Eds.), *Self-regulated learning: From teaching to self-reflective practice* (pp. 184–202). New York: Guilford.

Benjamin, L. T. (2007). *A brief history of modern psychology*. Malden, MA: Blackwell.

Berndt, T. J., & Burgy, L. (1996). Social self-concept. In B. A. Bracken (Ed.), *Handbook of self-concept: Developmental, social, and clinical considerations* (pp. 171–209). New York: Wiley.

Bertocci, P. A. (1945). The psychological self, the ego, and personality. *Psychological Review, 52*, 91–99.

Bickhard, M. H. (2004). The social ontology of persons. In J. I. M. Carpendale, & U. Muller, (Eds.), *Social interaction and the development of knowledge.* (pp. 111–132). Mahwah, NJ: Lawrence Erlbaum.

Bickhard, M. H. (2008). Are you social? The ontological and developmental emergence of the person. In U. Müller, J. I. M. Carpendale, N. Budwig, & B. Sokol (Eds.), *Social life and social knowledge: Toward a process account of development* (pp. 17–42). New York: Lawrence Erlbaum.

Biglan, A. (1987). A behavior-analytic critique of Bandura's self-efficacy theory. *Behavior Analyst, 10*, 1–15.

Blascovich, J., & Tomaka, J. (1991). Measures of self-esteem. In J. P. Robinson, P. R. Shaver and L. S. Wrightsman (Eds), *Measures of personality and social psychological attitudes* (Vol. 1, pp. 115–160). San Diego, CA: Academic Press.

Bledsoe, J. C. (1964). Self concepts of children and their intelligence, achievement, interests, and anxiety. *Journal of Individual Psychology, 20*(1), 55–58.

Bloom, A. (1979). Introduction. In J. R. Rousseau, *Émile* (pp. 3–28). New York: Basic Books.

Blumenfeld, P. C., Pintrich, P. R., Meece, J., & Wessels, K. (1982). The formation and role of self perceptions of ability in elementary classrooms. *Elementary School Journal, 82*, 401–420.

Blumer, J. (1969). *Symbolic interactionism: Perspective and method*. Englewood Cliffs, NJ: Prentice Hall.

Boekaerts, M., & Corno, L. (2005). Self-regulation in the classroom: A perspective on assessment and intervention. *Applied Psychology: An International Review, 54*, 199–231.

Boekaerts, M., Pintrich, P., & Zeidner, M. (2000). *Handbook of self-regulation*. San Diego, CA: Academic Press.

Borkovec, T. D. (1978). Self-efficacy: Cause or reflection of behavioral change? *Advances in Behaviour Research and Therapy, 1*, 163–170.

Bracken, B. A. (Ed.). (1996). *Handbook of self-concept: Developmental, social, and clinical considerations*. New York: Wiley.

Branden, N. (1984, August-September). In defense of self. *Association for Humanistic Psychology Newsletter*, 12–13.

Branden, N. (1995). *The six pillars of self-esteem*. New York: Bantam.

Bredo, E. (1994). Reconstructing educational psychology: Situated cognition and Deweyian pragmatism. *Educational Psychologist, 29*, 23–36.

Brennan, J. F. (1986). *History and systems of psychology*. (2nd ed.). Englewood Cliffs, NJ: Prentice Hall.

Bridgeman, B., & Shipman, V. C. (1978). Preschool measures of self-esteem and achievement motivation as predictors of third grade achievement. *Journal of Educational Psychology, 70*(1), 17–28.

Briggs, D. C. (1970). *Your child's self-esteem: The key to his life*. Garden City, NY: Doubleday.

British Columbia Children's Hospital. (2007). *Healthy buddies*. Retrieved on March 3, 2007 from http://www.bcchildrens.ca/KidsTeensFam/HealthyBuddies/

British Columbia Children's Hospital. (2010). *Healthy buddies*. Retrieved August 20, 2010, from http://www.bcchildrens.ca/KidsTeensFam/HealthyBuddies/

British Columbia Ministry of Education. (1989). *Statement of education policy order (Mandate for the school system)*. Retrieved June 2, 2008, from http://www.bced.gov.bc.ca/legislation/schoollaw/d/oic_1280-89.pdf

British Columbia Ministry of Education. (1999a). *Personal planning K to 7 integrated resource package*. Retrieved September 28, 2007, http://www.bced.gov.bc.ca/irp/pp/pptoc.htm

British Columbia Ministry of Education. (1999b). *Personal planning K to 7 recommended resources*. Retrieved August 2, 2005, from http://www.bctf.ca/cgi/LessonAidsDb.exe/get_entry?ne=mr=y,ol=n,x=ca,id=15

British Columbia Ministry of Education. (2001). *Social responsibility: A framework*. Retrieved July 10, 2008, from http://www.bced.gov.bc.ca/perf_stands/sintro.pdf

British Columbia Ministry of Education. (2004a). *Health and career education curriculum for grade 4*. Victoria, BC: Queen's Printer.

British Columbia Ministry of Education. (2004b). *Health and career education curriculum for grade 5*. Victoria, BC: Queen's Printer.

British Columbia Ministry of Education. (2004c). *Safe, caring, and orderly schools*. Retrieved July 10, 2008, from http://www.bced.gov.bc.ca/sco/guide/scoguide.pdf

British Columbia Ministry of Education. (2005). *English language arts K to 7 integrated resource package*. Retrieved March 10, 2006, from http://www.bced.gov.bc.ca/irp/drafts

British Columbia Ministry of Education. (2010). *The primary program: A framework for teaching*. Ministry of Education, student assessment and program evaluation branch, Province of British Columbia. Retrieved November 3, 2010, from http://www.bced.gov.bc.ca/primary_program/

British Columbia Ministry of Health Services. (2005). *Action schools! B.C.* Retrieved August 13, 2007 from http://www.healthservices.gov.bc.ca\prevent\actions_schools.html

Brown, J. S., Collins, A., & Duguid, P. (1989). Situated cognition and the culture of learning. *Educational Researcher, 18*, 32–42.

Brownlee, S., Leventhal, H., & Leventhal, E. A. (2000). In M. Boekaerts, P. R. Pintrich, & M. Zeidner (Eds.), *Handbook of self-regulation* (pp. 369–416). San Diego, CA: Academic Press.

Brubach, H. (2009, February 22). Enough about you: A little narcissism goes a long way. *New York Times*. Retrieved July 20, 2012 from http://www.nytimes.com/2009/02/22/style/tmagazine/22bruback.html

Bush, V. (2009, April 1). Review of "The narcissism epidemic." *Booklist*, *105*, p. 6.

Butler, D. L. (1998). The strategic content learning approach to promoting self-regulated learning: a report of three studies. *Journal of Educational Psychology*, *90*, 682–297.

Butler, D. L., & Winne, P. (1995). Feedback and self-regulated learning: A theoretical synthesis. *Review of Educational Research*, *65*, 245–281.

Butler, J. (1950). *Fifteen sermons*. New York: Liberal Art Press. (Original work published 1726.)

Butler, J. (1997). *The psychic life of power*. Stanford, CA: Stanford University Press.

Byrne, B. M. (1996). Academic self-concept: Its structure, measurement, and relation to academic achievement. In B. A. Bracken (Ed.), *Handbook of self-concept: Developmental, social, ad clinical considerations* (pp. 287–316). New York: Wiley.

Byrne, B. M., & Shavelson, R. J. (1986). On the structure of adolescent self-concept. *Journal of Educational Psychology*, *78*(6), 473–481.

Canfield, J. & Wells, H. C. (1976). *100 ways to enhance self-concept in the classroom: A handbook for teachers and parents*. Englewood Cliffs, NJ: Prentice Hall.

Canfield, J., & Wells, H. C. (1994). *100 ways to enhance self-concept in the classroom*. Upper Saddle River, NJ: Pearson Education.

Carpendale, J. I. M., & Lewis, C. (2006). *How children develop social understanding*. Oxford, UK: Blackwell.

Carver, C. S., & Scheier, M. F. (1998). *On the self-regulation of behavior*. Cambridge, UK: Cambridge University Press.

Center for Education Research and Innovation. (1988). *The social and economic integration of young people*. Retrieved July 10, 2008, from http://www.sba.gov/advo/research/proceedings_c05.pdf.

Chapman, M. (1991). The epistemic triangle: Operative and communicative components of cognitive competence. In M. Chandler, (Ed.), *Criteria for competence: Controversies in the conceptualization and assessment of children's abilities* (pp. 209–228). Hillsdale, NJ: Lawrence Erlbaum.

Charles, D. C. (1987). The emergence of educational psychology. In J. A. Glover & R. R. Ronning (Eds.), *Historical foundations of educational psychology* (pp. 17–38). New York: Plenum.

Cicirelli, V. G. (1971). Measures of the self-concept, attitudes, and achievement motivation of primary grade children. *Journal of School Psychology*, *9*(4), 383–391.

Cliff, N. (1982). What is and isn't measurement. In G. Keren (Ed.), *Statistical and methodological issues in psychology and social sciences research* (pp. 55–93). Hillsdale, NJ: Lawrence Erlbaum.

Cole, M. (1996). *Cultural psychology: A once and future discipline*. Harvard, MA: Harvard University Press.

Collaborative for Academic, Social, and Emotional Learning. (1998). *About CASEL: Overview*. Retrieved October 28, 2010, from http://www.casel.org/about/index.php

Collaborative for Academic, Social, and Emotional Learning. (2010). *HR4223. Academic, Social and Emotional Learning Act*. Retrieved November 12, 2010, from http://www.casel.org/policy.php

Combs, A. W. (1961). What can man become? *California Journal for Instructional Improvement*, *4*, 15–23.

Committee for Children. (2010). *Second step: a violence prevention curriculum*. Retrieved September 11, 2010, from http://www.cfchildren.org/programs/ssp/ms/

Cooley, C. H. (1902). *Human nature and the social order*. New York: Scribner's.

Coopersmith, S. (1967). *The antecedents of self-esteem*. San Francisco: W. H. Freeman.

Covington, M. V., & Beery, R. G. (1976). *Self-worth and school learning*. Oxford, UK: Holt, Rinehart & Winston.

Crain, R. M. (1996). The influence of age, race, and gender on child and adolescent multidimensional self-concept. In B. A. Bracken (Ed.), *Handbook of self-concept: Developmental, social, and clinical considerations* (pp. 395–420). New York: Wiley.

Craven, R. G., Marsh, H. W., & Burnett, P. (2003). Cracking the self-concept enhancement conundrum: A call and blueprint for the next generation of self-concept enhancement research. In H. W. Marsh, R. G. Craven, & D. M. McInerney (Eds.), *International advances in self research* (pp. 91–126). Greenwich, CT: Information Age.

Cushman, P. (1995). *Constructing the self, constructing America: A cultural history of psychotherapy*. Reading, MA: Addison-Wesley.

Damon, W. (1995). *Greater expectations: Overcoming the culture of indulgence in America's homes and schools*. New York: Free Press.

Danziger, K. (1990). *Constructing the subject: Historical origins of psychological research*. Cambridge, UK: Cambridge University Press.

Danziger, K. (1997a). *Naming the mind: How psychology found its language*. London: Sage.

Danziger, K. (1997b). The historical formation of selves. In R. D. Ashmore & L. Jussim (Eds.), *Self and identity: Fundamental issues* (pp. 137–159). New York: Oxford University Press.

Danziger, K. (2000). Making social psychology experimental: A conceptual history, 1920–1970. *Journal of the History of the Behavioral Sciences, 36*, 329–347.

Danziger, K. (2008). *Marking the mind: A history of memory*. Cambridge, UK: Cambridge University Press.

Das, J. P., & Gindis, B. (Eds.). (1995). Special issue: Lev S. Vygotsky and contemporary educational psychology. *Educational Psychologist, 30*, 55–104.

Davydov, V. V. (1990). *Types of generalization in instruction: Logical and psychological problems in the structuring of school curricula*. Reston, VA: National Council of Teachers of Mathematics.

Deegan, M. J. (1999). Play from the perspective of George Herbert Mead. In M. J. Deegan (Ed.), *Play, school, and society by George Herbert Mead* (xix–cxii). New York: Peter Lang.

DeGrandpre, R. (2000). *Ritalin nation: Rapid-fire culture and the transformation of human consciousness*. New York: Norton.

Department for Education, United Kingdom. (2010). *The national strategies*. Retrieved October 28, 2010, from http://nationalstrategies.standards.dcsf.gov.uk/node/65823

Descartes, R. (1960). *The meditations concerning first philosophy*. Indianapolis, IN: Bobbs-Merrill. (Original work published 1641.)

Dewey, J. (1938). *Experience and education*. New York: Macmillan.

Dilthey, W. (1989). *Selected works volume 1: Introduction to the human sciences* (R. A. Makkrell & Rodi, Trans.). Princeton, NJ: Princeton University Press. (Original work published 1883.)

Dineen, T. (2000). *Manufacturing victims: What the psychology industry is doing to people* (new edition). Montréal: Robert Davies.

Drummond, R. J., & McIntire, W. G. (1977). Evaluating the factor structure of self-concept in children: A cautionary note. *Measurement & Evaluation in Guidance, 9*(1), 172–176.

Duckworth, K., Akerman, R., MacGregor, A., Salter, E., & Vorhaus, J. (2009). *Self-regulated learning: Literature review*. Centre for research on the wider benefits of learning, Institute of Education. Retrieved September 11, 2010, from http://www.learningbenefits.net/Publications/ResRepIntros/ResRep33intro.htm

Duveen, G. (1997). Psychological development as a social process. In L. Smith, J. Dockrerll, & P. Tomlinson (Eds.), *Piaget, Vygotsky and beyond* (pp. 67–90). London: Routledge.

Eastman, C., & Marzillier, J. (1984). Theoretical and methodological difficulties in Bandura's self-efficacy theory. *Cognitive Therapy and Research, 8*, 213–229.

Edelman, G. (1987). *Neural Darwinism*. New York: Basic Books.

Engel, M., & Raine, W. J. (1963). A method for the measurement of the self-concept of children in the third grade. *Journal of Genetic Psychology, 102*(1), 125–137.

Erikson, E. H. (1950). *Childhood and society*. New York: Norton.

Erikson, E. H. (1959). Identity and the life cycle. *Psychological Issues, 1*, 18–164.

Erikson, E. H. (1968). *Identity, youth, and crisis*. New York: Norton.

Esteem Team. (2005). *Esteem team school resource*. Retrieved August 13, 2005, from http://www.esteemteam.com/index.php/article.131

Fagan, T. K. (1996). Witmer's contributions to school psychological services. *American Psychologist, 51*, 241–243.

Fairfield, P. (2000). *Moral selfhood in the liberal tradition*. Toronto: University of Toronto Press.

Fan, J., Meng. H., Gao, X., Lopez, F. J., & Liu, C. (2010). Validation of a U.S. adult social self-efficacy inventory in Chinese populations. *The Counseling Psychologist, 38*, 473–496.

Farmer, R. (1982). Children's rights and self-actualization theory. *Education, 103*(1), 82–89.

Fay, B. (1996). *Contemporary philosophy of social science*. Oxford, UK: Blackwell.

Fish, M. C., & Pervan, R. (1985). Self-instruction training: A potential tool for school psychologists. *Psychology in the Schools, 22*, 83–92.

Foucault, M. (1965). *Madness and civilization*. New York: Random House.

Foucault, M. (1970). *The order of things: An archeology of the human sciences*. London: Tavistock.

Foucault, M. (1977). *Discipline and Punish: The Birth of the Prison*. (A. Sheridan, Trans.). New York: Pantheon Books.

Foucault, M. (1980). *Power/knowledge: Selected interviews and other writings 1972–1977*. New York: Pantheon.

Foucault, M. (1984). *The Foucault reader* (M. Rabinow, Ed.). New York: Pantheon.

Foucault, M. (1986). *The care of the self: The history of sexuality* (Vol. 3). New York: Pantheon.

Foucault, M. (1988). Technologies of the self. In L. H. Martin, H. Gutman, & P. H. Hutton (Eds.), *Technologies of the self* (pp. 16–49). London: Tavistock.

Fowers, B. J. (2005). *Virtue in psychology: Pursuing excellence in ordinary practices*. Washington, DC: APA Press.

Friends for Life. (2008). *Friends in Canada*. Retrieved July 10, 2008, from http://www.friendsinfor.net/ca.htm

Freud, S. (1949). *An outline of psychoanalysis* (J. Strachey, Trans.). New York: Norton. (Original work published 1940.)

Freud, S. (1960). *The ego and the id* (J. Strachey, Trans.). New York: Norton. (Original work published 1923.)

Freud, S. (1961). *Civilization and its discontents* (J. Strachey, Trans.). New York: Norton. (Original work published 1930.)

Galton, F. (1973). *Inquiries into human faculty and its development*. New York: AMS Press. (Original work published 1883.)

Gauvain, M. (2001). Cultural tools, social interaction and the development of thinking. *Human Development, 44*(2–3), Special issue: Cultural minds, 126–143.

Gillespie, A. (2005). G. H. Mead: Theorist of the social act. *Journal for the Theory of Social Behaviour, 35,* 19–39.

Gillespie, A. (2006). Games and the development of perspective taking. *Human Development, 49,* 87–92.

Gillespie, A. (2012). Position exchange: The social development of agency. *New Ideas in Psychology, 30,* 32–46.

Goldstein, K. (1939). *The organism: A holistic approach to biology derived from pathological data in man.* Cincinnati, OH: American Book Company.

Goodenow, C. (1992). Strengthening the links between educational psychology and the study of social contexts. *Educational Psychologist, 27,* 177–196.

Government of Newfoundland and Labrador Department of Education. (2010a). *Social studies enterprise education 3205 curriculum guide.* Retrieved November 13, 2010, from http://www.ed.gov.nl.ca/edu/k12/curriculum/guides/enterprise/index.html

Government of Newfoundland and Labrador Department of Education. (2010b). *Elementary program 2010–2011.* Retrieved November 13, 2010, from http://www.ed.gov.nl.ca/edu/k12/curriculum/descriptions.html

Government of Newfoundland and Labrador Department of Education. (2010c). *Setting the stage: Self esteem and skill building activities.* Retrieved November 13, 2010, from http://www.ed.gov.nl.ca/edu/k12/curriculum/guides/enterprise/index.html

Greer, S. (2003). Self-esteem and the demoralized self: a genealogy of self research and measurement. In D. B. Hill, & M. J. Kral (Eds.), *About psychology: Essays at the crossroads of history, theory, and philosophy* (pp. 89–108). Albany, NY: State University of New York Press.

Greer, S. (2007). Is there a "self" in self research? Or, How measuring the self made it disappear. In A. C. Brock & J. Louw (Eds.), *History of psychology and social practice. Special Issue of Social Practice/Psychological Theorizing* (pp. 51–68). Retrieved November 4, 2007, from http://sspt-gulerce.bou.edu.tr/.

Gregory, R. L. (Ed.). (1987). *The Oxford companion to the mind.* Oxford, UK: Oxford University Press.

Grendler, P. F. (1989). *Schooling in renaissance Italy: Literacy and learning 1300–1600.* Baltimore, MD: Johns Hopkins University Press.

Guardo, C. J., & Bohan, J. B. (1971). Development of a sense of self-identity in children. *Child Development, 42*(6), 1909–1921.

Guignon, C. (2004). *On being authentic.* London: Routledge.

Gutmann, A. (1990). Democratic education in difficult times. *Teachers College Record, 92,* 7–20.

H & H Publishing (2010). *LASSI (Learning and Study Strategies Inventory).* Retrieved September 11, 2010, from http://www.hhpublishing.com/_assessments/LASSI/index.html

Hacker, P. M. S. (1986). *Insight and illusion: Themes in the philosophy of Wittgenstein.* Oxford: Clarendon.

Hacker, P. M. S. (2007). *Human nature: The categorial framework.* Oxford, UK: Blackwell.

Hacking, I. (1995). *Rewriting the soul. Multiple personality and the sciences of memory.* Princeton, NJ: Princeton University Press.

Hacking, I. (1998). *Mad travelers: Reflections on the reality of transient mental illnesses.* Charlottesville, VA: University Press of Virginia.

Hacking, I. (2002). *Historical ontology*. Cambridge, MA: Harvard University Press.

Hacking, I. (2006, April). *Kinds of people: Moving targets*. The Tenth British Academy Lecture, London.

Hall, G. S. (1896). Some aspects of the early sense of self. *American Journal of Psychology, 9,* 351–395.

Hall, G. S. (1906). *Youth: Its education, regimen, and hygiene*. Boston: Ginn.

Hall, G. S. (1970). *The contents of children's minds on entering school*. New York: E. L. Kellogg. (Original work published 1893.)

Harré, R. (1983). *Personal being: A theory for individual psychology*. Oxford, UK: Blackwell.

Harré, R. (1998). *The singular self: An introduction to the psychology of personhood*. Thousand Oaks, CA: Sage.

Harris, K. R. (1990). Developing self-regulated learners: The role of private speech and self-instructions. *Educational Psychologist, 25,* 35–49.

Harris, S., & Braun, J. R. (1971). Self-esteem and racial preference in black children. *Proceedings of the Annual Convention of the American Psychological Association, 6,* 259–260.

Harter, S. (1996). Historical roots of contemporary issues involving self-concept. In B. R. Bracken (Ed.), *Handbook of self-concept: Developmental, social, and clinical considerations* (pp. 1–37). New York: Wiley.

Harter, S. (1999). *The construction of the self: A developmental perspective*. New York: Guilford.

Harter, S., Waters, P. L., & Whitesell, N. R. (1997). Lack of voice as a manifestation of false self-behavior among adolescents: The school setting as a stage upon which the drama of authenticity is enacted. *Educational Psychologist, 32,* 153–173.

Hattie, J. (1992). *Self-concept*. Hillsdale, NJ: Lawrence Erlbaum.

Hattie, J. (2003). Getting back on the correct pathway for self-concept research in the new millennium: Revisiting misinterpretations of and revitalizing the contributions of James' agenda for research on the self. In H. W. Marsh, R. G. Craven, & D. M. McInerney (Eds.), *International advances in self research* (pp. 127–148). Greenwich, CT: Information Age.

Hauserman, N., Miller, J. S., & Bond, F. T. (1976). A behavioural approach to changing self-concept in elementary school children. *Psychological Record, 26,* 111–116.

Herman, E. (1995). *The romance of American psychology: Political culture in the age of experts*. Berkeley, CA: University of California Press.

Hickey, D. T., & Granade, J. B. (2004). The influence of sociocultural theory on our theories of engagement and motivation. In D. M. McInerney & S. Van Etten (Eds.), *Big theories revisited: Research on sociocultural influences on motivation and learning* (Vol. 4, pp. 223–248). Greenwich, CT: Information Age.

Hidi, S., & Renninger, K. A. (2006). The four-phase model of interest development. *Educational Psychologist, 41,* 111–127.

Hilgard, E. (1949). Human motives and the concept of the self. *American Psychologist, 4,* 374–382.

Hilgard, E. R., Leary, D., & McGuire, G. (1991). The history of psychology: A survey and critical assessment. *Annual Review of Psychology, 42,* 79–107.

Hobbes, T. (1962). *The English works of Thomas Hobbes* (W. Molesworth, Ed.). London: Scientia Aalen. (Original work published 1651.)

Hobson, P. (2002). *The cradle of thought*. Hampshire, UK: Macmillan Education.

Hock, R. R. (2002). *Forty studies that changed psychology: Explorations into the history of psychological research* (4th ed.). Upper Saddle River, NJ: Prentice Hall.

Hume, D. (1986). *A treatise of human nature* (E. C. Mossner, Ed.). New York: Penguin. (Original work published 1739.)

Humphrey, L. (1984). Children's self-control in relation to perceived social environment. *Journal of Personality and Social Psychology, 46*(1), 178–188.

Jacks, M. L. (1950). *Modern trends in education*. London: Melrose.

Jackson, T., Mackenzie, J., & Hobfoll, S. E. (2000). Communal aspects of self-regulation. In M. Boekaerts, P. R. Pintrich, & M. Zeidner (Eds.), *Handbook of self-regulation* (pp. 275–300). San Diego, CA: Academic Press.

James, W. (1890). *The principles of psychology*. New York: Henry Holt.

Jansz, J., & van Drunen, P. (Eds.). (2004). *A social history of psychology*. Oxford, UK: Blackwell.

Jayakar, R. (2009). *Self-efficacy and everyday problem solving performance*. Honour's thesis. Department of Psychology, Simon Fraser University, Burnaby, BC, Canada.

John-Steiner, V., & Mahn, H. (1996). Sociocultural approaches to learning and development: A Vygotskian framework. *Educational Psychologist, 31*, 191–206.

Jones, B. F., Valdez, G., Nowakowski, J., & Rasmussen, C. (1995). *Plugging in: Choosing and using education technology*. Oak Brook, IL: North Central Regional Educational Laboratory.

Jordan, T. J. (1981). Self-concepts, motivation, and academic achievement of Black adolescents. *Journal of Educational Psychology, 73*, 509–517.

Kamins, M. L., & Dweck, C. S. (1999). Person versus process praise and criticism: implications for contingent self-worth and coping. *Developmental Psychology, 35*, 835–847.

Kane, R. (Ed.). (2002). *The Oxford handbook of free will*. Oxford, UK: Oxford University Press.

Kazdin, A. E. (1978). Conceptual and assessment issues raised by self-efficacy theory. *Advances in Behaviour Research and Therapy, 1*, 177–185.

Keith, L. K. & Bracken, B. A. (1996). Self-concept instrumentation: A historical and evaluative review. In B. R. Bracken (Ed.), *Handbook of self-concept: Developmental, social, and clinical considerations* (pp. 91–170). New York: Wiley.

Kelly, J. M. (1970). Self-concept development in parent deprived children: A comparative study. *Graduate Research in Education & Related Disciplines, 6*(1), 30–48.

Kirschner, S., & Martin, J. (Eds.). (2010). *The sociocultural turn in psychology: The contextual emergence of mind and self*. New York: Columbia University Press.

Kirshner, D., & Whitson, J. A. (Eds.). (1997). *Situated cognition: Social, semiotic, and psychological perspectives*. Mahwah, NJ: Lawrence Erlbaum.

Kohn, A. (1994). The truth about self-esteem. *Phi Delta Kappan, 74*, 272–283.

Krantz, D. L. (2001). Reconsidering history of psychology's borders. *History of Psychology, 4*, 182–194.

Lamiell, J. T. (1987). *The psychology of personality: An epistemological inquiry*. New York: Columbia University Press.

Lamiell, J. T. (2003). *Beyond individual and group differences: Human individuality, scientific psychology, and William Stern's critical personalism*. Thousand Oaks, CA: Sage.

Lamiell, J. T. (2010, August). *Statisticism in personality psychologists' use of trait constructs: What is it? How was it contracted? Is there a cure?* Paper presented at the annual meetings of the American Psychological Association. San Diego, CA.

Lasch, C. (1978). *The culture of narcissism: American life in an age of diminishing expectations.* New York: Norton.

Lave, J., & Wenger, E. (1991). *Situated learning: Legitimate peripheral participation.* Cambridge, UK: Cambridge University Press.

Leahey, T. L. (1992). *A history of psychology: Main currents in psychological thought* (3rd ed.). Englewood Cliffs, NJ: Prentice Hall.

Lecky, P. (1945). *Self-consistency: A theory of personality.* New York: Island Press.

Lewin, K. (1935). *A dynamic theory of personality.* New York: McGraw-Hill.

Locke, J. (1959). *An essay concerning human understanding* (A. C. Fraser, Ed.). New York: Dover. (Original work published, 1693.)

Long, B. H., Henderson, E. H., & Ziller, R. C. (1967). Developmental changes in the self-concept during middle childhood. *Merrill-Palmer Quarterly, 13*, 201–215.

Luszczynska, A., Gutiérrez-Dona, B., & Schwarzer, R. (2005). General self-efficacy in various domains of human functioning: Evidence from five countries. *International Journal of Psychology, 40*, 80–89.

Lyons, J. (1978). *The invention of self: The hinge of consciousness in the eighteenth century.* Carbondale, IL: Southern Illinois University Press.

Mahoney, M. J., & Thoresen, C. E. (1972). Behavioral self-control: Power to the person. *Educational Researcher, 1*, 5–7.

Maraun, M. (2006). *Myths and confusions: Psychometrics and the latent variable model.* Unpublished manuscript, Department of Psychology, Simon Fraser University.

Markus, H. (1977). Self-schemata and processing information about the self. *Journal of Personality and Social Psychology, 35*, 63–78.

Marsh, H. W. (1986). Self-serving effect (bias?) in academic attributions: its relation to academic achievement and self-concept. *Journal of Educational Psychology, 78*(3), 190–200.

Marsh, H. W. (1990). A multidimensional, hierarchical self-concept: Theoretical and empirical justification. *Educational Psychology Review, 2*, 77–172.

Marsh, H. W. (1992). The content specificity of relations between academic achievement and academic self-concept. *Journal of Educational Psychology, 84*, 35–42.

Marsh, H. W., & Craven, R. G. (2005). A reciprocal effects model of the causal ordering of self-concept and achievement: New support for the benefits of enhancing self-concept. In H. W. Marsh, R. G. Craven, & D. M. McInerney (Eds.), *International advances in self research (Vol. 2): New frontiers for self research* (pp. 15–51). Greenwich, CT: Information Age.

Marsh, H. W., Craven, R. G., & Debus, R. (1991). Self-concepts of young children 5 to 8 years of age: Measurement and multidimensional structure. *Journal of Educational Psychology, 83*, 377–392.

Marsh, H. W., Craven, R. G., & McInerney, D. M. (Eds.). (2003). *International advances in self research.* Greenwich, CT: Information Age.

Marsh, H. W., Craven, R. G., & McInerney, D. M. (Eds.) (2005). *International advances in self research (Volume 2): New frontiers for self research.* Greenwich, CT: Information Age.

Marsh, H. W., & Hattie, J. (1996). Theoretical perspectives on the structure of self-concept. In B. R. Bracken (Ed.), *Handbook of self-concept: Developmental, social, and clinical considerations* (pp. 38–90). New York: Wiley.

Marsh, H. W., Hey, J., Roche, L., & Perry, C. (1997). Structure of physical self concept: Elite athletes and physical education students. *Journal of Educational Psychology, 89*(2), 369–380.

Marsh, H. W., & Köller, O. (2003). Bringing together two theoretical models of relations between academic self-concept and achievement. In H. W. Marsh, R. G. Craven, & D. M. McInerney (Eds.), *International advances in self research* (pp. 17–47). Greenwich, CT: Information Age.

Marsh, H. W., & Shavelson, R. J. (1985). Self-concept: Its multifaceted, hierarchical structure. *Educational Psychologist, 20*, 10.

Marsh, H. W., Smith, I., & Barnes, J. (1983). MTMM analysis of the Self-Description Questionnaire: Student-teacher agreement on multidimensional ratings of student self-concept. *American Educational Research Journal, 20*, 333–357.

Martin, J. (2004a). The educational inadequacy of conceptions of self in educational psychology. *Interchange: A Quarterly Review of Education, 35*, 185–208.

Martin, J. (2004b). Agency, self-regulation, and social cognitive theory. *Educational Psychologist, 39*, 135–145.

Martin, J. (2005a). Real perspectival selves. *Theory & Psychology, 15*, 207–224.

Martin, J. (2005b). Perspectival selves in interaction with others: Re-reading G. H. Mead's social psychology. *The Journal for the Theory of Social Behaviour, 35*, 231–253.

Martin, J. (2006a). Social cultural perspectives in educational psychology. In P. Alexander & P. H. Winne (Eds.), *Handbook of educational psychology* (2nd edition) (pp. 595–614). Mahwah, NJ: Erlbaum.

Martin, J. (2006b). Re-interpreting internalization and agency through G. H. Mead's perspectival realism. *Human Development, 49*, 65–86.

Martin, J. (2007). The selves of educational psychology. *Educational Psychologist, 42*, 79–89.

Martin, J., & Gillespie, A. (2010). A neo-Meadian approach to human agency: Relating the social and the psychological in the ontogenesis of perspective-coordinating persons. *Integrative Psychological and Behavioral Science, 44*, 252–272.

Martin, J., Sokol, B., & Elfers, T. (2008). Taking and coordinating perspectives: From pre-reflective interactivity, through reflective intersubjectivity, to meta-reflective sociality. *Human Development, 51*, 294–317.

Martin, J. & Sugarman, J. (1999). *The psychology of human possibility and constraint*. Albany, NY: State University of New York Press.

Martin, J., Sugarman, J., & Hickinbottom, S. (2010). *Persons: Understanding psychological selfhood and agency*. New York: Springer.

Martin, J., Sugarman, J., & Thompson, J. (2003). *Psychology and the question of agency*. Albany, NY: State University of New York Press.

Martin, R., & Barresi, J. (2006). *The rise and fall of soul and self: An intellectual history of personal identity*. New York: Columbia University Press.

Maslow, A. H. (1943). A theory of human motivation. *Psychological Review, 50*, 370–396.

Maslow, A. H. (1954). *Motivation and personality*. New York: Harper & Row.

Mattocks, A. L., & Jew, C. C. (1974). The teacher's role in the development of a healthy self-concept in pupils. *Education, 94*(3), 200–204.

Mayer, F. (1966). *A history of educational thought* (2nd ed.). Columbus, OH: Merrill.

Mayer, R. E. (2001). What good is educational psychology? The case of cognition and instruction. *Educational Psychologist, 36*, 83–88.

McCaslin, M. (2004). Co-regulation of opportunity, activity, and identity in student motivation: Elaborations on Vygotskian themes. In D. M. McInerney & S. Van Etten (Eds.), *Big theories revisited* (pp. 249–274). Greenwich, CT: Information Age.

McCaslin, M. (2009). Co-regulation of student motivation and emergent identity. *Educational Psychologist, 44*, 137–146.

McCulloch, G., & Richardson, W. (2000). *Historical research in educational settings.* Buckingham: Open University Press.

McDaniel, S., & Bielen, P. (1990). *Project self-esteem.* Austin, TX: Jalmar.

McLellan, A. (2008). *The educated self: Psychology's contribution to the education of children in twentieth-century North America.* Doctoral dissertation. Retrieved September 10, 2009 from ir.lib.sfu.ca/bitstream/1892/10407/1/etd4117.pdf

Mead, G. H. (1910/11). The philosophy of education. Chicago: *The George Herbert Mead Paper Archives, University of Chicago Library: Typescript of Student Notes By Juliet Hammond* (196 pages).

Mead, G. H. (1915). Natural rights and the theory of the political institution. *Journal of Philosophy, Psychology, and Scientific Methods, 12*, 141–155.

Mead, G. H. (1932). *The philosophy of the present* (A. W. Murphy, Ed.). LaSalle, IL: Open Court.

Mead, G. H. (1934). *Mind, self, & society from the standpoint of a social behaviorist* (C. Morris, Ed.). Chicago: University of Chicago Press.

Mead, G. H. (1938). *The philosophy of the act* (C. W. Morris, Ed.). Chicago: University of Chicago Press.

Mead, G. H. (1964). *Selected writings of George Herbert Mead* (A. Reck, Ed.). Chicago: University of Chicago Press.

Megill, A. (2007). *Historical knowledge, historical error: A contemporary guide to practice.* Chicago: University of Chicago Press.

Meirieu, P. (2005). *Lettre à un jeune professeur.* Paris: ESF Editeur.

Michell, J. (1999). *Measurement in psychology: A critical history of a methodological concept.* Cambridge, UK: Cambridge University Press.

Michael, W. B., Smith, R. A., & Michael, J. J. (1975). The factorial validity of the Piers-Harris Children's Self-Concept Scale for each of three samples of elementary, junior, high, and senior high school students in a large metropolitan school district. *Educational & Psychological Measurement, 35*(2), 405–414.

Miller, D. C., & Byrnes, J. P. (2001). To achieve or not to achieve: A self-regulation perspective on adolescents' academic decision making. *Journal of Educational Psychology, 93*, 677–685.

Miller, G. A., Galanter, E., & Pribram, K. H. (1960). *Plans and the structure of behavior.* New York: Holt, Rinehart, & Winston.

Mischel, H. N., & Mischel, W. (1983). The development of children's knowledge of self-control strategies. *Child Development, 54*(3), 603–619.

Mischel, W., Shoda, Y., & Rodriguez, M. L. (1989). Delay of gratification in children. *Science, 244*, 933–938.

Montmarquette, C. (1990). A legacy for learners: The report of the British Columbia Royal Commission on education—1988. *Canadian Public Policy, 16*(1). 91–96.

Morawski, J. G. (1987). After reflection: Psychologists' use of history. In H. Stam, T. B. Rogers, & K. Gergen (Eds.), *The analysis of psychological theory: Metaphysical perspectives* (pp. 157–169). Washington: Hemisphere.

Moses, L. J., & Carlson, S. M. (2004). Self-regulation and children's theories of mind. In C. Lightfoot, C. Lalonde, & M. Chandler (Eds.), *Changing conceptions of psychological life* (pp. 127–146). Mahwah, NJ: Lawrence Erlbaum.

Murphy, G. (1947). *Personality: A biosocial approach to origins and structure*. New York: Harper.

National Board for Professional Teaching Standards (2002). *What teachers should know and be able to do*. Retrieved Aug. 27, 2010, from http://www.nbpts.org/UserFiles/File/what_teachers.pdf

National Film Board of Canada. (1989). *Especially you. The growing up series*. Retrieved October 22, 2005, from http://www.bclc.bc.ca/download/national_film_board_of_canada.htm

National Life Work Centre (2005). *Destination 2020*. Retrieved August 12, 2005, from www.bctf.ca/cgi/LessonAidsDb.exe/get_Entry?ne=mr=y,ol=n,x=ca,id=15

Nicholson, I. A. M. (1998). Gordon Allport, character, and the "culture of personality." *History of Psychology, 1*, 52–68.

Nicholson, I. A. M. (2003). *Inventing personality: Gordon Allport and the science of selfhood*. Washington, DC: APA Books.

Norman, D. A., & Shallice, T. (1986). Attention to action: Willed and automatic control of behavior. In R. J. Davidson, G. E. Schwartz, & D. Shapiro (Eds.), *Consciousness and self regulation* (Vol. 4, pp. 4–18). New York: Plenum.

Nussbaum, M. C. (1994). *The therapy of desire: Theory and practice in Hellenistic ethics*. Princeton, NJ: Princeton University Press.

Nystul, M. S. (1984). Positive parenting leads to self-actualizing in children. *Individual Psychology: Journal of Adlerian Theory, Research & Practice, 40*(2), 177–183.

Obama, B. (2009). Remarks by the President in a National Address to America's schoolchildren. The White House: Office of the Press. Retrieved September 20, 2009, from http://www.whitehouse.gov/the_press_office/Remarks-by-the-President-in-a-National-Address-to-Americas-Schoolchildren

Olson, D. R. (2003). *Psychological theory and educational reform: How school remakes mind and society*. Cambridge, U.K.: Cambridge University Press.

Olson, D. R., & Bruner, J. S. (1996). Folk psychology and folk pedagogy. In D. R. Olson & N. Torrance (Eds.), *Handbook of education and human development* (pp. 9–27). Oxford, UK: Blackwell.

O'Mara, A. J., Marsh, H. W., Craven, R. B., & Debus, R. (2006). Do self-concept interventions make a difference? A synergistic blend of construct validation and meta-analysis. *Educational Psychologist, 41*, 181–206.

Ozehosky, R. J., & Clark, E. T. (1970). Children's self-concept and kindergarten achievement. *Journal of Psychology, 75*(2), 185–192.

Packer, M. J., & Goicoechea, J. (2000). Sociocultural and constructivist theories of learning: Ontology, not just epistemology. *Educational Psychologist, 35*, 227–241.

Pajares, F. & Schunk, D. H. (2002). Self and self-belief in psychology and education: An historical perspective. In J. Aronson (Ed.), *Improving academic achievement: Impact of psychological factors on education* (pp. 3–21). San Diego, CA: Academic Press.

Pajares, F., & Schunk, D. H. (2005). Self-efficacy and self-concept beliefs: Jointly contributing to the quality of human life. In H. W. Marsh, R. G. Craven, & D. M. McInerney (Eds.), *International advances in self research (Volume 2): New frontiers for self research* (pp. 95–121). Greenwich, CT: Information Age.

Parish, T. S., & Philip, M. K. (1982). The self-concepts of children from intact and divorced families: Can they be affected in school settings? *Education, 103*(1), 60–63.

Partnership for 21st Century Skills (2009). *P21 framework definitions*. Retrieved September 20, 2010, from http://www.p21.org/documents/P21_Framework.pdf

Pereboom, A. (1979). Bandura's self system: Some reservations. *American Psychologist, 34,* 438–439.

Pfister, J. (1997). Glamorizing the psychological: The politics of the performances of modern psychological identities. In J. Pfister & N. Schnog (Eds.), *Inventing the psychological: Toward a cultural history of emotional life in America* (pp. 167–216). New Haven, CT: Yale University Press.

Pfister, J., & Schnog, N. (Eds.). (1997). *Inventing the psychological: Toward a cultural history of emotional life in America.* New Haven, CT: Yale University Press.

Phillips, A. S. (1964). Self concepts in children. *Educational Research, 6*(2), 104–109.

Piaget, J. (1965). *The child's conception of the world.* Paterson, NJ: Littlefield, Adams.

Piers, E., & Harris, D. B. (1964). Age and other correlates of self-concept in children. *Journal of Educational Psychology, 55,* 91–95.

Pintrich, P. R., & Blumenfeld, P. C. (1985). Classroom experience and children's self-perceptions of ability, effort, and conduct. *Journal of Educational Psychology, 77,* 646–657.

Pintrich, P. R., & DeGroot, E. V. (1990). Motivational and self-regulated learning components of classroom academic performance. *Journal of Educational Psychology, 82,* 33–40.

Plato. (1980). *The laws of Plato* (T. L. Spangle, Trans.). Chicago: University of Chicago Press. (Original published 360 BCE.)

Popkewitz, T. S. (1991). *A political sociology of educational reform: Power/knowledge in teaching, teacher education, and research.* New York: Teachers College Press.

Popkewitz, T. S. (1998). The culture of redemption and the administration of freedom in educational research. *Review of Educational Research, 68,* 1–34.

Popkewitz, T. S., Pereyra, M. A., & Franklin, B. M. (2001). History, the problem of knowledge, and the new cultural history of schooling. In T. S. Popkewitz, B. M. Franklin, & M. A. Pereyra (Eds.), *Cultural history and education: Critical essays on knowledge and schooling* (pp. 3–44). New York: Routledge/Flamer.

Poser, E. G. (1978). The self-efficacy concept: Some theoretical, procedural and clinical implications. *Advances in Behaviour Research and Therapy, 1,* 193–202.

Prawat. R. S. (1995). Misreading Dewey: Reform, projects, and the language game. *Educational Researcher, 24* (7) 13–22.

Purkey, W. W. (1970). *Self concept and school achievement.* Englewood Cliffs, NJ: Prentice Hall.

Ramey, V. C. (1948). Self-reference in counseling interviews. *Journal of Consulting Psychology, 12,* 153–163.

Randi, J., & Corno, L. (2000). Teacher innovations in self-regulated learning. In M. Boekaerts, P. R. Pintrich, & M. Zeidner (Eds.), *Handbook of self-regulation* (pp. 651–685). San Diego, CA: Academic Press.

Reeve, J., Deci, E. L., & Ryan, R. M. (2004). Self-determination theory: A dialectical framework for understanding sociocultural influences on student motivation. In D. M. McInerney & S. Van Etten (Eds.), *Big theories revisited* (pp. 31–60). Greenwich, CT: Information Age.

Renger, P. (1992). George Herbert Mead's contribution to the philosophy of American education. In P. Hamilton (Ed.), *George Herbert Mead: Critical assessments* (Vol. 4, pp. 146–169). New York: Routledge.

Richardson, F. C., Fowers, B. J., & Guignon, C. (1999). *Re-envisioning psychology: Moral dimensions of theory and practice.* San Francisco: Jossey-Bass.

Richmond, B. O., & White, W. F. (1971). Sociometric predictors of the self concept among fifth and sixth grade children. *Journal of Educational Research, 64*(9), 425–429.

Rilke, R. M. (1954). *Letters to a young poet* (M. D. Herter Norton, Trans.). New York: Random House. (Original published 1903–1908.)

Roeser, R. W., Peck, S. C., & Nasir, N. S. (2006). Self and identity processes in school motivation, learning, and achievement. In P. A. Alexander & P. H. Winne (Eds.), *Handbook of educational psychology* (2nd ed.) (pp. 391–424). Mahwah, NJ: Lawrence Erlbaum.

Rogers, C. R. (1957). The necessary and sufficient conditions of therapeutic personality change. *Journal of Consulting Psychology, 21,* 95–103.

Rogers, C. R. (1969). *Freedom to learn.* Columbus, OH: Merrill.

Rohrkemper, M. M. (1989). Self-regulated learning and academic achievement: A Vygotskian view. In B. J. Zimmerman, & D. H. Schunk (Eds.), *Self-regulated learning and academic achievement: Theory, research, and practice* (pp. 143–167). New York: Springer-Verlag.

Roid, G. H., & Fitts, W. H. (1988). *Tennessee Self-Concept Scale: Revised Manual.* Los Angeles: Western Psychological Services.

Rose, N. (1998). *Inventing ourselves: Psychology, power, and personhood.* Cambridge, UK: Cambridge University Press.

Rose, N. (1999). *Governing the soul: The shaping of the private self* (2nd ed.). London: Free Association Books.

Rousseau, J. J. (1979). *Émile or on education* (A. Bloom, Trans.). New York: Basic Books. (Original work published 1762.)

Russell, J. (1996). *Agency: Its role in mental development.* Hove, UK: Erlbaum.

Russon, J. (2003). *Human experience: Philosophy, neurosis, and the elements of everyday life.* Albany, NY: State University of New York Press.

Rychlak, J. (1979). A nontelic teleology? *American Psychologist, 34,* 435–438.

Ryle, G. (1949). *The concept of mind.* Chicago: University of Chicago Press.

Salomon, G. (1995). Reflections on the field of educational psychology by the outgoing journal editor. *Educational Psychology, 30,* 105–108.

Samuels, S. C. (1977). *Enhancing self-concept in early childhood: Theory and practice (Early Education Series).* New York: Human Sciences Press.

Sandoval, W. A., & Bell, P. (Eds.). (2004). Special issue: Design-based research methods for studying learning in context. *Educational Psychologist, 39,* 199–260.

Scherbaum, C. A., Cohen-Charash, Y., & Kern, M. J. (2008). Measuring general self-efficacy: A comparison of three measures using item response theory. *Educational and Psychological Measurement, 66,* 1047–1063.

Schunk, D. H. (1981). Modeling and attributional effects on children's achievement: A self-efficacy analysis. *Journal of Educational Psychology, 73,* 93–105.

Schunk, D. H. (1982). Effects of effort attributional feedback on children's perceived self-efficacy and achievement. *Journal of Educational Psychology, 74,* 548–556.

Schunk, D. H., & Ertmer, P. A. (2000). Self-regulation and academic learning: Self-efficacy enhancing interventions. In M. Boekaerts, P. R. Pintrich, & M. Zeidner (Eds.), *Handbook of self-regulation* (pp. 631–649). San Diego, CA: Academic Press.

Schunk D. H., & Hanson, A. R. (1985). Peer models: Influence on children's self-efficacy and achievement. *Journal of Educational Psychology, 77,* 313–322.

Schunk, D. H., & Pajares, F. (2004). Self-efficacy in education revisited: Empirical and applied evidence. In D. M. McInerney & S. Van Etten (Eds.), *Big theories revisited* (pp. 115–138). Greenwich, CT: Information Age.

Schunk, D. H., & Zimmerman, B. J. (Eds.). (1994). *Self-regulation of learning and performance: Issues and educational applications*. Hillsdale, NJ: Lawrence Erlbaum.

Schunk, D. H., & Zimmerman, B. J. (Eds.). (1998). *Self-regulated learning: From teaching to self-reflective practice*. New York: Guilford.

Schutz, A. (2000). Teaching freedom: Postmodern perspectives. *Review of Educational Research, 70*, 215–251.

Schwarzer, R., & Jerusalem, M. (1995). Generalized Self-Efficacy Scale. In J. Weinman, S. Wright, & M. Johnston (Eds.), *Measures in health psychology: A user's portfolio. Causal and control beliefs* (pp. 35–37). Windsor, UK: NFER-Nelson.

Sears, R. R. (1970). Relation of early socialization experiences to self-concepts and gender role in middle childhood. *Child Development, 41*(2), 267–289.

Seigel, J. (2005). *The idea of the self: Thought and experience in Western Europe since the seventeenth century*. Cambridge, UK: Cambridge University Press.

Selman, R. L. (1980). *The growth of interpersonal understanding: Developmental and clinical analyses*. New York: Academic Press.

Selman, R. L. (2003). *The promotion of social awareness: Powerful lessons from the partnership of developmental theory and classroom practice*. New York: Russell Sage Foundation.

Shain, B. A. (1994). *The myth of American individualism: The protestant origins of American political thought*. Princeton, NJ: Princeton University Press.

Shavelson, R. J. (2003). Preface. In H. Marsh, R. G. Craven, & D. M. McInerney (Eds.), *International advances in self research* (ix–xv). Greenwich, CT: Information Age.

Shavelson, R. J., & Bolus, R. (1982). Self-concept: the interplay of theory and models. *Journal of Educational Psychology, 74*(1), 3–17.

Shavelson, R. J., Hubner, J. J., & Stanton, G. C. (1976). Self-concept: validation of construct interpretations. *Review of Educational Research, 46*(3), 407–441.

Shavelson, R. J., & Marsh, H. W. (1986). On the structure of self-concept. In R. Schwarzer (Ed.), *Anxiety and cognitions* (pp. 305–330). Hillsdale, NJ: Lawrence Erlbaum.

Sherer, M., Maddux, J. E., Mercandante, B., Prentice-Dunn, S., Jacobs, B., & Rogers, R. (1982). The self-efficacy scale: Construction and validation. *Psychological Reports, 51*, 663–671.

Simon, H. A. (1979). *Models of thought*. New Haven, CT: Yale University Press.

Skinner, B. F. (1968). *The technology of teaching*. New York: Appleton-Century-Crofts.

Smedslund, J. (1978). Bandura's theory of self-efficacy: A set of common sense theorems. *Scandinavian Journal of Psychology, 19*, 1–14.

Smedslund, J. (1988). *Psycho-logic*. New York: Springer-Verlag.

Smith, A. (1976). The theory of the moral sentiments. In D. D. Raphael & A. L. Macfie (Eds.). *The Glasgow edition of the works and correspondence of Adam Smith* (Vol. 1, pp. 47–343). Oxford, UK: Oxford University Press. (Original work published 1759.)

Snygg, D., & Coombs, A. W. (1959). *Individual behavior: A perceptual approach to behavior* (rev. ed.). New York: Harper.

Soares, A. T., & Soares, L. M. (1969). Self-perceptions of culturally disadvantaged children. *American Educational Research Journal, 6*, 31–45.

Sorabji, R. (2006). *Self: Ancient and modern insights about individuality, life, and death*. Chicago: University of Chicago Press.

Starobinski, J. (1988). *Jean-Jacque Rousseau: Transparency and obstruction* (A. Goldhammer, Trans.). Chicago: University of Chicago Press

Stelzig, E. (2000). *The romantic subject in autobiography: Rousseau and Goethe*. Charlottesville, VA: University of Virginia Press.

Stokes, D. (1986). Chance can play key role in life, psychologist says. *Stanford Campus Report, 8*, 1–2.

Stout, M. (2000). *The feel-good curriculum: The dumbing down of America's kids in the name of self-esteem*. Cambridge, MA: Da Capo.

Stright, A. D., & Supplee, L. H. (2002). Children's self-regulatory behaviors during teacher-directed seat-work and small-group instructional contexts. *Journal of Educational Research, 95*, 235–244.

Tappan, M. B. (1998). Sociocultural psychology and caring pedagogy: Exploring Vygotsky's "hidden curriculum." *Educational Psychologist, 33*, 23–34.

Taylor, C. (1985). Self-interpreting animals. In *Philosophical papers: Vol. 1. Human agency and language* (pp. 45–76). Cambridge, UK: Cambridge University Press.

Taylor, C. (1989). *Sources of the self: The making of modern identity*. Cambridge, MA: Harvard University Press.

Taylor, C. (1991). *The malaise of modernity*. Concord, Ontario, Canada: Anansi.

Taylor, C. (1995). *Philosophical arguments*. Cambridge, MA: Harvard University Press.

Teasdale, J. D. (1978). Self-efficacy: Toward a unifying theory of behavioural change? *Advances in Behaviour Research and Therapy, 1*, 211–215.

Teo, T., & Febbraro, A. R. (2003). Ethnocentrism as a form of intuition in psychology. *Theory & Psychology, 13*, 673–694.

Texas A&M University (2010). Student counselling service. Retrieved November 12, 2010, from http://scs.tamu.edu/calendar/ac.asp

Thorndike, E. L. (1903). *Educational psychology*. New York: Lemcke and Buechner.

Tolman, E. C. (1932). *Purposive behavior in animals and men*. New York: Appleton-Century-Crofts.

Tomasello, M. (1999). *The cultural origins of human cognition*. Cambridge, MA: Harvard University Press.

Tomasello, M. (2008). *Origins of human communication*. Cambridge, MA: MIT Press.

Toulmin, S. (1977). Self-knowledge and knowledge of the "self." In T. Mischel (Ed.), *The self: Psychological and philosophical issues* (pp. 291–317). Oxford, UK: Blackwell.

Trowbridge, N. (1972). Self-concept and socio-economic status in elementary school children. *American Educational Research Journal, 9*, 525–537.

Trowbridge, N. (1974). Self-concept and IQ in elementary school children. *California Journal of Educational Research, 25*(1), 37–49.

Twenge, J. M. (2006). *Generation me: Why today's young Americans are more confident, assertive, entitled—and more miserable than ever before*. New York: Free Press.

Twenge, J. M., & Campbell, W. K. (2009). *The narcissism epidemic: Living in the age of entitlement*. New York: Free Press.

U.S. Department of Education (2009a). *Lead and manage my school. President Barack Obama makes historic speech to America's students*. Retrieved September 12, 2009, from http://www2.ed.gov/admins/lead/academic/bts.html

U.S. Department of Education (2009b). *Menu of Classroom Activities. President Obama's Address to Students Across America (Grades 7–12)*. Retrieved September 12, 2009 from http://www2.ed.gov/teachers/how/lessons/7–12.pdf

Usher, R., & Edwards, R. (1994). *Postmodernism and education*. London: Routledge.

Vadeboncoeur, J., & Portes, P. (2002). Students "at risk": Exploring identity from a sociocultural perspective. In D. M. McInerney & S. Van Etten (Eds.), *Research on sociocultural influences on motivation and learning* (Vol. 2, pp. 89–127). Greenwich, CT: Information Age.

Vallacher, R. R., & Nowak, A. (1997). The emergence of dynamical social psychology. *Psychological Inquiry, 8*, 73–99.

Valsiner, J. & van der Veer, R. (2000). *The social mind: Construction of the idea.* Cambridge, UK: Cambridge University Press.

van Drunen, P. & Jansz, J. (2004). Child-rearing and education. In J. Jansz & P. van Drunen (Eds.), *A social history of psychology* (pp. 45–92). Oxford, UK: Blackwell.

Vohs, K. D., & Baumeister, R. F. (2004). Understanding self-regulation: An introduction. In R. F. Baumeister & K. D. Vohs (Eds.), *Handbook of self-regulation: Research, theory and applications* (pp. 1–9). New York: Guilford.

Vygotsky, L. S. (1978). *Mind in society: The development of higher psychological processes* (M. Cole, V. John-Steiner, S. Scribner, & E. Souberman, Eds.). Cambridge, MA: Harvard University Press.

Vygotsky, L. S. (1986). *Thought and language* (A. Kozulin, Trans.). Cambridge, MA: Harvard University Press. (Original work published 1934)

Walker, R., Pressick-Kilborne, K., Sainsbury, E., & McCallum, J. (2010). A sociocultural approach to motivation: A long time coming but here at last. In T. C. Urdan, & S. A. Karabenick (Eds.), *Advances in motivation and achievement (volume 16A). The decade ahead: Applications and contexts of motivation and achievement* (pp. 1–42). Bingley, UK: Emerald.

Wang, M.C., & Stiles, B. (1976). An investigation of children's concept of self-responsibility for their school learning. *American Educational Research Journal, 13*(3), 159–179.

Weinstein, C. E., Goetz, E. T., & Alexander, P. A. (1988). Design and development of the LASSI. In C. E. Weinstein, E. T., Goetz, & P. A. Alexander (Eds.). *Learning and Study Strategies: Issues in Assessment, Instruction, and Evaluation* (pp. 137–162). New York: Academic Press.

Weinstein, C. E., Husman, J., & Dierking, D. R. (2000). Self-regulation interventions with a focus on learning strategies. In M. Boekaerts, P. R. Pintrich, & M. Zeidner (Eds.), *Handbook of self-regulation* (pp. 728–747). San Diego, CA: Academic Press.

Wenger, E. (1998). *Communities of practice: Learning, meaning, and identity.* Cambridge, UK: Cambridge University Press.

Wentzel, K. R., & Berndt, T. J. (Eds.). (1999). Special issue: Social influences on school adjustment: Families, peers, neighborhoods, and culture. *Educational Psychologist, 34*, 1–69.

Wertsch, J. V. (1998). *Mind as action.* New York: Oxford University Press.

White, W. F., & Bashaw, W. L. (1971). High self-esteem and identification with adult models among economically deprived children. *Perceptual and Motor Skills, 33*(3, 2), 1127–1130.

Wiener, N. (1948). *Cybernetics: Control and communication in the animal and the machine.* Cambridge, MA: MIT Press.

Wigfield, A., & Karpathian, M. (1991). Who am I and what can I do? *Educational Psychologist, 26*, 233–261.

Williams, R. N. (2005). The language and methods of science: Common assumptions and uncommon conclusions. In B. D. Slife, J. S. Reber, & F. C. Richardson (Eds.), *Critical thinking about psychology: Hidden assumptions and plausible alternatives* (pp. 235–250). Washington, DC: APA Books.

Williams, R. L. & Cole, S. (1968). Self concept and school adjustment. *Personnel and Guidance Journal, 46*, 478–481.

Winne, H. P., & Walsh, J. (1980). Self-concept and participation in school activities reanalyzed. *Journal of Educational Psychology, 72*(2), 161–166.

Winne, P. H., & Hadwin, A. F. (1998). Studying as self-regulated learning. In D. J. Hacer, J. Dunlosky, & A. C. Graesser (Eds.), *Metacognition in educational theory and practice* (pp. 279–306). Hillsdale, NJ: Lawrence Erlbaum.

Winne, P. H., & Perry, N. E. (1994). Educational psychology. *Encyclopedia of Human Behavior, 2*, 213–223.

Winne, P. H., & Perry, N. E. (2000). Measuring self-regulated learning. In M. Boekaerts, P. R. Pintrich, & M. Zeidner (Eds.), *Handbook of self-regulation* (pp. 532–629). San Diego, CA: Academic Press.

Winston, A. S. (1990). Robert Sessions Woodworth and the "Columbia Bible": How the psychological experiment was redefined. *American Journal of Psychology, 103*, 391–401.

Wittgenstein, L. (1953). *Philosophical investigations*. (G. E. M. Anscombe, Trans.). Oxford, UK: Blackwell.

Woolfolk, A. E., Winne, P. H., & Perry, N. E. (2010). *Educational psychology* (4th ed.). Toronto: Pearson Canada.

Wordsworth, W. (1966). *The prelude: With a selection from the shorter poems, the sonnets, the recluse, and the excursion, and three essays on the art of poetry*. (C. Baker, Ed.). New York: Holt, Rinehart and Winston.

Wylie, R. C. (1974). *The self-concept* (rev. ed., Vol. 1). Lincoln, NB: University of Nebraska Press.

Wylie, R. C. (1979). *The self-concept* (Vol. 2). Lincoln, NB: University of Nebraska Press.

Wylie, R. C. (1989). *Measures of self-concept*. Lincoln, NB: University of Nebraska Press.

Zeidner, M., Boekaerts, M., & Pintrich, P. R. (2000). Self-regulation: Directions and challenges for future research. In M. Boekaerts, P. R. Pintrich, & M. Zeidner (Eds.), *Handbook of self-regulation* (pp. 750–768). San Diego, CA: Academic Press.

Zimmerman, B. J. (1989). Models of self-regulated learning and academic achievement. In B. J. Zimmerman & D. H. Schunk (Eds.). *Self-regulated learning and academic achievement: Theory, research, and practice* (pp. 1–25). New York: Springer-Verlag.

Zimmerman, B. J. (1997). Developmental phases in self-regulation: Shifting from process goals to outcome goals. *Journal of Educational Psychology, 89*, 29–36.

Zimmerman, B. J., & Schunk, D. H. (Eds.) (1989). *Self-regulated learning and academic achievement: Theory, research, and practice*. New York: Springer Verlag.

Zimmerman, B. J., & Schunk, D. H. (2003). Albert Bandura: The scholar and his contributions to educational psychology. In B. J. Zimmerman & D. H. Schunk (Eds.), *Educational psychology: A century of contributions* (pp. 431–458). Mahwah, NJ: Lawrence Erlbaum.

Zirkel, P.A., & Moses, E. (1971). Self-concept and ethnic group membership among public school students. *American Educational Research Journal, 8*(2), 253–265.

Index

Note: Page numbers followed by "*f*" indicate figures; page numbers followed by "*n*" indicate footnotes.